The Syntax Handbook:

Everything You Learned About Syntax . . . But Forgot

The Syntax Handbook
Everything You Learned About Syntax... But Forgot

SECOND EDITION

Laura M. Justice
Helen K. Ezell

800-897-3202   Fax 800-397-7633
www.proedinc.com

© 2016, 2008 by PRO-ED, Inc.
1301 W. 25th St., Suite 300
Austin, TX 78705-4248
800/897-3202   Fax 800/397-7633
www.proedinc.com

All rights reserved. Except as indicated below, no part of the material protected by this copyright notice may be reproduced or used in any form or by any means, electronic or mechanical, including photocopying, recording, or by any information storage and retrieval system, without prior written permission of the copyright owner.

Library of Congress Cataloging-in-Publication Data

Justice, Laura M., 1968–
  The syntax handbook : everything you learned about syntax — but forgot / Laura M. Justice, Helen K. Ezell. — Second Edition.
     pages cm
  Includes bibliographical references.
  ISBN 978-1-4164-0998-4 (Print)
  ISBN 978-1-4164-0999-1 (e-book PDF)
  1. English language—Syntax—Handbooks, manuals, etc. I. Ezell, Helen K., 1951- II. Title.
  PE1365.J87 2016
  428.2—dc23
                                                        2015025885

Art Director: Jason Crosier
Designer: Lissa Hattersley
This book is designed in Minion and Neutra Text.

Printed in the United States of America
5 6 7 8 9 10 11 12 13 14   30 29 28 27 26 25 24 23 22 21

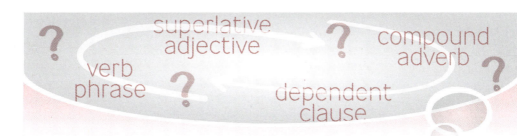

Contents

Preface   vii
Introduction   ix

Part I: *Syntactic Form*   1

ONE	Nouns	3
TWO	Pronouns	17
THREE	Verbs	31
FOUR	Adjectives	55
FIVE	Adverbs	73
SIX	Determiners	87
SEVEN	Conjunctions	101
EIGHT	Prepositions	111

Part II: *Syntactic Function*   125

NINE	Sentence Structure	127
TEN	Phrases	145
ELEVEN	Clauses	165
TWELVE	Sentence Types	179
THIRTEEN	Complex Syntax	197
	by Contributing Author Mary Beth Schmitt	

APPENDICES   209

   A: Major Syntactic Accomplishments in Child Language Acquisition Arranged by Brown's (1973) Stages   211
   B: Examples of Major Syntactic Forms   213
   C: Examples of Major Syntactic Functions   217

Glossary   219
References   231
About the Authors   237

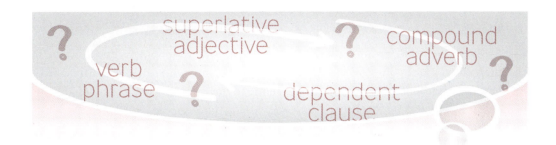

Preface

Our reason for writing this text is straightforward: In our experience working with preprofessional language interventionists, at both the undergraduate and graduate levels, we found that many students struggled with syntactic terminology and analysis in classroom and clinical tasks. For example, many students had difficulties analyzing the syntactic structures present (or absent) in clients' language. Likewise, these students had problems devising educational or clinical goals specifically related to syntax. We heard their frustration when we asked them to analyze clause or sentence structure in the narratives of school-age children. And we weren't alone. Several of our colleagues who also teach courses in language development and disorders had made similar observations.

Our students believed that their lack of such a basic understanding of syntax was hindering their ability to participate in higher-level clinical activities. Consequently, a number of these students asked us for materials that they could use to help them better understand syntactic forms and functions and their relationship to syntactic analysis. We also received similar requests from advanced professionals working in the field. Despite our searching, we were unable to find materials directed at helping preprofessional and professional language interventionists increase their knowledge of syntax and apply this knowledge to their work. That's where we came in. We wrote *The Syntax Handbook* to fill this void in our profession and to help ease the frustration of learning about syntax. We tried to make this book both educationally relevant to the speech-language reader and at the same time keep it friendly and fun (as friendly and fun as the topic of syntax can get, anyway). We hope *The Syntax Handbook* remains a handy reference tool for you long after you have mastered the basics.

Given the topic addressed in this book, there have been relatively few major changes made to this updated second edition. (In other words, there isn't too much regarding syntax that has changed in the last decade!) While we have made some refinements to this second edition of the book—including the addition of Chapter 13, which covers more complex syntactic issues—many of the original concepts and examples are still applicable and thus have remained the same.

A number of individuals played important roles of support and encouragement in the generation of the initial draft of this work: Sarah Thurs and Linda Schreiber of Thinking Publications (the publisher of the first edition); Lucille Hess, Vicki Lord Larson, LaRae McGillivray, Kristine Retherford, and Heidi Benson for their initial reviews;

Elizabeth Stroud and Caron Causey, who assisted in the development and critique of the chapter exercises; Norman Garber and Richard Dean, who critiqued early drafts; Stephanie Curenton, for allowing us to use many of the child language samples appearing in this book; and Ian Mykel and Craig Ezell, for their ongoing support and never-ending encouragement of our time-consuming endeavors.

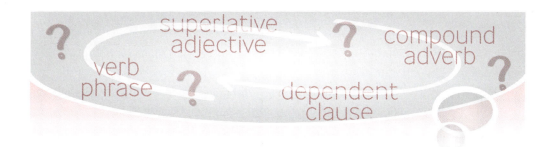

Introduction

OVERVIEW

The Syntax Handbook: Everything You Learned About Syntax . . . But Forgot (Second Edition) provides you with an updated and reader-friendly review of the syntactic terms most frequently encountered and used by language interventionists. With eight chapters devoted to syntactic form and five to syntactic function, plus developmental data on children's attainment of significant syntactic structures, this text was written especially for professionals concerned with language development and disorders. Exercises (with answer keys) are provided to review key vocabulary and to practice applying the information from each chapter to your work as a language interventionist. A glossary and a number of helpful appendices are also included for your convenience. This practical book simplifies syntax for the beginning university student, yet offers insight and quick reference to the seasoned professional.

Target Audience

People who may find this work particularly useful include:

- Speech-language pathologists and special educators working with individuals with language disorders
- Undergraduate students completing coursework in language development and disorders
- Graduate students completing coursework and clinical requirements for certification in speech-language pathology or special education
- Instructors of language development, language disorders, and other courses requiring students to have a basic understanding of syntactic structures and analysis
- Individuals who desire to enhance their working knowledge of syntactic forms and functions

Throughout this text, we use the term *language interventionist* to refer to the wide array of professionals who work with children and adults exhibiting language disorders.

These professionals include (but are not limited to) speech-language pathologists, special educators, general educators, and psychologists. We recognize that some of the terminology used within this text, such as *client, clinical goal,* and *service delivery,* may not represent the terms most commonly used by some of these professionals. Our choice of terms stems from our own experiences as speech-language pathologists, and hence our familiarity with the vernacular of our profession.

Background

Broadly speaking, *syntax* refers to "the architecture of phrases, clauses, and sentences" in a language (Shapiro, 1997, p. 254). In other words, syntax is the combination of words into sentences on the basis of rules inherent to a language. A consideration of syntax must take into account two distinct levels of analysis: syntactic form and syntactic function (Williams, 1999). *Syntactic form* refers to the grammatical category in which a particular word falls, which is generally independent of the word's role in a sentence. Syntactic forms are also known as the "parts of speech" (noun, pronoun, verb, and so on), which most of us remember learning about in elementary school, though the details of each probably escape us now. *Syntactic function,* on the other hand, refers to the role of a word or a group of words in relation to the rest of the elements in a phrase, clause, or sentence. Take the word *apple,* for instance. The word *apple* nearly always has the same syntactic form (i.e., noun) across different sentences, but its function can differ based on its role in a particular sentence. In the sentence *The apple is rotten, apple* functions as the subject. Contrast this with the function of *apple* in *I picked the apple for you,* in which *apple* is no longer the subject, but rather the object of the sentence.

A discussion of syntactic form uses terms such as *noun, pronoun, verb, adjective,* and *adverb.* A discussion of syntactic function uses terms such as *subject, object, predicate, clause,* and *phrase.* Opdycke (1965) provides a lively rationale for students of language to understand both the parts of speech (form) as well as the parts of sentences (function):

> The sentence is the unit of speech, that is, of expression. The isolated word or part of speech is, in the main, a detached tool only, to be kept handy and ready for use in association or relation with other words or parts of speech. . . . The word—the part of speech—in and of itself is indeed nothing but a cold combination of letters. It usually needs the society of other words—other parts of speech—to give it vital spark. (p. 219)

Organization

This text is organized to consider both syntactic form and function. The first eight chapters (Part I) of *The Syntax Handbook* focus predominantly on elements of form.

The last five chapters (Part II) focus primarily on elements of function, with the newly added Chapter 13 providing an overview of complex syntax. Each chapter within these two parts is organized so as to provide:

- A description of key syntactic terms and structures pertinent to the chapter's content
- A section of "Developmental Notes" containing a brief description of children's attainment of the syntactic structures covered in the chapter (In these sections, we often use Roger Brown's [1973] stages of early language development as an organizational scheme for describing specific syntactic advances. Brown's seminal work organized children's major linguistic advances in the preschool period into a five-stage process.)
- Exercises to review the chapter's vocabulary and to tie the material covered to the process of syntactic analysis (The first several exercises in each chapter have you review key syntactic terms and concepts. The rest are application exercises, in which you apply your knowledge of syntax to activities common to the work of language interventionists.)
- An answer key for selected exercises (Answers to some exercises are not included, particularly those that focus on application. The answers are not always definitive, due to the dynamic nature of syntactic analysis.)

Appendix A provides a useful overview of Brown's (1973) stages, as well as major syntactic advances occurring during these stages, as presented in Retherford (2000). You may find it useful to study this appendix if you are unfamiliar with Brown's stages of linguistic growth. Appendix B is a table of the major syntactic forms addressed in this book, and Appendix C is a table of the major syntactic functions covered in this text; these appendices may prove helpful when working through each chapter's exercises. A glossary of important terms is included at the end of the text for quick reference as needed.

Given the overall magnitude of the topic of syntax, this text does not encompass all aspects of form and function, but rather may serve as a foundational work to broaden interventionists' capabilities in using syntactic terminology and analysis within the context of service delivery. It should also be noted that theories of syntax are not addressed. Readers interested in syntactic theory should refer to Shapiro (1997) for a brief overview of this topic and to Williams (1999) for a more comprehensive discussion.

Rationale

Speech-language pathologists, special educators, and other professionals who provide educational services, clinical services, or both to individuals with language disorders require a sophisticated knowledge of syntax. Although many individuals exhibiting disordered language experience difficulties transcending the array of linguistic domains (e.g., pragmatics, semantics, and phonology), language disorders nearly always have an adverse impact on individuals' syntactic or grammatical systems.

Consider, for instance, a 4-year-old child with specific language impairment (a language disorder with no known etiology). The child may speak with a "telegraphic quality," such that key syntactic structures are omitted. For instance, the child might say, *Me go* instead of *I am going, Give me cat* for *Give me the cat,* or *That girl* in place of *That is a girl.* Analysis of the child's expressive language would suggest difficulties with using nominative pronouns (using *me* for *I*), auxiliary verbs (omitting *am*), verb tense inflections *(go* for *going),* articles (omitting *the* and *a*), and copular *be* (omitting *is*). This type of analysis is a commonplace activity for the language interventionist and is an important tool for preventing, identifying, and remediating language disorders. Familiarity with key syntactic structures is thus a clear requisite to being an effective language interventionist.

Knowledge of syntax is required for assessing an individual's language abilities, for formulating short-term objectives and long-term educational or clinical goals, for monitoring progress, and for evaluating the outcomes of language intervention. To illustrate (using examples from the field of communication disorders), short-term clinical objectives for children or adults with language disorders may look something like this:

- (Child) will use the present tense copular form of *be (is, am, are)* in 90% of obligatory contexts given an eliciting prompt by the interventionist.
- (Child) will use 10 complex noun phrases joined by the conjunction *and* in each of six consecutive sessions given models by the interventionist.
- Given an array of objects, (child) will act out irreversible passive present tense sentences spoken by the interventionist with 90% accuracy.
- (Child) will produce a third-person regular present tense verb in 9 out of 10 trials given an eliciting prompt by the interventionist.
- (Child) will use articles and conjunctions during conversational speech with 80% accuracy.
- (Child) will use compound and complex sentences in spontaneous speech during classroom activities with 90% accuracy.
- (Child) will inflect verbs to denote past and future tense with 75% accuracy.

Likewise, a long-term goal for a school-age child with a language disorder, as stated in the individualized education program (IEP), may emphasize the child's development of "age-appropriate syntactic structures."

Because syntactic terms are so frequently used to establish and monitor educational or clinical goals, language interventionists must be prepared to define and illustrate these terms for caregivers of children or adults with a language disorder so that syntactic acquisition may be facilitated in the home or caregiving environment. Likewise, language interventionists must also be able to explain the use of these terms and their reference to educational or clinical goals and intervention outcomes to other professionals, including occupational and physical therapists, psychologists, teachers, nurses, and physicians. *The Syntax Handbook* can help you master your understanding of important syntactic terms, making it easier for you to discuss syntactic goals and objectives with parents, caregivers, and colleagues.

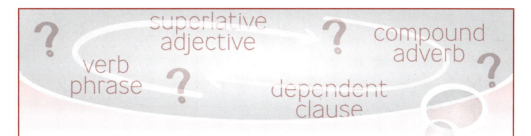

PART I

Syntactic Form

ONE: **Nouns**
TWO: **Pronouns**
THREE: **Verbs**
FOUR: **Adjectives**
FIVE: **Adverbs**
SIX: **Determiners**
SEVEN: **Conjunctions**
EIGHT: **Prepositions**

CHAPTER ONE

Nouns

Chapter at a Glance

What Is a Noun?

Simple and Compound Nouns

Noun Classes
- Common and Proper Nouns
- Concrete and Abstract Nouns
- Count and Noncount Nouns
- Collective Nouns

Noun Forms
- Number
- Gender
- Case

Developmental Notes

Chapter Exercises

Answer Key

What Is a Noun?

We all learned in elementary school that nouns are persons, places, or things. But this definition, while certainly accurate, needs to be broadened to include words like *July, liberty, language, sadness,* and *solitude,* which don't really fit into the neat categories of persons, places, or things. For example, is *July* a thing? It most certainly is not a person or a place. But can *July* be best characterized, then, as a thing? Given this conundrum, it is best to define nouns as those words that represent persons, places, things, or *abstractions* (Kessler & McDonald, 1991). *July* better fits in this definition, given that its meaning is more consistent with that of an abstraction. (The concept of time is certainly abstract and rather esoteric, wouldn't you agree?)

Nouns could even be defined as the "labels we use to classify the world and our experiences in it" (Williams, 1999, p. 14). Given this definition, *July* could be thought of as a label that we use to classify the world around us, and more specifically, to classify a particular period of time within our world.

Regardless of which definition of *noun* you choose, it is widely agreed that nouns can be simple or compound and that nouns can be sorted into noun classes and noun forms. These categories are delineated in the sections that follow.

Simple and Compound Nouns

Simple nouns consist of a single word (e.g., *man, key, hope*). **Compound nouns** consist of more than one word and can occur in several forms (Dodds, 1998). Closed compounds, such as *swimsuit, chalkboard,* and *wristwatch,* are compound nouns in which two words are combined to form a single word. Compound nouns may also consist of separate words, as in *vice president, Ohio River,* and *high school*. These nouns are called *open compounds*. A third category of compound noun is the hyphenated compound, which includes nouns like *brother-in-law, president-elect,* and *ex-wife*.

Noun Classes

Using either of the above definitions of nouns, it is probably obvious that nouns are abundant in the English language—given that nouns are what we use to classify the entities (persons, places, things, or abstractions) within our environment. It should not be surprising, then, for you to learn that nouns may be characterized into different classes, given the types of things (or persons or places or abstractions) to which they refer. These classes include common and proper nouns, concrete and abstract nouns, count and noncount nouns, and collective nouns.

Common and Proper Nouns

One way to classify nouns is by differentiating between common nouns and proper nouns. A **common noun** refers to a "general group or class of indefinite animal, condition, material, object, person, place, [or] quality" (Opdycke, 1965, p. 17), such as *cat, stability, linen, box, friend, street,* and *beauty*. In writing, common nouns are typically not capitalized. **Proper nouns**, on the other hand, are nearly always capitalized in writing. Proper nouns refer to specific entities, such as *Louisiana, Homer,* and *The Ohio State University*. Table 1.1 provides additional examples of these two noun classes.

Concrete and Abstract Nouns

Nouns may also be divided into concrete and abstract nouns. Concrete nouns refer to tangible, physical entities, whereas abstract nouns refer to intangible, nonphysical entities (i.e., entities unable to be discerned by the five senses). Abstract nouns are often words that we use when describing our ideas, emotions, senses, and the situations in which we find ourselves. Table 1.2 provides several examples of concrete and abstract nouns.

With respect to the previous section on common and proper nouns, note that common nouns may be either concrete (e.g., *cereal*) or abstract (e.g., *logic*), although some common nouns (e.g., *language*) are open for debate regarding their categorization. Nearly all proper nouns, however, are concrete (e.g., *Pennsylvania Boulevard*), although there are some exceptions (e.g., *Dadaism*, as shown in Table 1.2).

Count and Noncount Nouns

Nouns that represent countable objects are count nouns. Count nouns refer to entities that are viewed as individual elements or units (Jacobs, 1995), such as *letter, pizza,* and *minute*. If you have more than one letter, pizza, or minute, you can count each one. On the other hand, noncount nouns (sometimes called *mass nouns*) refer to entities that are not usually viewed as having individual elements; they have "no specific shape or boundary" (Jacobs, p. 108), or they simply cannot be counted (Dodds, 1998)—like *mathematics, corn, honesty,* and *fortitude*. You cannot, for example, have one or more

TABLE 1.1
Examples of Common and Proper Nouns

COMMON NOUNS	PROPER NOUNS
monkey	Curious George
car	Chevrolet
restaurant	McDonald's
teacher	Mrs. Ross
state	Pennsylvania

TABLE 1.2
Examples of Concrete and Abstract Nouns

CONCRETE NOUNS	ABSTRACT NOUNS
camera	fear
curtain	love
iPad	Dadaism
Eiffel Tower	reason
pencil	youth

"honesties," now can you? A helpful tip for remembering these is that count nouns in their plural form may be modified by the word *many,* and noncount nouns in their plural form may be modified by the word *much.* Try out this tip on the words in Table 1.3.

Some nouns can be either count or noncount depending on context. For example, *stone* is a count noun in *Each stone was polished to perfection,* but it is a noncount noun in *My house is made of stone.* Proper nouns are even more confusing since it can be argued that a proper noun is the name of a unique entity. And if it is truly unique, there cannot be more than one, making it neither a count noun nor a noncount noun, but a unique noun (A. Rubrecht, personal communication, September 21, 2001).

Collective Nouns

One final group of nouns requiring mention is collective nouns. Collective nouns are those that can name a "group acting as a unit" (Dodds, 1998, p. 54). Examples include *jury, group, neighborhood, audience, staff, The Beatles, committee,* and *flock.* These nouns may be either singular or plural in meaning, as the context dictates. For instance, the noun *group* can be used in a sentence like *The group is going to California* when meaning the group members as a unit are going to California, or it can be used with a plural verb in a sentence like *The group have all had chicken pox already* to place emphasis on the individual members of the group. Collective nouns can be plural in form (e.g., *families* and *choirs*), but there are some collective nouns that are always singular in form (e.g., *luggage* and *china*). (You'll learn more about singular and plural noun formation in the next section.)

Noun Forms

Each noun can generally be characterized by three dimensions that represent its form: number (Is it singular or plural?), gender (Is it masculine, feminine, indefinite, or neuter?), and case (Is it nominative [subjective], possessive, or objective?).

TABLE 1.3
Examples of Count and Noncount Nouns

COUNT NOUNS	NONCOUNT NOUNS
desk	progress
leg	mail
clock	wheat
bowl	courage
banana	cement

Number

Many nouns can change form to denote the number of entities to which they are referring, such as *pan* → *pans*. A noun that denotes one entity (e.g., *pan*) is singular, whereas a noun denoting two or more entities (e.g., *pans*) is plural. Often, the plural of a noun is formed by adding *-s* or *-es* to the singular form. For example, the plural form of the noun *bat* is *bats*, and the plural form of the noun *bench* is *benches*. Irregular nouns, however, have a unique plural form that does not follow the above formation rule. Some examples include *mice* (the plural form of *mouse*), *syllabi* (the plural form of *syllabus*), *feet* (the plural form of *foot*), and *data* (the plural form of *datum*). In fact, some nouns do not have plural forms at all, a circumstance that occurs more often with proper nouns. For example, there is only one *Mississippi River* and only one *Noam Chomsky*. (The speech-language world couldn't handle more than one Noam Chomsky, anyway!)

Gender

Many nouns can be characterized in terms of gender, a classification set that includes masculine, feminine, indefinite, and neuter. Masculine nouns characteristically apply to males (e.g., *man, bishop, bull, prince,* and *gentleman*). Feminine nouns usually apply to females (e.g., *woman, princess, nun, empress,* and *lady*). Nouns that are indefinite generally apply to both or either gender (e.g., *child, doctor, sibling,* and *parent*). And nouns that are neuter carry no gender connotation at all (e.g., *molecule, chair, screen,* and *arrow*).

Case

Noun forms can also be characterized as nominative (sometimes called *subjective*), objective, or possessive, depending on the noun's case (its role in a clause or sentence). Although no longer true in English, nouns in many other languages (e.g., Latin) change in form from the nominative to the objective case. The nominative case is used when nouns are serving as the subject in a sentence; the objective case is used when nouns are serving as the object in a sentence. In *Jenny wrote the note*, the proper noun *Jenny* is in the nominative case and the common noun *note* is in the objective case. In English, the forms of these two nouns would not change even if their roles in the sentence were reversed to form *The note was written by Jenny*.

Most nouns are not case sensitive, meaning that their form does not change as a function of case. That is, of course, unless they are in the possessive case. A noun in the possessive case is usually marked by the possessive *'s* (e.g., *children's, Mexico's,* and *alligator's*). Possessive case nouns denote ownership, as in *The children's dog is still ill*. (As you will learn in Chapter 2, pronouns are case sensitive for all three cases.)

Developmental Notes

Most children who are typically developing speak their first word at about 12 months of age, give or take a few months on either side. This first word represents the beginning of the expressive lexicon. From age 12 months (or the occurrence of the first word) to about 18 months, children typically amass approximately 50 words in their spoken repertoire. Many of the earliest words spoken by children during this period represent common, concrete nouns that are salient features of the child's environment, such as *ball, kitty, book,* and *doggy*. Some experts suggest that children's lexical development is, in fact, *initiated* by the acquisition of nouns (Weiss & Lillywhite, 1976). From this period forward, with the occurrence of the first spoken word, nouns continue to play an important role in the lexical development of young children.

Throughout the second year of life, nouns represent at least half of children's early vocabulary acquisition (McDonough et al., 2011). These early nouns are frequently referred to as *nominals* and allow the child to name objects occurring in the environment. Common categories for early nominals include the names of food items, animals, clothes, toys, and vehicles (Turnbull & Justice, 2011).

Language researchers have traditionally examined the composition of children's emergent vocabularies—with particular interest in the rise of nominals—by focusing on attainment of general nominals versus specific nominals. General nominals refer to general entities (e.g., *ball, girl,* and *juice*), whereas specific nominals refer to specific entities (e.g., *Fluffy, Granny,* and *Tommy*). In the early lexicon, general nominals tend to constitute a substantially larger percentage of words than specific nominals do (Rescorla & Alley, 2001). In fact, general nominals may represent about half of the total words acquired by children in their early vocabulary. In contrast, specific nominals may comprise only about 15% of total words. Taken together, these figures indicate that the early vocabularies of young children contain a large percentage of nominals, or nouns. This pattern may even be universal, if the experience of children acquiring sign language is any indication. For children who are deaf and acquiring sign language as their first language, general nominals comprise about 60% of their early words, whereas specific nominals comprise only about 7% (Orlansky & Bonvillian, 1988).

There are some general patterns to young children's acquisition of nouns. First, common nouns tend to be acquired before proper nouns. As previously noted, common nouns constitute a larger proportion of the early lexicon as compared to proper nouns. Children's earliest proper nouns often refer to family members or the names of family pets. Second, concrete nouns are acquired prior to abstract nouns. That is, early nouns tend to refer to real, tangible entities that are important in the child's life, such as food and toys, rather than abstractions, such as emotions, feelings, or time. Third, young children tend to acquire new nouns at the basic level rather than the superordinate or subordinate level. What this means is that words such as *dog* or *cookie,* which are basic-level nouns, are acquired prior to nouns at the superordinate (e.g., *animal* or *dessert*) or subordinate (e.g., *poodle* or *macaroon*) levels.

As children mature into the preschool period, the proportion of nouns comprising everyday language tends to decrease as other syntactic forms begin to be used more frequently. By 4 years of age, nouns account for about 20% of use, whereas verbs comprise 25% and adjectives comprise 15%. These proportions tend to stay relatively stable. For example, a classic study showed that at 9 years of age, nouns account for 18% of words used, verbs account for 27%, and adjectives account for 20% (Davis, 1938).

Into adolescence (beginning at age 10–12), nouns account for about 20% of the total words used and children continue to acquire more sophisticated labels to describe their environment. There are several significant developments in language learning with respect to nouns. First, adolescence is marked by an increased understanding and expression of abstract terms. Adolescents learn the meaning of such abstract nouns as *confusion, debt,* and *rebellion*. Even during this period, however, children's understanding of concrete nouns is stronger than their understanding of abstract nouns (McGhee-Bidlack, 1991). Second, and on a similar note, adolescents gradually acquire increased knowledge about the multiple and sometimes ambiguous meanings of some nouns (e.g., *foot* and *club*), which provides ripe opportunities for playing with nouns on a literal and figurative level, as with the following example (Wallach & Butler, 1994).

Q: Why can't your nose be 12 inches long?

A: Because then it would be a foot.

CHAPTER EXERCISES

Exercise 1A

Identify each noun as either concrete or abstract by placing an *X* in the appropriate box.

	Concrete	Abstract
1. lemon	☐	☐
2. epiphany	☐	☐
3. danger	☐	☐
4. jacket	☐	☐
5. hope	☐	☐
6. Marilyn	☐	☐
7. liquid	☐	☐
8. cafeteria	☐	☐
9. attitude	☐	☐
10. school	☐	☐

Exercise 1B

Provide two examples for each of the following noun categories.

1. Common   _____   _____
2. Proper   _____   _____
3. Concrete   _____   _____
4. Abstract   _____   _____
5. Count   _____   _____
6. Noncount   _____   _____
7. Collective _____   _____
8. Masculine   _____   _____
9. Feminine   _____   _____
10. Neuter   _____   _____

Exercise 1C

The following are 10 examples of nouns for which conventional pluralizing rules (adding -*s* or -*es*) do not apply. Pluralize these nouns, using a dictionary if necessary.

1. *cactus* _____
2. *thesis* _____
3. *syllabus* _____
4. *sheep* _____
5. *child* _____
6. *diagnosis* _____
7. *analysis* _____
8. *stimulus* _____
9. *ox* _____
10. *foreperson* _____

Exercise 1D

Circle each common noun and underline each proper noun in the following parent–child book reading of *Top Cat*, by Lois Ehlert.

MOTHER: You know the book with the snow dad and the snow that I was showing Mary the other day?

CHILD: Yeah.

MOTHER: This is by the same lady, Lois Ehlert.

MOTHER: See any letters you know there?

MOTHER: What letters are there in your name?

CHILD: T, o, p.

MOTHER: You are right.

MOTHER: That's a funny *a*, isn't it?

MOTHER: Whose name starts with that?

CHILD: Todd.

MOTHER: Uncle Todd, you're right!

Exercise 1E

1. Underline each noun in the following utterances produced by Zachary, a 5-year-old boy with a language disorder.

   - cut my pie up
   - me make pie
   - me make star
   - me cut all piece
   - me not push red piece
   - so now me make star
   - don't make car
   - you pushing the red piece
   - me make bear
   - me want scissor

2. Now write a statement that characterizes the types of nouns that predominate in Zachary's conversational language.

   _____
   _____

Exercise 1F

Identification of specific linguistic goals is an important part of the assessment/intervention process when working with children and adolescents who have language disorders. For this exercise, pretend that you are working with two clients; both have specific language impairment. The first, Allison, is a 4-year-old girl; the second, James, is a 10-year-old boy. Complete the following.

1. **Goal: Allison will name pictures of concrete nouns with 90% accuracy given 10 opportunities.**

   List a few possible target words for Allison.

   _____   _____
   _____   _____
   _____   _____

2. **Goal: James will define 10 abstract nouns with 90% accuracy.**

   List a few possible target words for James.

   _____   _____
   _____   _____
   _____   _____

3. **Goal: Allison will name 10 objects representing proper nouns in each session.**

   List a few possible target words for Allison.

   _____   _____
   _____   _____
   _____   _____

4. Goal: James will correctly define 5 masculine nouns with 90% accuracy across sessions.

   List a few possible target words for James.

   _____   _____
   _____   _____
   _____   _____

Exercise 1G

1. As you read the following transcript representing an interaction between a language interventionist (LI) and Robby (a 5-year-old boy with a language disorder), underline each noun used by Robby. The LI and Robby are using a book in a vocabulary-building exercise.

   LI: Do you know what that's called? An iron.
   ROBBY: A iron.
   LI: What are those?
   ROBBY: A spider and a spider and a spider and a spider.
   LI: What's that?
   ROBBY: A apple.
   LI: What color is the apple?
   ROBBY: Red.
   LI: How does it taste?
   ROBBY: Red.
   LI: How does it taste? Is it sweet or sour?
   ROBBY: Sweet.
   LI: Sweet. Very good.
   ROBBY: It's for pirates!
   ROBBY: What is it?
   LI: An anchor.
   ROBBY: A anchor.
   LI: Can you tell me something you see?
   ROBBY: It's red.
   LI: OK, it's red. What do you see on top of it?
   ROBBY: It's a triangle.
   LI: You throw it in the air. It's called an arrow.
   ROBBY: Arrow.
   ROBBY: A ant.
   ROBBY: It's purple.
   LI: It is purple.

2. Determine the proportion of words that are nouns in comparison to all the other types of words Robby produced.
   - Count the total number of nouns used and write it in the blank below.
   - Count the total number of words produced and write it in the blank below.
   - Divide the total number of nouns used by the total number of words produced.
   - Multiply this total by 100 to obtain the percent of nouns Robby used.

Calculating the Proportion of Nouns

_____ ÷ _____ = _____ × 100 = _____ % Nouns
Total number   Total number
of nouns   of words

3. What proportion of nouns would you expect for a child of Robby's age?

   _____

ANSWER KEY

Exercise 1A

1. Concrete
2. Abstract
3. Abstract
4. Concrete
5. Abstract
6. Concrete
7. Concrete
8. Concrete
9. Abstract
10. Concrete

Exercise 1C

1. *cacti*
2. *theses*
3. *syllabi*
4. *sheep*
5. *children*
6. *diagnoses*
7. *analyses*
8. *stimuli*
9. *oxen*
10. *forepeople*

Exercise 1D

MOTHER: You know the (book) with the (snow)* (dad) and the (snow) that I was showing <u>Mary</u> the other (day)?

CHILD: Yeah.

MOTHER: This is by the same (lady), <u>Lois Ehlert</u>.

MOTHER: See any (letters) you know there?

MOTHER: What (letters) are there in your (name)?

CHILD: (t)(o)(p).

MOTHER: You are right.

MOTHER: That's a funny (a), isn't it?

MOTHER: Whose (name) starts with that?

CHILD: <u>Todd</u>.

MOTHER: <u>Uncle Todd</u>, you're right!

*While *snow* may seem like an adjective, the child is most likely using *snow dad* as an open compound noun.

Exercise 1E

1.
   - cut my <u>pie</u> up
   - me make <u>pie</u>
   - me make <u>star</u>
   - me cut all <u>piece</u>
   - me not push red <u>piece</u>
   - so now me make <u>star</u>
   - don't make <u>car</u>
   - you pushing the red <u>piece</u>
   - me make <u>bear</u>
   - me want <u>scissor</u>

2. Zachary's conversation is characterized by concrete, common, singular nouns.

Exercise 1G

1.
    LI: Do you know what that's called? An iron.
ROBBY: A <u>iron</u>.
    LI: What are those?
ROBBY: A <u>spider</u> and a <u>spider</u> and a <u>spider</u> and a <u>spider</u>.
    LI: What's that?
ROBBY: A <u>apple</u>.
    LI: What color is the apple?
ROBBY: Red.
    LI: How does it taste?
ROBBY: Red.
    LI: How does it taste? Is it sweet or sour?
ROBBY: Sweet.
    LI: Sweet. Very good.
ROBBY: It's for <u>pirates</u>!
ROBBY: What is it?
    LI: An anchor.
ROBBY: A <u>anchor</u>.
    LI: Can you tell me something you see?
ROBBY: It's red.
    LI: OK, it's red. What do you see on top of it?
ROBBY: It's a <u>triangle</u>.
    LI: You throw it in the air. It's called an arrow.
ROBBY: <u>Arrow</u>.
ROBBY: A <u>ant</u>.
ROBBY: It's purple.
    LI: It is purple.

2. $11 \div 36 = .31 \times 100 = 31\%$ Nouns

3. At least 20%

CHAPTER TWO

Pronouns

Chapter at a Glance

What Is a Pronoun?
Pronoun Classes
- Personal Pronouns
- Demonstrative Pronouns
- Indefinite Pronouns
- Relative Pronouns
- Interrogative Pronouns

Developmental Notes
Chapter Exercises
Answer Key

What Is a Pronoun?

Pronouns are a finite group of words that can take the place of nouns. The term *finite* means that the group of pronouns has a relatively unchanging number of words. Nouns, on the other hand, represent a class of words with relatively infinite boundaries. This is because new nouns are constantly being created (e.g., *selfie*, *Katniss Everdeen*, and *humblebrag*) while, at the same time, other words are fading away from disuse (e.g., *typewriter*, *gauchos*, and *buggy*). Another way of saying this is that pronouns represent a closed-class group of words, since we do not create new pronouns as we do new nouns.

The role of the pronoun is important: Pronouns remove the reduplication or repetitiveness that would occur if we constantly had to rename a noun each time we referenced it. Consider the following sentence:

I grabbed the shiny, green apple Susan wanted, and then **I** threw **it** to **her**.

This sentence includes four instances of pronouns (*I, I, it, her*). Without pronouns, the sentence would read something like this:

Laura grabbed the shiny, green apple Susan wanted, and then **Laura** threw **the shiny, green apple** to **Susan**.

As can be seen from this example, pronouns allow us to be more efficient in our communication. The above example also illustrates the importance of ensuring that one make clear which noun a particular pronoun is referring to (e.g., it = shiny, green apple); these relations between nouns and pronouns create cohesion in our communication, whether we are talking or writing. When this reference isn't clear, sentences become ambiguous and lack cohesion. Therefore, a key requirement for using most pronouns is that the antecedent (sometimes called the *referent*) for the pronoun is identified, either directly or indirectly, and so is shared (known) information by the communication partners. In the previous example, the antecedent for *it* is *apple* and the antecedent for *her* is *Susan*. The antecedent for *I* is more subtle, given our distance from the actual event, as this pronoun represents the speaker of the sentence.

The finite group of pronouns that exist in the English language may be categorized into various classes: personal, demonstrative, indefinite, relative, and interrogative. These pronoun classes are described in the sections that follow.

Pronoun Classes

Personal Pronouns

Personal pronouns replace nouns that represent persons or entities. They are generally categorized into three cases: the nominative (also referred to as *subjective*) case, the objective case, and the possessive case. (Ah, yes . . . It's all coming back to you now, right? Remember how we told you in Chapter 1 that contrary to nouns, pronouns are case sensitive for all three cases? Well, here's where we back that up. Read on!) The characterization of pronouns into either the nominative or objective case depends primarily on the entity to which the pronoun is referring. That is, you must ask yourself if the pronoun is referring to the person or thing *doing* the action or the person or thing *receiving* the action. The third case, the possessive case, is used to signify ownership. Furthermore, personal pronouns can also be classified as reflexive. Details of these distinctions follow.

Nominative pronouns (or subject pronouns) are those pronouns that are used when the pronoun serves as the subject. They are *I, you, he, she, it, we,* and *they*. In contrast, **objective pronouns** are those pronouns that are used when the pronoun serves as the object. They are *me, you, him, her, it, us,* and *them*. Consider the following examples in which the personal pronouns are highlighted:

He will not leave.

Lisa told Susan that **she** doesn't want to go.

Jack hit **her** on the head.

Why won't Susan talk to **him**?

Notice that in the first two examples above, the nominative pronouns *he* and *she* are used. In both cases, the pronouns are serving as the doers of the action. In the latter two examples, the objective pronouns *her* and *him* are used because they are serving as the recipients of the action.

Possessive pronouns are used to signify possession or ownership. They are *my, mine, your, yours, his, her, hers, its, our, ours, their,* and *theirs*. Here are some examples of their use:

That is not **yours**; it's **mine**.

Our parents will not be attending, will **yours**?

Theirs is a love like no other.

When possessive pronouns are used to clarify information about a noun that immediately follows (as in the pronoun *our* above, which explains which parents), they are also called *determiners*. More specific information about determiners is presented in Chapter 6.

The form of the pronoun changes as a function of whether the pronoun encompasses the speaker (first person) or other people (second person and third person) and also as a function of the number of entities being encompassed by the pronoun (e.g., *I* versus *we*).

As with nouns (see Chapter 1), some pronouns also differ in form as a function of gender: masculine, feminine, or neuter. Specifically, the third person singular pronouns (*he, him, his; she, her, hers;* and *it, its*) vary depending on the gender of the entities to which they refer. The first and second person singular pronouns (*I, me, my, mine* and *you, your, yours*) do not change their form in this manner.

Table 2.1 depicts all the personal pronouns for the three cases. Note that the pronouns are further classified in terms of number (singular and plural) and person (first, second, and third person).

Reflexive pronouns are a special type of personal pronoun used when a person or entity performs an action on his-, her-, or itself. Consider the following:

Jack wrote **Jack** a note.

TABLE 2.1
Personal Pronouns Categorized by Case, Number, and Person

	CASE		
NUMBER	**NOMINATIVE**	**OBJECTIVE**	**POSSESSIVE**
Singular			
First Person	I	me	my/mine
Second Person	you	you	your/yours
Third Person (Masculine)	he	him	his
Third Person (Feminine)	she	her	her/hers
Third Person (Neuter)	it	it	its
Plural			
First Person	we	us	our/ours
Second Person	you	you	your/yours
Third Person	they	them	their/theirs

The preceding sentence indicates that Jack is writing a note to himself, as many of us do when we want to remember something important (like the difference between nominative and objective pronouns, right?). The personal pronoun *him* cannot be used, as it would create an ambiguous construction, as follows:

Jack wrote **him** a note.

By using the personal pronoun *him*, the sentence suggests that Jack wrote someone else a note. Consequently, a reflexive personal pronoun must be used for accurate interpretation of this situation:

Jack wrote **himself** a note.

Reflexive pronouns are formed by adding the singular suffix *-self* or the plural suffix *-selves* to personal pronouns (see Table 2.2). For this reason, they are sometimes called *compound personal pronouns*.

Demonstrative Pronouns

Demonstratives can function as pronouns or as adjectives (as you'll learn in Chapter 4). **Demonstrative pronouns** identify or highlight a particular antecedent. In other words, they demonstrate. (Yeah, that's right. Demonstrative pronouns demonstrate. You didn't see that coming, did you?) The demonstrative pronouns are *this* and *that*. Each of these pronouns has a plural form (see Table 2.3). Some scholars argue that there are, in fact, four demonstrative pronouns (*this*, *that*, *these*, and *those*), but since this is our book, we're going to give you *our* opinion on the matter!

TABLE 2.2
Reflexive Pronouns

SINGULAR REFLEXIVE PRONOUNS	PLURAL REFLEXIVE PRONOUNS
myself	*ourselves*
yourself	*yourselves*
itself	*themselves*
himself	
herself	

TABLE 2.3
Demonstrative Pronouns

	SINGULAR	PLURAL
Near the Speaker	*this*	*these*
Away From the Speaker	*that*	*those*

This and its plural form, *these*, refer to entities that are near the speaker. *That* and its plural form, *those*, refer to entities that are away from the speaker. These pronouns are called *deictic* because their meaning shifts with respect to the location of the speaker (e.g., *here* can mean anywhere, with its specificity changed by where the speaker is).

The antecedent for demonstrative pronouns may be in the same sentence as the pronoun, may be in a previous sentence, or may be unstated due to context. In the following examples, the antecedents for the demonstratives are unstated:

This is broken.

Will you grab those for me, please?

Indefinite Pronouns

Indefinites can function as pronouns or as adjectives (as you'll learn in Chapter 4). **Indefinite pronouns** have general, unstated referents, whereas other types of pronouns have specific antecedents (even if the reference is established only through context). An example is the indefinite pronoun *nobody*, which does not refer to a specific person or group of people, but rather a general (and nonexistent) group. There are many indefinite pronouns in the English language (see some common ones listed in Table 2.4). Some carry an implicit plurality to them, such as *everyone* and *several*, and others are intrinsically singular, such as *one* and *each*. Here are some examples of indefinite pronouns as used in sentences:

I doubt if anybody is coming.

Nothing ever goes right on Mondays.

Relative Pronouns

Relative pronouns have two roles: (1) They refer to a noun or a pronoun, as do the other pronoun types, and (2) they embed or conjoin a portion of a sentence to the rest of the sentence via subordination (e.g., *Lynn told her who was coming*). We have not yet discussed relative (or dependent/subordinate) clause structure (that comes in Chapter 11), so a quick explanation of this important syntactic device is needed here in order to describe relative pronouns (several of which are listed in Table 2.5).

A **relative clause** is a component of a complex sentence that includes its own subject and its own predicate (verb structure), but cannot exist by itself outside of the sentence; it must be linked to an independent clause. In the sentence *Lynn told her who was coming*, the relative clause is *who was coming*. It cannot logically stand alone; it must be joined to an independent clause, like *Lynn told her*. The relative pronoun *who* has the role of making this connection happen. (If you feel confused, you may wish to preview Chapter 11.)

TABLE 2.4
Common Indefinite Pronouns

all	either	nothing
any	every	one
anybody	everyone	other
anyone	everything	several
anything	many	some
both	much	something
each	nobody	such

TABLE 2.5
Common Relative Pronouns

that
what / whatever
who / whom / whose / whoever / whomever
which / whichever

Relative pronouns are important for the construction of relative clauses, because they are what link relative clauses to the rest of a sentence. Let's look at the following two sentences:

We have Mrs. Pena for class.

Mrs. Pena is supposed to be very demanding.

The relative pronoun *who* can be used to embed, or conjoin, the second sentence with the first sentence, as in the example that follows.

We have Mrs. Pena, **who** is supposed to be very demanding, for class.

This example shows the dual role of the relative pronoun. First, *who* takes the place of the noun *teacher*. (This is the primary role of pronouns.) Second, in a role that is somewhat unique to relative pronouns, *who* serves to conjoin the second sentence to the first sentence. You might think, then, that relative pronouns would be easy to identify when analyzing syntactic form. However, relative pronouns are often omitted and simply assumed, as we see when comparing the following two sentences:

The money **that** I used to pay her was not mine.

The money I used to pay her was not mine.

In the first sentence, the relative pronoun *that* stands in place of its antecedent (*the money*) and begins the clause *that I used to pay her*. In the second sentence, however, the pronoun is omitted. This "disappearing act" of the relative pronoun can sometimes make identification of the relative pronoun—and the relative clause that it introduces—elusive. (Not as elusive as, say, spotting Bigfoot, but elusive nonetheless.)

Here are three examples of relative pronouns (highlighted) serving to embed relative clauses (marked with brackets) within the greater sentence structure:

That man [**whom** I do not like] will be coming.

I saw the woman [**who** lives on the corner].

Tell her [**whatever** you want].

Interrogative Pronouns

Interrogatives can be used as pronouns or as adjectives (as you will learn in Chapter 4). **Interrogative pronouns** are used to ask *wh-* questions. They include words like *who, whose, whom, why, what,* and *which*. As you may have noticed, several of these were classified as relative pronouns in the previous section. However, when words such as *who* and *why* are used for the purpose of asking a question (e.g., *Why are these called* interrogative pronouns *when they were just referred to as* relative pronouns?), they are called *interrogative pronouns* (sometimes also referred to as *question words* or *wh- words*).

Whatever you call them, this special class of pronouns is used to ask questions like the following:

    Which do you prefer?

    What are you doing with my pen?

Developmental Notes

During Brown's Stage I (between 12 and 26 months of age), most children begin to use pronouns, and by age 2 years, nearly all children are using personal pronouns to refer to themselves (Lewis & Ramsay, 2004). By this time, children move from using nominals (e.g., *baby eat cookie* and *help baby*) to using pronominal forms (e.g., *I eat cookie* and *help me*); that is, children move from using only nominal forms (nouns) to using other words in place of these nouns (pronominals). From 15 months forward, children show gradual but consistent use of pronouns in their conversations (Lewis & Ramsay, 2004).

The earliest pronouns typically acquired include *I, it, my, me, mine*, and *you*, which are all personal pronouns. The general order of acquisition is reference to the self (e.g., *me*) followed by references to another person in proximity (e.g., *you*). Acquisition of later terms (e.g., *they, us, our, him, myself,* and *yourself*) do not appear to follow an obvious order for English-speaking children, although many of these forms will be evident in children's speech by Brown's (1973) Stage V (41–46 months of age). In terms of case, subjective pronouns usually emerge first, followed by objective pronouns. Possessives follow, as do reflexives (see summary in Turnbull & Justice, 2011).

By about 3 years of age, pronouns tend to represent approximately 20% of the words spoken by children (Davis, 1938). According to Davis's research, this figure remains fairly constant throughout early childhood and adolescence. At 9 years of age, for instance, pronouns constitute 17% of total words spoken.

Children's understanding and use of pronouns continues to advance throughout the adolescent years. In fact, although pronouns represent a fairly large percentage of children's spoken language, mastery of pronouns is not usually evident until early adolescence. Research into pronoun acquisition at these later ages generally considers children's refined understanding of pronouns in relation to their antecedents, such as using 'him' to refer to a boy already mentioned in a conversation. Children at 5 and 6 years of age are only just beginning to develop certain skills in assessing and understanding the relationship between pronouns and their references in varying circumstances.

Karmiloff-Smith (1986) examined children's use of pronouns in narrative production tasks and asserted that children go through three developmental stages with respect to pronoun use. In Stage One (2–5 years), children rarely use pronouns to link utterances. In Stage Two (5–8 years), children refer to a main character in a story with a pronoun (e.g., *he* and *she*), but do not refer to subordinate characters with pronouns. In

Stage Three (8 years and beyond), children use pronouns more liberally to refer to the full range of characters within a narrative context.

Most children acquire pronouns with relative ease, although several groups of children do have difficulties with pronoun comprehension and production. For example, young children with autism often make pronoun reversals, such as the reversal of *you* and *I*, as depicted in the following examples from deVilliers and deVilliers (1978):

You get hurt! [child jerks hand away from stove]

You want to take a walk. [child wants to take a walk]

Although pronoun reversals may be observed in children with typical development at about 2 years of age, this tends to be a brief developmental stage (Rispoli, 1998). For children with autism, such pronoun reversals will be less transient and may require intervention. Difficulties with the use and comprehension of pronouns has also been demonstrated in other groups of children exhibiting language disorders, such as children with specific language impairment and children with Down syndrome. The difficulties for both groups may occur because pronoun use requires awareness of the communication partner's knowledge and perspective. Further, the variety of personal pronoun forms (nominative, objective, possessive, and reflexive) used for any referent complicates the learning of them. For example, the name of a person is one noun, but that noun can have a variety of pronouns that replace it.

Children's pronoun use at the discourse level, as within conversations and storytelling, is of particular interest to many researchers (e.g., Curenton & Justice, 2004; Levy & McNeill, 2013) and practitioners in the field of language assessment and intervention. This is because of the importance of pronoun use within these contexts; that is, pronouns are used to reduce repetitiveness (e.g., "Once upon a time there was a princess named Anne. She was very sad.") and to create cohesion among the various discourse units (i.e., the use of *she* to reference Anne creates cohesion between the two sentences). In the example above, cohesion between the two sentences is built by having a shared referent, which is referred to in the first sentence by the proper noun *Anne* and referred to in the second sentence by the personal pronoun *she*.

Cohesion refers to the dependency between two elements of discourse, such as the relations between "him" (a pronoun) and "Tom," the person to which the pronoun is referring. Going back to our original example of Princess Anne, the interpretation of *she* in the second sentence is dependent on the identification of Anne as the corresponding referent in the first sentence. The relationship between *Anne* and the pronoun *she* is called a *cohesive tie* (or *cohesive link*), and more specifically, one based on reference (Halliday & Hasan, 1976). In this particular example, the cohesive tie is "complete," meaning the relationship between the pronoun and its referent is clear. If the tie was not clear, the tie would be "incomplete," as in the following: "Once upon a time, she was a princess. And she was sad." In this example, the pronoun *she* occurs on two occasions, but no clear identification of the person to which they refer has been identified.

Researchers and practitioners are interested in the production and comprehension of cohesive ties, specific to use of pronouns, because it is an area in which children with language impairment (LI) tend to have great difficulty. This can lead to breakdowns in both written and oral communication. For instance, a study of Finnish-speaking children with and without LI examined the accuracy with which children used pronouns to refer to characters when telling a story. Whereas children with typical language skills were, on average, accurate in their production of cohesive references 62% of the time, those with LI were accurate only 37% of the time (Mäkinen, Loukusa, Laukkanen, Leinonen, & Kunnari, 2014). These data suggest that children with language impairments use reference cohesion less accurately than children with typical language do, and that their cohesive ties are often incomplete.

CHAPTER EXERCISES

Exercise 2A

Underline each pronoun that occurs in this story produced by a 6-year-old child.

Once upon a time, there was a little boy named Bobby. Bobby told a bunch of friends to come over for a party. Everybody came. Jamie, Scott, Annie, and other kids too. They had cake and ice cream. Then they opened the presents. Bobby didn't know what to open first. So he picked the biggest one. It was Jamie's present. And it was a truck! Like the one Bobby's grandma gave him. So now he had two trucks! He loved that. After the presents, they went outside for fireworks.

Exercise 2B

Identify each underlined pronoun as one of the following types: Personal (P), Demonstrative (D), Indefinite (ID), Relative (RL), or Interrogative (IR).

_____ 1. She told us to clean it <u>ourselves</u>.

_____ 2. I wish <u>he</u> would tell us if he is coming.

_____ 3. Janie doesn't think <u>that</u> anybody is going to do it.

_____ 4. The cat acts like the dog's bone is <u>hers</u>.

_____ 5. Don't throw <u>those</u> away.

_____ 6. They swore <u>everyone</u> to secrecy.

_____ 7. Even after <u>they</u> sprayed, the swarm came back to its hive.

_____ 8. The psychologist warned <u>him</u> about too much stress.

_____ 9. <u>Those</u> don't look much different than diamonds.

_____ 10. <u>Why</u> don't you think that behavior is inappropriate?

Exercise 2C

Identify each underlined pronoun as one of the following types: Personal Nominative (PN), Personal Objective (PO), Personal Possessive (PP), Personal Reflexive (PR), Demonstrative (D), Indefinite (ID), Relative (RL), or Interrogative (IR).

_____ 1. <u>These</u> have got to go!

_____ 2. The women <u>who</u> are known as "Jack's girls" were roommates in college.

_____ 3. Will you please bring <u>me</u> the shortbread cookies?

_____ 4. Becky did not enjoy the movie as much as <u>we</u> did.

_____ 5. There is <u>nothing</u> I like more than sipping sweet tea.

_____ 6. <u>Something</u> has got to give!

_____ 7. <u>That</u> is Julia's favorite book.

_____ 8. Carol is going to the beach by <u>herself</u>.

_____ 9. <u>Why</u> in the world did he go to Antarctica?

_____ 10. <u>Yours</u> is the one next to mine.

Exercise 2D

A child client (5 years of age) consistently uses objective personal pronouns in place of nominative personal pronouns. Give three examples of utterances the child might produce in spontaneous conversation.

- _____
- _____
- _____

Provide one example activity a language interventionist might use to encourage the child's production of nominative personal pronouns:

_____

_____

Exercise 2E

1. Assume that the following samples are indicative of the children's typical pronoun usage in spontaneous speech. Indicate the type of pronoun they appear to be struggling with.

   - *her is little* _____
   - *he wants to do it by hisself* _____
   - *me like to buy chocolate if me go to the store* _____
   - [pointing to the chalkboard across the room]
     them bears are scary looking! _____
   - *Josh is putting the pencil in Josh's book bag* _____
   - *Kelly and I, us went to the mall* _____

2. Describe an activity you could do to help the children improve one of the above types of pronoun usage.

   _____
   _____

ANSWER KEY

Exercise 2A

Once upon a time, there was a little boy named Bobby. Bobby told a bunch of friends to come over for a party. <u>Everybody</u> came. Jamie, Scott, Annie, and other kids too. <u>They</u> had cake and ice cream. Then <u>they</u> opened the presents. Bobby didn't know <u>what</u> to open first. So <u>he</u> picked the biggest <u>one</u>. <u>It</u> was Jamie's present. And <u>it</u> was a truck! Like the <u>one</u> Bobby's grandma gave <u>him</u>. So now <u>he</u> had two trucks! <u>He</u> loved <u>that</u>. After the presents, <u>they</u> went outside for fireworks.

Exercise 2B

1. P
2. P
3. RL
4. P
5. D
6. ID
7. P
8. P
9. D
10. IR

Exercise 2C

1. D
2. RL
3. PO
4. PN
5. ID
6. ID
7. D
8. PR
9. IR
10. PP

Exercise 2E

- Personal (third person nominative)
- Personal Reflexive
- Personal (first person nominative)
- Demonstrative
- Personal Possessive
- Personal (first person nominative)

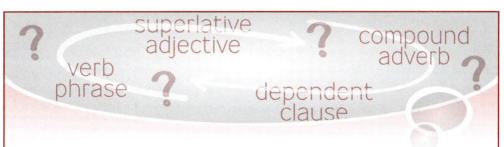

CHAPTER THREE

Verbs

Chapter at a Glance

What Is a Verb?

Verb Classes
- Main and Auxiliary Verbs
- Transitive and Intransitive Verbs

Verb Forms
- Number
- Person
- Tense
- Voice
- Mood

Verbals
- Infinitives
- Gerunds
- Participles

Developmental Notes

Chapter Exercises

Answer Key

What Is a Verb?

Verbs, as we learned in elementary school, are the action words of sentences that serve to "signify an action or state of being" (Williams, 1999). We can think of verbs as the "muscles" of our sentences in that they represent what is happening. That said, what is a verb, really? Verbs are those words that describe what nouns and pronouns do and what is done to nouns and pronouns. (You haven't forgotten what nouns and pronouns are already, have you? If you have, skim through Chapters 1 and 2 for a quick refresher.) Verbs are what allow us to request, command, prompt, and cue. Consider the following "conversation" between a woman and her dog (the woman is doing the talking):

Wait! [no response]

Sit! [also no response]

Stay! [still no response]

Kiss! [Ah, a response. Who doesn't like getting licked by a dog?]

These four sentences consist solely of verbs. What these examples demonstrate is that a verb, unlike a noun or a pronoun, is strong enough to serve as a sentence all by itself. This is why we can think of verbs as the muscles of sentences. The above commentary does not, however, explain the verbs in the following sentences:

Louie **is** my dog.

Louie **is** black and white.

The verb in both of these sentences is *is*. But *is* doesn't really describe what a noun (in this case, the proper noun *Louie*) is doing or what is being done to a noun. In other words, the verb *is* does not signify an action. But if you look again at the earlier definitions of verbs in the opening paragraph, you will see that verbs can also signify a state of being or mirror existence. These definitions of verbs may help explain the role of *is* in the two example sentences. That is, *is* serves as a connector between *Louie* and his "state of being" my pet dog.

Verb Classes

Main and Auxiliary Verbs

Generally speaking, verbs can be divided into two major categories: main verbs and auxiliary verbs. **Main verbs** serve as the principle descriptor of an action or a state of being. They include words like *eat, walk,* and *stand up* (note that *stand up* is a prepositional verb—which you'll learn more about in Chapter 8). Auxiliary verbs (sometimes called *helping verbs*) are conjoined with main verbs to clarify the action or state of being that is depicted by the main verb. **Auxiliary verbs** provide additional information about person, tense, mood, and so forth. For example, in the sentences *I will help* and *They shall come, will* and *shall* are auxiliary verbs indicating that the action of the main verbs (*help* and *come*) will occur at some time in the future. Auxiliary verbs cannot stand alone; main verbs can.

Consider the following examples of auxiliary verbs and how they are used to clarify what Katherine is doing. Notice that the meaning of each sentence subtly differs from the others, and that these shifts in meaning are signaled by the auxiliaries. Also note that the subject (*Katherine*) and the main verb (*talk*) remain the same across sentences:

Katherine **will** talk.

Katherine **may** talk.

Katherine **can** talk.

Katherine **should** talk.

In English, *be, have,* and *do* are three commonly used auxiliary verbs. These auxiliaries are often used to denote person and tense for main verbs. These three are not, however, the only auxiliary verbs, as can be seen in the list presented in Table 3.1.

Modals

Modals are a special class of auxiliary verbs. Like all auxiliaries, they cannot stand alone (they have no meaning by themselves) and they are used to clarify the action or state of being expressed by a main verb. Generally speaking, *modal* means "mood," and as such, **modal auxiliaries** provide information about certainty, intention, command, and emphasis (Master, 1995). For example, one's intention to lend a friend money changes dramatically given the use of different modal auxiliaries, as can be seen with these examples:

Jenny said she **will** lend me the down payment.

Jenny said she **might** lend me the down payment.

The modals in the above examples (*will* and *might*) provide specific information regarding the likelihood of your receiving money from Jenny. If you're the one in need of the loan, you would clearly prefer that she use the modal *will* instead of *might*.

The "core modals" in the English language (according to Jacobs, 1995) are starred in Table 3.1. These core modals are the most commonly used modals for representing mood. In addition to the core modals, other verbs can be used as modals, such as *have*

TABLE 3.1
Common Auxiliary Verbs

am	did	may*	should*
are	get	might*	was
be	had	must*	were
been	has	need	will*
can*	have	ought	would*
could*	is	shall*	

Starred items are core modals.

to, want to, and *got to*. These are often referred to as *semimodals*. When analyzing children's speech, we often see informal variations of these kinds of modals (*hafta, wanna,* and *gotta*), called *catenatives*, as can be seen in the following sentences:

> We **hafta** go now.
>
> You **wanna** use the blue one?
>
> They **gotta** go to the store first.

It is important to be able to identify catenatives because they are an early use of auxiliary verbs (that are easier for the child to say). In analysis, catenatives should be recognized as an early-developing linguistic structure (a one-word semiauxiliary), rather than a later developing structure.

Be Verbs

A special consideration of the verb *be* is warranted. The verb *be* has special importance to the work of the language interventionist: It appears especially vulnerable to difficulty for children and adults exhibiting language disorders. Therefore, in language evaluation and intervention, we often focus specific attention on this verb.

The verb *be* takes many forms, including not only *be,* but also *am, is, are, was, being, were,* and *been.* All of these *be* forms (except *being* and *been*) can serve both as a main verb—known as a **copula**—and as an auxiliary (or helping) verb. "The term *copula* refers to the verb *be,* and copular verbs [also known as **linking verbs**] are those verbs [including *appear, feel,* and *become*] . . . which are functionally equivalent to the copula" (Quirk, Greenbaum, Leech, & Svartvik, as cited in Burchfield, 1996). You'll learn more about the role of copular verbs under "The Subject Complement" section in Chapter 9. Go there now if you need more explanation.

Since the copula serves as the main verb, it can stand alone. Auxiliary verbs, as you recall, work in concert with main verbs. It is important for language interventionists to recognize the difference between the copula and the auxiliary forms of *be.* Consider the difference in the following sentences, in which the first in each pair contains *be* as a copula and the second in each pair contains *be* as an auxiliary verb:

> I **am** happy.
>
> I **am** leaving.
>
> Sally **is** not my friend.
>
> Sally **is** not planning to be there.
>
> We **are** late.
>
> We **are** taking the test early.
>
> The light **was** red.

The light **was** blinking on and off.

We **were** furious.

We **were** married in December.

The verb *be,* like all other English verbs, can be conjugated (inflected) across the 12 tenses (Master, 1995), as presented in Table 3.2.

Many of the copula and auxiliary forms of *be* can occur in uncontracted and contracted forms. Examples of copula *be* forms include *She is happy* (uncontracted) and *She's happy* (contracted). Examples of auxiliary *be* forms include *He is helping* (uncontracted) and *He's helping* (contracted). In some cases, the form must be uncontracted for the full meaning of the verb to be recognized, making them uncontractible. For example, the auxiliary verb in *He was working* cannot be contracted, because then it would be *He's working,* which loses the tense information provided by the auxiliary *was.* Other reasons for uncontractible forms include that the contraction cannot be pronounced without dropping the syllable (e.g., *The dog is barking* → *The dog's barking*) and that a contracted form cannot be used with an elliptical utterance. For instance, when being asked *"Who would like to go to the store?"* one can answer with an elliptical *I would,* but not *I'd* (Retherford, 2000).

Recognizing the difference between these various forms of *be* is important for analyzing several of the "Big 14" grammatical morphemes (Brown, 1973). That is, the 10th, 11th, 12th, and 13th grammatical morphemes to emerge in children's language production are the contractible copula, contractible auxiliary, uncontractible copula, and uncontractible auxiliary, respectively. Table 3.3 provides examples of these various forms of *be.*

TABLE 3.2
Tenses of the Verb *Be*

TENSE	EXAMPLE(S)
Simple present	*is, am, are*
Simple past	*was, were*
Simple future	*will be, shall be*
Present progressive	*is being, are being*
Past progressive	*was being, were being*
Present perfect	*have been, has been*
Past perfect	*had been*
Future perfect	*will have been, shall have been*

TABLE 3.3
Contractibility of Be

BE FORM	EXAMPLE
Uncontracted copula	I am happy.
Uncontracted auxiliary	I am helping.
Contracted copula	I'm happy.
Contracted auxiliary	I'm helping.
Uncontractible copula	I was there.
Uncontractible auxiliary	He was asking.

Transitive and Intransitive Verbs

Verbs can also be divided into the two general classes of transitive and intransitive verbs. **Transitive verbs** require an object. When a transitive verb is used, it means that the action or state of a subject carries over to an object, as in: *Jonathan* **kicked** *the ball.*

In this example, the verb *kicked* is transitive, and thus requires an object. Jonathan's action of kicking carries over to the object being kicked (*the ball*). Additional examples of transitive verbs include *admire, cut, like, put, send, want,* and *watch.* (Hint: You can often tell if a verb is transitive if you can logically put the word *something* after it, as in *You send* something *and I want* something.)

In contrast, **intransitive verbs** may stand by themselves without needing an object. No action or state is carried over from a verb to an object, as in the following examples.

He **sleeps**.

She **dreams**.

In the first sentence, *sleep* is intransitive and does not require an object (you cannot *sleep something*; you just *sleep*). Examples of other intransitive verbs include *dream, bark, flow, remain, go, smile, sit,* and *look.* The sentences *Gracie barks* and *The Hocking River flows* do not require an object to convey their meaning, although they may be supplemented by prepositional or adverbial information, as in *Gracie barks at the squirrel* or *The Hocking River flows quickly.*

Some verbs are both transitive and intransitive (e.g., *ask, eat, hit, drink, open, read,* and *stop*), depending on their use in a particular sentence. In the first sentence in the next example, the verb *open* requires an object (*the door* is what you cannot open), and so it is transitive. In the second sentence, however, the verb *open* does not require an object and is instead followed by a prepositional phrase (*with this*), making it intransitive:

You cannot **open** the door. (transitive)

The garage door does not **open** with this. (intransitive)

The general rule of thumb in deciding whether a verb is transitive or intransitive is asking whether the action or state depicted by the verb needs to have an object to receive the action or state.

Verb Forms

Verbs are a notably complex class of words in that they have other important jobs beyond signifying actions and states of being. Verbs, in fact, have a critical role in sentence structure. They provide us with information about such things as time (e.g., *He walks, He walked, He will walk*), intention (e.g., *He may walk, He might walk, He must walk*), and number (e.g., *He is walking, They are walking*). Specifically, verb inflections (modifications to the verb form itself) give us clues about number, person, tense, voice, and mood. These five important elements of verb structure are described in the following sections.

Number

Verb forms reflect whether the nouns or pronouns they describe in the subject of the sentence are singular or plural; hence, a particular verb form can also be characterized as singular or plural. Consider the following sentences:

Jeremy **sleeps**.

Jeremy and Jessica **sleep**.

In the first sentence, the noun in the subject of the sentence is singular. In the second sentence, two nouns together make up a plural subject. Note that the verbs used to describe what is happening to the subjects in these sentences reflect the number represented by the nouns (although it could also be argued that it's the other way around: that nouns reflect the number of the verb). The verb in the first example sentence is singular, whereas the verb in the second sentence is plural. The previous examples contain only main verbs, but the same is true of sentences that contain auxiliary (sometimes called *helping*) verbs and main verbs, as in these two sentences:

Jeremy **is sleeping**.

Jeremy and Jessica **are sleeping**.

In the first sentence above, the auxiliary verb (*is*) is singular, and in the second sentence, the auxiliary verb (*are*) is plural. In the above examples, the singular and plural forms of the auxiliary verbs differ as a function of number. However, this is not always the case, as the following examples illustrate:

Jeremy **will go**.

Jeremy and Jessica **will go**.

The verb forms in these last two sentences, which are in the future tense, appear identical, but do, in fact, differ in number. The auxiliary verb in the first sentence is singular and the auxiliary verb in the second sentence is plural. We know this is true because the verb number must be consistent with the number of entities to which it's referring. Our knowledge of this can only be inferred, however, as there are no structural changes in the auxiliary verb *will* based on number.

Person

Verb forms also contain information related to **person**, thereby reflecting who or what is completing the action or state of being. English pronouns, as discussed in Chapter 2, vary in their form to reflect first person (e.g., *I* and *we*), second person (e.g., *you* and *your*), and third person (e.g., *she* and *they*). This, too, is the case for verbs. Consider how the verb forms coordinate with the person (as expressed by the nouns and pronouns) to which they are referring in the following sentences:

> **He is** working.
>
> **They are** working.

You wouldn't say *He are working* or *They is working*, because the person reflected by the verb must coordinate with the person reflected by the noun or pronoun. Table 3.4 demonstrates how a particular verb form reflects person in the present tense.

Tense

Verb **tense** refers to the time of an action or state of being. English has three basic tenses: present, past, and future.

Present tense verbs denote actions or states of being occurring right now; **past tense** verbs denote actions or states of being that occurred previously; and **future tense** verbs describe actions or states of being that will occur. The verb stem (which is typically the simple first and second person present tense form of the verb) is usually modified to express tense—by changing its spelling (e.g., *hide* → *hid*), by changing its ending (e.g., *hide* → *hiding*), or by adding auxiliary verbs (e.g., *do, have,* and *will*). So, for ex-

TABLE 3.4
First, Second, and Third Person for the Present Tense Verb *Work*

PERSON	NUMBER	
	SINGULAR	PLURAL
First	*I work.*	*We work.*
Second	*You work.*	*You work.*
Third	*He/She/It works.*	*They work.*

ample, if I said to you *Tom sleeps,* you would probably think I meant that Tom is sleeping at this very moment. The reason you would think this is because of the verb tense I used (present). In contrast, if I said *Tom slept* or *Tom will sleep,* you would think that Tom is not sleeping now, but that he slept at some time in the past or is likely to be sleeping at some time in the future. Again, your knowledge of when Tom did or will do all this sleeping (not that it's any of *your* business) is guided by changes in tense to the main verb from *sleep* to *slept* (for past tense) or by the addition of the auxiliary verb *will* (for future tense).

Each of the three basic tenses (present, past, and future) can occur along three dimensions: simple, progressive, and perfect. This means that there are three types each for:

- Present tense verbs (simple present, present progressive, present perfect)
- Past tense verbs (simple past, past progressive, past perfect)
- Future tense verbs (simple future, future progressive, future perfect)

All of these tenses are described in the following sections.

Simple

Simple present verbs describe actions or states of being that exist now. The simple present tense is typically indicated using the verb stem for first and second person (e.g., *I walk, you walk*) and by adding *-s* or *-es* to the verb stem for third person (e.g., *he walks*). On occasion, a minor spelling change occurs (e.g., *study* → *studies*).

Simple past verbs convey actions or states of being that occurred at one particular time. The simple past tense for first, second, and third person is typically formed by adding *d* or *ed* to the verb stem (e.g., *I walked, you walked,* and *he walked*); verbs that follow this pattern are called *regular verbs.* Occasionally, regular verbs have a minor spelling change to form the past tense (e.g., *swat* → *swatted*). Other verbs are irregular, because their past tense is instead formed by a more significant spelling change (e.g., *break* → *broke, run* → *ran,* and *take* → *took*). Interestingly (yes, syntax can be interesting), some verbs have both regular and irregular past tense forms. Consider *burn* (*burned* or *burnt*), *leap* (*leaped* or *leapt*), and *dive* (*dived* or *dove*).

Simple future verbs describe actions or states of being that will occur at one particular time in the future. The future tense (unlike the present and past tenses) is viewed by some as a compound tense, meaning that two or more words are needed to reflect the time of the action or the state of being. In English, we use the auxiliary verbs *will* or *shall* with the present tense of the verb to form the simple future tense (e.g., *I will walk; I shall walk*). The following examples illustrate all three simple forms for the regular verb *rain* and the irregular verb *eat:*

Simple Present It **rains** every Sunday. The bear **eats** bark.

Simple Past It **rained** every Sunday. The bear **ate** bark.

Simple Future It **will rain** every Sunday. The bear **will eat** bark.

Progressive

The **progressive** (sometimes called *continuous*) **tense** of a verb is used to denote the duration of an ongoing action or state of being. The present participle form of a verb is used to form the present, past, and future progressive tenses. The present participle is formed by adding *-ing* (and sometimes making a minor spelling change) to the verb stem (e.g., *lifting, calling,* and *riding*). (More information on participles is coming up!) **Present progressive** verbs are formed by combining *am, is,* or *are* and the present participle; they reference actions or states of being that are still happening right now. **Past progressive** verbs are formed by combining *was* or *were* and the present participle; they reference actions or states of being that were in progress in the past. **Future progressive** verbs are formed by combining *will be* or *shall be* and the present participle; they reference actions or states of being that will be or shall be continuously happening in the future. The following examples illustrate all three progressive forms for the regular verbs *jump* and *cry*:

Present Progressive	Carlos **is jumping**. The children **are crying** again.
Past Progressive	Carlos **was jumping**. The children **were crying** again.
Future Progressive	Carlos **will be jumping**. The children **will be crying** again.

Perfect

Verbs in the **perfect tense** describe actions or states of being that happened in the past, and they generally suggest that the action or state of being happened before some other action or state of being. The present, past, and future perfect tenses are formed using the past participle form of a verb. The past participle is typically formed by adding *-d* or *-ed* (and sometimes making a minor spelling change) to the verb stem (e.g., *fired, walked, swatted*); however, there are also irregular past participles formed by a more significant spelling change (e.g., *know* → *known, eat* → *eaten*). **Present perfect** verbs are formed by combining *have* or *has* and the past participle form of a verb; they reference action or states of being that were started in the past and have recently been completed or are continuing up to the present time. **Past perfect** verbs are formed by combining *had* and the past participle form of a verb; they indicate actions or states of being that were completed before another action or state of being that occurred in the past. **Future perfect** verbs are formed by combining *will have* or *shall have* and the past participle; they convey actions or states of being that will be or shall be completed before a particular time in the future. The following examples illustrate all three perfect forms for the regular verb *miss* and the irregular verb *eat*.

Present Perfect	Linda **has missed** the plane.
	They **have eaten**.
Past Perfect	By the time she got to the airport, Linda **had missed** the plane.
	They **had eaten** before they left the house.

Future Perfect By the time she gets to the airport, Linda **will have missed** the plane.

They **will** already **have eaten** when they leave the house.

As a review, Table 3.5 provides an overview of the English tense system. It shows the simple, progressive, and perfect forms of the present, past, and future tenses of the verb *study* across both person and number.

Voice

There are two voices used in the English language: active and passive. The **voice** of a verb is modified to indicate whether the subject (the noun[s] or pronoun[s]) to which it

TABLE 3.5
English Tense System for the Verb *Study*

		SIMPLE	PROGRESSIVE	PERFECT
SINGULAR	**First Person**			
	Present	I study.	I am studying.	I have studied.
	Past	I studied.	I was studying.	I had studied.
	Future	I will study.	I will be studying.	I will have studied.
	Second Person			
	Present	You study.	You are studying.	You have studied.
	Past	You studied.	You were studying.	You had studied.
	Future	You will study.	You will be studying.	You will have studied.
	Third Person			
	Present	He studies.	He is studying.	He has studied.
	Past	He studied.	He was studying.	He had studied.
	Future	He will study.	He will be studying.	He will have studied.
PLURAL	**First Person**			
	Present	We study.	We are studying.	We have studied.
	Past	We studied.	We were studying.	We had studied.
	Future	We will study.	We will be studying.	We will have studied.
	Second Person			
	Present	You study.	You are studying.	You have studied.
	Past	You studied.	You were studying.	You had studied.
	Future	You will study.	You will be studying.	You will have studied.
	Third Person			
	Present	They study.	They are studying.	They have studied.
	Past	They studied.	They were studying.	They had studied.
	Future	They will study.	They will be studying.	They will have studied.

refers is doing the action or receiving the action. When the emphasis of a sentence is on the subject as the doer of an action, the sentence is said to be in the **active voice**. In the examples that follow, the subjects (*Miguel* and *the bear*) are performing an action (*eating* and *grabbed*). Neither Miguel nor the bear is receiving an action.

>Miguel is eating the apple.

>The bear grabbed the boy.

In contrast, the following sentences are in the **passive voice**, such that the emphasis of the subjects (*apple* and *boy*) is on them as recipients of an action.

>The apple is being eaten by Miguel.

>The boy was grabbed by the bear.

Notice that the subjects in the earlier two example sentences (*Miguel* and *the bear*) moved to the end of the sentences in this second set of examples. Likewise, the objects in the two earlier examples (*the apple* and *the boy*) moved to the beginning of the sentences in these later examples for emphasis. In other words, the word order has reversed. The speaker's choice of emphasis drives the syntax of the sentence.

These examples also demonstrate the concept of reversible and irreversible passive sentences. The first sentence is considered irreversible because, obviously, the apple cannot eat Miguel. (After all, it doesn't have a mouth!) The apple must be the recipient, rather than the performer, of the action. In this case, regardless of voice and the position of *Miguel* in the sentence, it is clear that Miguel must be the performer.

The second sentence, however, is less straightforward and represents a reversible passive sentence. Both the boy and the bear could serve as the performers and the recipients of the action since both boys and bears are known to grab things. Therefore, you must rely solely on your knowledge of verb and sentence structure to understand who is doing what to whom: Is the boy or the bear in fear for its life? Of the two types of passive sentences—irreversible and reversible—guess which one is more difficult for young children to comprehend. You're right! Reversible. (We'll talk more about this under the "Developmental Notes" section in this chapter.)

Mood

Verbs also contain information about **mood**, which depicts the speaker's state of mind (level of intention). Language interventionists tend not to focus on mood in analysis, but one should be aware that verbs can indicate such information. The three moods include indicative, imperative, and subjunctive.

Generally speaking, the **indicative mood** is used when one is stating a fact or requesting information, as in the following example:

>That dog **is** a terrier.

The **imperative mood** is used to give a command or to make a request. Often the *you* is simply implied, not stated, as the following example illustrates:

Tell that terrier to stop barking!

The **subjunctive mood** is used in dependent clauses (which are covered in Chapter 11) that follow independent clauses (also covered in Chapter 11) expressing wishes and demands (as in the examples below) or conditions that are improbable, doubtful, or contrary to fact. The subjunctive mood often reflects fantasizing and hypothesizing, as in:

I wish I **were** a little bit taller.

We demand that we **be** heard.

Verbals

Verbs are very malleable; they can take a variety of forms (as you may have noticed). **Verbals** are derived from verbs, but they function in different ways. They include infinitives, gerunds, and participles.

Infinitives

The **infinitive** form is characterized by "*to* + verb" (e.g., *to go* or *to call*). Infinitives can be used as nouns, adjectives, and adverbs. Infinitives are used for efficiency; they allow you to avoid repeating the subject in a sentence. They also allow you to embed one sentence into another, which helps clarify meaning, as seen in the following examples:

John is calling. (sentence 1)

John is telling us about the class. (sentence 2)

John is calling **to tell** us about the class. (An infinitive is used to embed sentence 2 into sentence 1.)

The structure of *to* followed by a verb (e.g., *to write*) is a useful clue for recognizing an infinitive. Sometimes, however, the word *to* is omitted and the infinitive becomes what is known as a *bare infinitive*, making an infinitive tricky to spot, as in these two examples:

Help Ruby **get** the coffee ready.

Help Heather **prepare** the manuscript.

Gerunds

Gerunds use the form of the present participle (the *-ing* form of a verb) to take the place of a noun or a pronoun in a sentence. You can tell the difference between present participles and gerunds because gerunds can be preceded by *the* and followed by *of* (which are sometimes present in the sentence and sometimes simply assumed). In the following examples, the gerund is highlighted and the entire gerund phrase is indicated in brackets. Note how the gerunds can be preceded by *the* and followed by *of*:

[The **handling** of wild animals] is for experts.

[**Cleaning**] is not my favorite activity.

The only thing he doesn't like is [**cooking**].

She never thinks about [**watching** television].

Participles

Participles can occur in either the present or the past tense. Both tenses are formed using a verb stem. The **present participle** is formed by adding *-ing* to the verb stem (e.g., *buy* + *-ing* = *buying*) and is used to form the progressive tenses. The **past participle** is used to form the perfect tenses. For regular verbs, the past participle is formed by adding *-d* or *-ed* to the verb stem (e.g., *hire* + *-d* = *hired*, *lift* + *-ed* = *lifted*). For irregular verbs, the past participle is formed with a spelling change (e.g., *buy* → *bought*). Some verbs have both regular and irregular past participle forms (e.g., *burned* or *burnt*, *kneeled* or *knelt*, and *leaped* or *leapt*).

Gerunds and participles, especially the present participle, can take the identical form. For instance, *reading* could be either a gerund or a participle, depending on the way it is used. It can be very tricky to differentiate between these. As a rule, try to remember that gerunds are *-ing* forms that are a kind of noun, whereas present participles are *-ing* forms that are a kind of verb. The examples below show *reading* as a gerund serving as the noun in a sentence versus *reading* as a present participle serving as the verb in a sentence:

Reading is important, so I like to take careful notes to help me recall important points. (Gerund: *reading* is a noun)

Reading the text, I paused regularly to make careful notes about important points. (Present Participle: *reading* is a verb)

While this chapter seems to have explained quite a bit about verbs, there are many more details that were not covered. You might refer to Master (1995) for a more comprehensive description of the English verb system.

Developmental Notes

Children's earliest words typically include a variety of simple verbs, often referred to at this stage as *action words*. The acquisition of these action words follows shortly after children's development of nouns (Rescorla, Alley, & Christine, 2001), and is a very prominent part of early language (Yuan, Fisher, & Snedeker, 2012). Common action words occurring in the first 50 words of young children include *sit, see, eat,* and *go.* Although nouns (nominals) tend to dominate the lexicon of very young children in their transition to symbolic communication, verbs increasingly gain ground in the second year. Braunwald (1995) described the developmental trajectory of proportion of verbs in the early speech of two young girls: For one girl, the percentage of verbs in total vocabulary increased from 6% at 17 months to 24% at 24 months. For the other girl, the pattern of verb accumulation was similar, with the percentage of verbs increasing from 6% at 19 months to 29% at 23 months. These findings demonstrate the rapid accumulation of verbs in the second year of life and show how verbs begin to take on a more important role in everyday language use.

The appearance of two-word utterances, which begin to occur at approximately 18 months of age, often features the combination of an action word (a verb) with a noun: *hug baby, Mommy go, Daddy eat,* and so on. Other examples of these forms of early utterances include *Mommy go, kitty jump, eat cookie,* and *see baby.* Note the combinations of Agent + Action and Action + Object in these examples. During these stages of acquisition (the one- and two-word utterance stages, transcending the second year of life for most children), children's verbs are not yet inflected and typically only one main verb is observed per utterance. However, this may be a language-specific phenomenon, for young Korean children at only 15 months of age have been observed using inflected verbs (Gopnik & Choi, 1995).

A comprehensive overview of children's verb acquisition is depicted in Miller (1981) and Retherford (2000), resources we invite you to consult. The following paragraphs provide a broad overview of children's attainment of the verb system; much is drawn from these two references.

At approximately 2½ years of age, when children's mean length of utterance (MLU) moves beyond 2.0, the use of inflected verb forms first begins to appear. The earliest verb inflection is use of the present participle form, depicted by the adding of the suffix *-ing* to the main verb (e.g., *running*). Shortly thereafter, at approximately 31–34 months of age, present and future tense auxiliary forms begin to appear, including *can, do, will, am,* and *be.* Examples of these more complex verb forms include *I can do it* and *Jenny will help.* However, as noted by Owens (2012), children's use of these auxiliary forms may not always accurately reflect agreement between person and tense. Constructions such as *he am helping* and *they is walking* are therefore not surprising when heard in the everyday speech of young children.

Between the ages of 35 and 40 months of age, children typically begin to use regular past tense verbs (e.g., *I walked*) and modals such as *could, would, should, must,* and *might* in combination with main verbs (e.g., *I might walk*). Also at this time, children begin to use auxiliary forms of *"be + present progressive -ing"* (e.g., *I am walking*) in the majority of obligatory contexts (contexts in which the form is required). It should be noted that throughout these years (between the ages of 3 and 5 years), children frequently overextend the rules for constructing regular past tense verbs (adding *-ed*) to irregular verbs, and thus such interesting forms as *goed* and *eated* may occur. Between the ages of 4 and 5 years, most children begin to use the past tense of *be* forms as the copula and auxiliary verbs (e.g., *John was sad* and *I was walking*).

Children's expressive and receptive understanding of verbs continues to evolve at a more gradual but continuous pace over the later preschool and elementary years. There is also some evidence that the use of verbs in children's conversational language increases—albeit modestly—in the transition from childhood into adolescence. Specifically, during the preschool period, verbs constitute about 25% of the total words used by children; by adolescence (about 9–10 years of age), about 30% of the total words used by children are verbs (Davis, 1938).

There are, of course, some developmental trends that have been observed with respect to children's preference or use of particular types of verbs, and specifically with their use of auxiliary and copular verbs (Davis, 1938). Let's take the verb *be* (in all its permutations), for example. For 5-year-old children, *be* is used as an auxiliary (e.g., *I am walking*) only about 28% of the time; by 9 years of age, *be* is used as an auxiliary 42% of the time. Children's use of *be* verbs as auxiliaries increases with age.

Children's understanding of verbs in a lexical sense also continues to grow during the early period of adolescence. Children tend to understand simple action words before they understand those that describe more complex actions or states of being. By 5 years of age, for example, many children understand the verb *hit*. In contrast, it is not until approximately 12 years of age that most children will accurately comprehend the verb *direct*.

An interesting area of research has focused on children's understanding of metalinguistic verbs, or verbs that are used to reflect on aspects of thought and language (Nippold, 2007). Metalinguistic verbs include, for example, *assess, conclude, imply,* and *predict*. Such research has indicated that even by high school, children's understanding of such verbs, specifically those used to discuss language and thought processes, is not fully complete. In fact, over the broad course of childhood, children continually show a preference for using verbs that denote action versus those that refer to sensory or thought states (e.g., *think, know,* and *suppose*) (Davis, 1938).

Between 7½ and 8 years of age, 90% of children comprehend reversible passive sentences (Carlson, 1977) and 80% of children produce reversible passive sentences (Baldie, 1976). Baldie also observed a marked increase in the number of irreversible passive sentences produced at this age; however, by age 9, children generally produced irreversible sentences. Clearly by age 11, children can produce both reversible and irreversible sentences.

An area of language development that is of particular interest to interventionists is the child's achievement of negatives. This is important because we often strive to enhance children's abilities to make their needs known (e.g., *I don't want it!* or *Mommy don't do that!*). Children move gradually (although some parents would contend that the movement occurs rather rapidly!) from extralinguistic means for expression negation (e.g., shaking their heads No) to linguistic means (using words). Embedded within children's first 50 words is usually the word *no* (Nelson, 1974). Soon thereafter, when children begin to use two-word combinations, *no* and *not* are often (and quite imaginatively) combined with other words: *no baby, no kitty, no shoe, not puppy, not Daddy*, and so forth. It is also in this time frame that we first see negative elements attached to verbs (e.g., *not go, no eat, not want, no sit*, and *no up*).

Hoff-Ginsberg (1997) described three general stages to the child's achievement of negation sentence forms. In Stage I, children's negative markers (e.g., *no* and *not*) are located at the peripheral of sentences, which she calls "external negative markers": *no want it, eat bite no,* and *not go Mommy.*

In Stage 2, children's negative markers are moved internally, and negation is marked without the use of auxiliaries. Primary markers are *no, not, can't,* and *don't: I don't want it,* or *I no eat it.* Note that it is in this stage (usually at about 30 months) that children begin to use contracted verbs to express negation, primarily *can't* and *don't*. Interestingly, these negative contractions emerge prior to the child's use of *can* and *do* (Owens, 2012). *Won't* emerges soon thereafter, at about 34 months.

In Stage 3, children's negative markers are marked with auxiliaries and more diverse contractions. It is in this time frame, in the months shortly after the child turns 3, that children's use of negated verbs (contracted or uncontracted) takes on a more sophisticated feel (e.g., *I can't do it, I won't help,* or *I will not do it*). The increased repertoire of contracted negatives include *aren't, isn't, doesn't,* and *didn't*. The last negative contractions to emerge, from about 40–46 months, include *wouldn't, couldn't,* and *shouldn't*, all of which involve modal auxiliaries (Miller, 1981).

CHAPTER EXERCISES

Exercise 3A

Identify each underlined verb as one of the following: Copula *be* (C), Auxiliary *be* (A), Gerund (G), or Infinitive (I).

_____ 1. People don't like to eat bones.
_____ 2. She was not coming until we asked her.
_____ 3. It is uncertain whether the wedding day will be sunny.
_____ 4. He is sure my condition will not improve.
_____ 5. You need to focus on keeping it warm.
_____ 6. To eat to my heart's content is my plan for the day.
_____ 7. The truck driver slammed the door and swore never to return.
_____ 8. They were not happy about having to take care of the bill.
_____ 9. Purchasing the ring made her forget about what was to come.
_____ 10. Tell him that anxiety is a natural phenomenon.

Exercise 3B

Conjugate the following two verbs (*talk* and *grow*) in the first person singular tense.

	talk	*grow*
1. Simple present	I _____.	I _____.
2. Simple past	I _____.	I _____.
3. Simple future	I _____.	I _____.
4. Present progressive	I _____.	I _____.
5. Past progressive	I _____.	I _____.
6. Future progressive	I _____.	I _____.
7. Present perfect	I _____.	I _____.
8. Past perfect	I _____.	I _____.
9. Future perfect	I _____.	I _____.

Exercise 3C

Underline all the auxiliary verbs that occur in the following paragraph. Indicate those that are modals by marking them with an asterisk.

If you are hearing rumors that an employee at the hospital is bored, you know they are not referring to the speech-language pathologist. For, from day to day, she is quite busy and her work is never the same. She may do three language evaluations in one day and might never do another for three weeks. One week, she was meeting with a new parent who found out that her child had cleft palate. Another week, she gave a presentation to the facility's medical students. She also has to prepare for several upcoming IEP meetings. In addition, she is scheduled for training several graduate students on the use of stroboscopy in voice examinations. Most days, she has to begin work early in the morning so that she can observe patients eating their breakfast. Were she to see signs of swallowing difficulties, she would ask the patient's physician for a referral to do a more objective evaluation. While she could rely on traditional textbooks for therapy sessions, she must tailor her instruction to meet the various needs of each and every patient. Even though she has been to graduate school and was given clinical supervision, she is always seeking opportunities to further her education in order to be the best clinician she can be. While there are many other hospital employees who may complain of a dull job, you know that you will never have a speech-language pathologist who resigns from her job on the premise that "I am so bored."

Exercise 3D

1. Underline each verb that occurs in the following child utterances. The transcript represents an interaction between a parent and her 4-year-old child during a shared-reading session.

   ADULT: I want to know why there are bones on it.

   CHILD: **Oh, because dogs like bones.**

   ADULT: [reads from book]

   CHILD: **But the mouse helped, the mouse helped by putting the shells in.**

   ADULT: He sure did.

   CHILD: **I don't know why the dogs thought it was delicious. It had shells in it.**

   ADULT: Because dogs are silly.

   CHILD: **Yeah. And dogs don't like the same things that people like.**

Adult: They like different things.
Child: **Yeah.**
Adult: Like bones.
Child: **We only like bones with chicken on them.**
Adult: And chicken and what else?
Child: **We like to eat some things that are off bones, like chicken.**
Adult: Yeah.
Child: **I like chicken off bones. Like drumsticks.**

2. Examine the child utterances in Step 1 and determine if there are any examples of the following verb forms. If so, list one or two examples for each. If no examples occur for a particular category, write *None*.

   - Simple present tense verb   _____   _____
   - Simple past tense verb   _____   _____
   - Simple future tense verb   _____   _____
   - Transitive verb   _____   _____
   - Intransitive verb   _____   _____
   - Infinitive   _____   _____
   - Gerund   _____   _____
   - Auxiliary   _____   _____
   - Contractible copular *be*   _____   _____
   - Uncontractible copular *be*   _____   _____

3. Determine the proportion of verbs the child produced in comparison to the other types of words in the shared-reading interaction presented previously.

   - Count the total number of verbs (encompassing all types) that you underlined in Step 1; count contractions (e.g., *don't*) as only one verb. Write this number in the blank below.
   - Count the total number of words produced and write this number in the blank below.
   - Divide the total number of verbs used by the total number of words produced.
   - Multiply this total by 100 to obtain the percent of verbs the child used.

Calculating the Proportion of Verbs

_____ ÷ _____ = _____ × 100 = _____ % Verbs
Total number   Total number
of verbs   of words

4. What proportion of verbs would you expect for a child of this age?

   _____

Exercise 3E

Preschool children with language disorders often demonstrate delayed acquisition of key verb structures, such as copula *be* and infinitive forms (Leonard, Eyer, Bedore, & Grela, 1997). For example, children may omit the copula and auxiliary forms of *be* in obligatory contexts in spontaneous speech. For this exercise, give examples of utterances that might be observed in the speech of a preschool child with a language disorder, in which the obligatory use of a target structure is omitted.

1. Infinitive
Intact Form: _____

Child: _____

Intact Form: _____

Child: _____

2. Auxiliary *Be*
Intact Form: _____

Child: _____

Intact Form: _____

Child: _____

3. Copular *Be*
Intact Form: _____

Child: _____

Intact Form: _____

Child: _____

ANSWER KEY

Exercise 3A

1. I   2. A   3. C   4. C   5. G
6. I   7. I   8. C   9. G   10. C

Exercise 3B

		talk	*grow*
1.	Simple present	*I talk.*	*I grow.*
2.	Simple past	*I talked.*	*I grew.*
3.	Simple future	*I will talk.*	*I will grow.*
4.	Present progressive	*I am talking.*	*I am growing.*
5.	Past progressive	*I was talking.*	*I was growing.*
6.	Future progressive	*I will be talking.*	*I will be growing.*
7.	Present perfect	*I have talked.*	*I have grown.*
8.	Past perfect	*I had talked.*	*I had grown.*
9.	Future perfect	*I will have talked.*	*I will have grown.*

Exercise 3C

If you <u>are</u> hearing rumors that an employee at the hospital is bored, you know they <u>are</u> not referring to the speech-language pathologist. For, from day to day, she is quite busy and her work is never the same. She <u>may</u>* do three language evaluations in one day and <u>might</u>* never do another for three weeks. One week, she was meeting with a new parent who found out that her child had cleft palate. Another week, she gave a presentation to the facility's medical students. She also has to prepare for several upcoming IEP meetings. In addition, she <u>is</u> scheduled for training several graduate students on the use of stroboscopy in voice examinations. Most days, she has to begin work early in the morning so that she <u>can</u>* observe patients eating their breakfast. Were she to see signs of swallowing difficulties, she <u>would</u>* ask the patient's physician for a referral to do a more objective evaluation. While she <u>could</u>* rely on traditional textbooks for therapy sessions, she <u>must</u>* tailor her instruction to meet the various needs of each and every patient. Even though she <u>has</u> been to graduate school and <u>was</u> given clinical supervision, she <u>is</u> always seeking opportunities to further her education in order to be the best clinician she <u>can</u>* be. While there are many other hospital employees who <u>may</u>* complain of a dull job, you know that you <u>will</u>* never have a speech-language pathologist who resigns from her job on the premise that "I am so bored."

Exercise 3D

1.
   ADULT: I want to know why there are bones on it.
   CHILD: Oh, because dogs <u>like</u> bones.
   ADULT: [reads from book]
   CHILD: But the mouse <u>helped</u>, the mouse <u>helped</u> by <u>putting</u> the shells in.
   ADULT: He sure did.
   CHILD: I <u>do</u>n't <u>know</u> why the dogs <u>thought</u> it <u>was</u> delicious. It <u>had</u> shells in it.
   ADULT: Because dogs are silly.
   CHILD: Yeah. And dogs <u>don't</u> <u>like</u> the same things that people <u>like</u>.
   ADULT: They like different things.
   CHILD: Yeah.
   ADULT: Like bones.
   CHILD: We only <u>like</u> bones with chicken on them.
   ADULT: And chicken and what else?
   CHILD: We <u>like to eat</u> some things that <u>are</u> off bones, like chicken.
   ADULT: Yeah.
   CHILD: I <u>like</u> chicken off bones. Like drumsticks.

2.
• Simple present tense verb	*like*	*know*
• Simple past tense verb	*helped*	*thought*
• Simple future tense verb	None	
• Transitive verb	*like*	
• Intransitive verb	*help(ed)*	
• Infinitive	*to eat*	
• Gerund	*putting*	
• Auxiliary	*do(n't)*	*had*
• Contractible copular *be*	None	
• Uncontractible copular *be*	*was*	*are*

3. 15 ÷ 71 = .21 × 100 = 21% Verbs

4. 25%

CHAPTER FOUR

Adjectives

Chapter at a Glance

What Is an Adjective?

Simple and Compound Adjectives

Positive, Comparative, and Superlative Forms

Descriptive Adjectives

Limiting Adjectives

- Proper Adjectives
- Possessive Adjectives
- Demonstrative Adjectives
- Cardinal Adjectives
- Ordinal Adjectives
- Nouns Used as Adjectives
- Definite and Indefinite Articles
- Indefinite Adjectives
- Interrogative Adjectives

Sequencing Adjectives

Developmental Notes

Chapter Exercises

Answer Key

What Is an Adjective?

Adjectives are an important class of words that serve as the descriptors in a language. They provide information about nouns and pronouns and may generally be referred to as **modifiers** and more specifically as *adjectival modifiers*. (Adverbs are another type of modifier and will be discussed in the next chapter.) In terms of their role as modifiers, adjectives are important for narrowing down the qualities and properties of the nouns and pronouns to which they refer. Here are some examples of common adjectives:

> The long and winding road is the famous Deadman's Drive.
>
> The test is lousy for specifying degree of impairment.

Now pay attention to the different types of information provided by the adjectives highlighted in the following couple's conversation.

> JESSIE: Let's go to **that** restaurant we went to **last** week.
>
> STEPHEN: **Which** one?
>
> JESSIE: You know, **the** one where we had **that delicious red** wine; **the** one with **the huge** buffet?
>
> STEPHEN: You mean Cutler's?
>
> JESSIE: No. **That** place with **the** really **nice** waitress, she had **long, blonde** hair. You left **a** really **big** tip for her.
>
> STEPHEN: Oh, you mean Northern Exposure!

Jessie's adjectives (e.g., *that, last, the, delicious, red, huge, nice, long, blonde, a,* and *big*) helped Stephen along here. (Yes, demonstratives and articles can be adjectives—that is, limiting adjectives. You'll learn about them later in the chapter.) Clearly, adjectives help us all along when we are trying to distinguish some nouns from others.

Like nouns, adjectives come in infinite proportions. In other words, adjectives are an open class of words because words move in and out of this class. Some adjectives, such as *delightful, exhausted,* and *bitter,* seem to be enduring, whereas adjectives like *groovy, cheesy,* and *rad* represent slang that varies in popularity. New adjectives are frequently created (e.g., *buzzworthy* and *tweetable*) or common adjectives attain new meanings (e.g., *heavy* and *thirsty*), some of which may become popular parlance.

Adjectives are the third largest group of words, following nouns and verbs. Adjectives are generally grouped into two categories: descriptive adjectives and limiting adjectives. Descriptive adjectives describe a quality of the noun or pronoun they modify and come in two types of their own: attributive adjectives and predicate adjectives. Likewise, limiting adjectives come in nine types: proper adjectives, possessive adjectives, demonstrative adjectives, cardinal adjectives, ordinal adjectives, nouns used as adjectives, definite and indefinite articles, indefinite adjectives, and interrogative adjectives. All of these types will be discussed in detail later in this chapter.

Simple and Compound Adjectives

A large number of adjectives occur as single words; these are **simple adjectives**. Examples include *tacky, experimental,* and *shrill.* The English language also makes use of a variety of **compound adjectives**, which are formed in one of three ways: (1) by combining two words into one word (e.g., <u>pickup</u> *truck,* <u>ballpoint</u> *pen,* and <u>hardcover</u> *book*); (2) by hyphenating two words (e.g., <u>mobile-friendly</u> *website,* <u>low-income</u> *households,* and <u>no-nonsense</u> *woman);* or (3) by using two closely related words together without combining or hyphenating them (e.g., <u>child development</u> *center,* <u>Supreme Court</u> *ruling,* and <u>high school</u> *graduate*).

Positive, Comparative, and Superlative Forms

The **positive form** of adjectives can be inflected to create the comparative and superlative forms. Adjectives that can be modified to compare two or more entities along a continuum (e.g., *smart, smarter, smartest*) are referred to as **gradable** adjectives. The **comparative degree** reflects a comparison of two nouns or pronouns and is typically formed by adding *-er* to the positive form. The **superlative degree** reflects a comparison of three or more nouns or pronouns and is typically formed by adding *-est* to the positive form. When an adjective cannot be modified with *-er,* the comparative form is made by adding either *more* or *less* before the positive form. When an adjective cannot be modified with *-est,* the superlative form is made by adding either *most* or *least* before the positive form (see the examples in Table 4.1). Some common exceptions to these rules are *good, better, best* and *bad, worse, worst.*

Some adjectives are non-gradable (e.g., *perfect, square,* and *plastic*). These adjectives cannot be modified into comparative or superlative forms, because they typically describe all or no qualities of entities. That is, something either is or isn't perfect, square, or plastic; it can't be more perfect or less square than another object and can't be the least plastic item in a group of three or more items. (Kind of depressing to learn you'll never again say *I had the <u>most perfect</u> night of my life,* huh?)

TABLE 4.1
Examples of the Three Adjective Forms

POSITIVE	COMPARATIVE	SUPERLATIVE
sleepy	sleepier	sleepiest
serious	more serious	most serious
studious	less studious	least studious

Descriptive Adjectives

Descriptive adjectives describe a quality of the noun or pronoun they modify and come in two types: attributive adjectives and predicate adjectives. **Attributive adjectives** most often precede nouns (e.g., *The tall girl is in my class*). **Predicate adjectives** can follow a copula (e.g., *The girl in my class is tall*) and can follow intransitive verbs (e.g., *She seems sad*) to modify nouns and pronouns serving as subjects. (For a review of the copula and intransitive verbs, see the section "Verb Classes" in Chapter 3). When adjectives follow a copula or an intransitive verb, they can also be referred to as **complements**—specifically **subject complements**—or as **nominal predicates**.

Some descriptive adjectives occur in a simple unmodified form (e.g., *long*, *tall*, and *green*), but a large number of descriptive adjectives can be readily recognized by the presence of an adjectival suffix and by considering their meaning and what they are modifying. Several of the more common adjectival suffixes (according to Leech, 1991) are presented in Table 4.2.

Although most descriptive adjectives are easily recognized due to their frequent position in front of a noun (e.g., *endemic* proportions), descriptive adjectives can directly follow the noun they modify, as in *She only drinks her soda cold* and *She keeps her office organized*. In some cases, adjectives can even occur without a noun, typically following the article *the*, as in *Feed the hungry* and *Pay attention to the obvious*.

TABLE 4.2
Common Adjectival Suffixes

SUFFIX	EXAMPLES
-al	actual, adjectival
-ous	conscious, glorious, serious, wondrous
-y	easy, blurry, freaky, savory
-ful	beautiful, plentiful, wonderful
-ish	foolish, pinkish, selfish, feverish
-less	blameless, bottomless, selfless
-ive	expensive, native, pensive, plaintive
-ial	presidential, inferential, influential
-ent	excellent, intelligent, belligerent
-ic	caloric, endemic
-like	childlike, catlike
-en	frozen, brazen, waxen

Limiting Adjectives

Limiting adjectives modify nouns by focusing on how much, how many, whose, and so on. Limiting adjectives can include other parts of speech (e.g., nouns and pronouns) that take on an adjectival role, causing language interventionists difficulty when trying to determine an individual's adjective use in syntactic analysis. To make matters even more confusing, some scholars call most limiting adjectives *determiners,* which we will cover in Chapter 6. The following sections provide you with a brief overview of the nine types of limiting adjectives: proper adjectives, possessive adjectives, demonstrative adjectives, cardinal adjectives, ordinal adjectives, nouns used as adjectives, definite and indefinite articles, indefinite adjectives, and interrogative adjectives.

Proper Adjectives

Common adjectives are descriptive and general in their meaning (e.g., *blue, tall,* and *long*). Proper adjectives, however, are limiting and refer to distinct entities (e.g., <u>Shakespearean</u> *style,* <u>Spanish</u> *class,* and <u>Android</u> *phone*). They are often—though not always—modified from their proper noun counterparts by the addition of a suffix (e.g., *Japan + -ese = Japanese*). Like proper nouns, proper adjectives are typically capitalized (though there are a few exceptions—like *french dressing, bunsen burner,* and *manila envelope*—which have taken on common meanings and are therefore often lowercased). A few examples of proper adjectives include:

> They took a **Disney** vacation.
>
> I really admire the discipline of **Tibetan** monks.
>
> Dr. Shea is my **English** professor.

Possessive Adjectives

When common and proper nouns (see Chapter 1) and pronouns (see Chapter 2) are used to signify possession, they become adjectival in function and thus can be considered **possessive adjectives**. Here are some examples.

> The **man's** ferret escaped over the weekend. (possessive common noun used as an adjective)
>
> Please don't eat all of **Janet's** cookies. (possessive proper noun used as an adjective)
>
> **His** hair is a wreck! (possessive pronoun used as an adjective)

In the last example above, the possessive *his* is used to modify the noun *hair* and thus may be categorized as an adjective (specifically, a possessive adjective). Consider how this example differs from how the possessive *his* is used in the sentence *It is his,* in which *his* is not directly modifying a noun (it is taking the place of a noun) and is therefore functioning as a possessive pronoun, not as a possessive adjective.

When possessive adjectives precede a noun, they are commonly referred to as *determiners*. Determiners will be discussed more thoroughly in Chapter 6.

Demonstrative Adjectives

Demonstratives may also serve an adjectival role. Recall from Chapter 2 that the demonstrative pronouns include *this, that, these,* and *those* (with *this* and *these* referring to entities close to the speaker and *that* and *those* referring to entities away from the speaker). Examples of their use in sentences as demonstrative adjectives modifying nouns include the following:

> Please help her hang **this** wallpaper.
>
> **That** one is the best.
>
> **These** shoes are too tight.
>
> Scott disagrees with **those** rules.

In the second example above, the demonstrative *that* is modifying the word *one*, and thus can be classified as an adjective (specifically, a demonstrative adjective). Think about how this example differs from the demonstrative *that* in the sentence *That's cool*, in which *that* is not directly modifying a noun and is functioning as a demonstrative pronoun, not as a demonstrative adjective.

Demonstrative adjectives are also a type of determiner, which, as we've already told you, will be covered in Chapter 6. (It's only two chapters away. You can make it till then, can't you?)

Cardinal Adjectives

Often when numbers are used in language, they are used to denote a specific attribute of a noun or pronoun, such as *six apples* or *one Taco Bell*. The words *six* and *one* in these phrases are adjectival since *six* modifies the common noun *apples* and *one* modifies the proper noun *Taco Bell*. This type of numeric adjective is a cardinal adjective. **Cardinal adjectives** are the "counting numbers," such as *one, two,* and *three*. They modify a noun or pronoun by stating how many. Cardinal adjectives are also a type of determiner, although as determiners, they are referred to as **quantifiers**. Here are a few examples:

> It was only **thirty-three** cents!
>
> I need **two** yellow spools and **one** black one for the costume.

Ordinal Adjectives

Another type of numeric adjective is the ordinal adjective. **Ordinal adjectives** are those numbers that denote the order of a noun or pronoun in a series, such as *first, second,* and *third.* And you guessed it! Ordinal adjectives can also be considered a quantifier type of determiner. Some examples are:

> Jason came in **fourth** place.
>
> This is the **millionth** time I've reminded you what an ordinal adjective is!

Nouns Used as Adjectives

A number of nouns can be used as adjectives (e.g., *my computer class, that kitchen gadget,* and *the porch light*). Note that they are identical in form to their noun counterparts. Consequently, they are not as easily recognizable as adjectives since they do not contain one of the common adjectival suffixes (listed in Table 4.2). Here are two examples of nouns used as adjectives:

> It's in my top **desk** drawer.
>
> Could you hand me my **coffee** cup?

Definite and Indefinite Articles

Articles include *the, a,* and *an. The* is definite, and *a* and *an* are indefinite. Below are some example sentences illustrating each kind of article:

> **The** boy is on his way.
>
> I need **a** paintbrush for this.
>
> It is not **an** issue.

Although both **definite articles** and **indefinite articles** can serve an adjectival role, they are considered as articles (or sometimes determiners) in syntactic analysis. We discuss them as a type of limiting adjective here.

Indefinite Adjectives

In addition to indefinite articles, indefinites can also be a type of limiting adjective. **Indefinite adjectives** include, for instance, *all, enough, few, much, many, more, most, never,* and *some* (for a more comprehensive list, see Table 2.3 in Chapter 2). These words can serve as either a pronoun or an adjective, based on their function in a sentence. When one of these words takes the place of a noun or pronoun, it is an indefinite pronoun.

When one of these words modifies a noun or pronoun, it is an indefinite adjective. Here are several examples:

>Nancy has **several**. (indefinite pronoun)

>Nancy has **several** dogs. (indefinite adjective)

>Please share **both**. (indefinite pronoun)

>Please share **both** pieces of information. (indefinite adjective)

Note that the indefinite adjective in each of the examples above provides additional information about the nouns that they modify. In the second example, *several* provides details about the number of dogs that Nancy has; in the fourth example, *both* provides details about how many pieces of information should be shared. It is important to note that indefinites can serve many purposes and that when they are not modifying nouns, they are not indefinite adjectives.

Interrogative Adjectives

Whose, which, and *what* are interrogatives that can serve an adjectival role when they modify nouns. Again, note the difference between the use of the interrogative pronoun and the interrogative adjective, as demonstrated in the following examples:

>**Whose** is this? (interrogative pronoun)

>**Whose** pencil is this? (interrogative adjective)

>**Which** did you say you wanted? (interrogative pronoun)

>**Which** hat did you say you wanted? (interrogative adjective)

Sequencing Adjectives

Adjectives are frequently strung together to modify nouns and pronouns. Although the sequence is not necessarily fixed, a general sequence does exist and is as follows (Darling, 2001; Master, 1995):

>Limiting Adjective/Determiner + Opinion/Quality + Size + Shape + Condition/Age + Color + Pattern + Material + Origin + Noun Used as an Adjective

Can you imagine how long a sentence would be if it used all the adjectives in the sequence above? You probably couldn't say it without running out of breath! For the most part, only two or three adjectives are used at one time. And don't worry—you don't have to carry the above adjective-order chart with you in your pocket. Most people order adjectives appropriately without giving it a thought. Consider the following sentence:

Two scary, old, American men came into the diner.

In this example, *two* is the limiting adjective/determiner, *scary* is an opinion/quality, *old* describes age, and *American* references origin. You would be taken aback if someone said *American old, scary two men came into the diner,* wouldn't you? Here are a few other examples:

He's such a nice, young man. (determiner + opinion/quality + age)

We replaced **the dirty, old, green** shingles last year. (determiner + opinion/quality + age + color)

My favorite blanket is **the blue, checkered, fleece** one. (determiner + color + pattern + material)

Developmental Notes

Children's first 50 words typically contain several modifiers; these may be considered the earliest adjectives acquired. Commonly occurring modifiers in the speech of very young children frequently include descriptive adjectives like *big, hot, dirty,* and *cold.* Overall, however, modifiers may constitute only a small percentage of children's earliest words (approximately 10%, according to Nelson, 1973), especially as compared to nouns (nominals) and verbs (action words). In fact, studies of infants and toddlers show that adjectives are rarely contained in children's vocabularies until after they have acquired at least 100 words (Caselli et al., 1995).

Children's early two-word combinations, which begin to emerge at approximately 18 months of age, reflect moderate use of early adjectives, which are often referred to during this stage as *attributes*. Examples of adjectives seen in this period—in combination with early nominals—may include *big candy, dirty sock,* and *Mommy pretty*.

The emergence of three-word combinations follows a similar pattern (e.g., *eat big candy, wash dirty sock,* and *Mommy look pretty*). Common modifiers children might use at this time include *big, tall, soft,* and *heavy,* which often emerge at approximately 30 months of age. Their opposites, such as *little, short, hard,* and *light,* are typically acquired a short time later, between the ages of 36 and 48 months of age (Kent, 1994). Within this time period, several new phrase-level patterns emerge with respect to children's use of adjectival modifiers (Crystal, Fletcher, & Garman, 1974). Specifically, children's three-word utterances reflect the following formats:

Noun + Adjective + Noun (e.g., *Mommy pretty hat*)

Adjective + Adjective + Noun (e.g., *big, black dog*)

Demonstrative + Adjective + Noun (e.g., *that pretty kitty*)

As children begin to produce four-word utterances, even more complex patterns emerge, such as "Preposition + Article/Determiner + Adjective + Noun" (e.g., *in the little house*). Common pairs of adjectives acquired during this period, beginning at about 3 years of age, include *same* and *different, empty* and *full,* and *high* and *low*. Children's noun phrase elaboration occurs for nouns in the subject and object positions (Crystal et al., 1974).

Children's elaboration of noun phrases through adjectival use continues through the preschool years, and during this period children refine their understanding of joining adjectives in a series (e.g., *the old, cranky woman*) and of the positioning of adjectives within complex noun phrases, as in *I only want that other green one*. Throughout the course of early childhood, descriptive adjectives comprise about 15% of children's spoken language. Some evidence suggests that this percentage increases only slightly, to about 20%, as children move into school age (Davis, 1938). At 9 years of age, for example, descriptive adjectives comprise about 19% of children's spontaneous speech. As children age, their comprehension of adjectives systematically improves (see Nippold & Sun, 2008). In fact, by about age 9, the child begins to understand (at a 60% level) the meaning of the derivational suffixes *-ette, -ize, -ful, -like,* and *-able,* but has full understanding of the suffix *-less*. The child at this age produces these suffixes at a level that is half as accurate as what an adult would produce. By about age 13, however, the adolescent comprehends these derivational suffixes at a level approaching adult understanding, but use of these suffixes is still less accurate than adult accuracy (Windsor, 1994).

CHAPTER EXERCISES

Exercise 4A

Underline all the descriptive and limiting adjectives in the following sentences.

1. Missy's story was a fascinating account of her father's life.
2. Plan to find a well-paying job after you graduate.
3. Please call Jeffrey's mom about the used clothing.
4. The story was told by a very well-known folk singer.
5. Rabbits always look after their young.
6. Please clean your room.
7. I study for this class.
8. She is applying for the modeling position.
9. You can go to the new exhibition; however, I will not pay.
10. The preschool children were excited about the substitute teacher.

Exercise 4B

List the comparative and superlative forms of the following positive adjective forms.

Positive	Comparative	Superlative
1. *good*	_____	_____
2. *bad*	_____	_____
3. *new*	_____	_____
4. *scared*	_____	_____
5. *shiny*	_____	_____
6. *far*	_____	_____
7. *concerned*	_____	_____
8. *few*	_____	_____
9. *prestigious*	_____	_____
10. *ugly*	_____	_____

Exercise 4C

Consider the following narrative produced by a 4-year-old child while looking at a wordless picture book. Underline all the descriptive adjectives.

Well, the boy's dog got the jar on his head. The little boy's looking for the little green froggie. The dog being mean to that little boy. The dog fell out the window. He's looking in that deep, deep hole. It's dark. Dog's trying to climb that big tree. The boy falls out the tree. The dog runs. The little boy climbs that big tall rock. And he howls. And that big moose knocks them off. He's in the cold water. That water is cold. He climbs on that broken log. He sees a lot of baby frogs. He sees them sitting on the log. The end.

Exercise 4D

1. Examine the following narrative produced by a 7-year-old child. Underline all the descriptive adjectives.

   Once there was a beautiful girl and she had a rich, mean father. Her mean father wouldn't let the beautiful girl get married. Then there was a handsome young prince and he said, "Will you marry me?" The girl said she couldn't because of her mean dad. The prince went very fast to talk to her dad. It took a long time, but the dad finally said yes. The prince and the pretty lady got married in a big, white castle. And they went far away to a new country, where they lived in a big house the prince's dad gave them.

2. Determine the proportion of words that are adjectives in comparison to all the other types of words produced in the above narrative.

   - Count the total number of adjectives used and write it in the blank below.
   - Count the total number of words produced and write it in the blank below.
   - Divide the total number of adjectives used by the total number of words produced.
   - Multiply this total by 100 to obtain the percent of adjectives used.

Calculating the Proportion of Adjectives

_____ ÷ _____ = _____ × 100 = _____ % Adjectives
Total number   Total number
of adjectives   of words

---

3. Compare this child's proportion of adjectives to what you would expect of a typical 7-year-old child.

   _____

Exercise 4E

1. A preschooler with a language disorder may demonstrate delayed acquisition of adjectival modifiers. A language goal for such a child may look something like this:

   Given a verbal model, the child will produce three-word utterances in the form of "Verb + Adjective + Noun" or "Article + Adjective + Noun." (For the latter, use *a*, *an*, or *the* as articles.)

   Provide examples of utterances a child might produce that would meet these goals.

   Verb + Adjective + Noun

   _____

   _____

   Article + Adjective + Noun (use *a*, *an*, or *the* for the article)

   _____

   _____

2. What activity could you do to elicit these types of utterances?

   _____

   _____

Exercise 4F

A language interventionist (LI) is working with a 3-year-old child with a language disorder. An analysis of the child's spontaneous language indicated the presence of very few adjectival modifiers. The interventionist wants to model the use of select adjectives for the child so that the child might increase her receptive understanding of these terms.

The particular strategy that the LI decides to use to increase this child's exposure to adjectival modifiers is that of expanding. (An *expansion* is when utterances produced by the child are repeated and embellished by the LI to provide additional grammatical and/or lexical information.) In this case, the LI will expand by adding adjectival modifiers to the child's utterances. For example, if the child says *blue ball*, the LI might say *big, blue ball*.

For each of the child's utterances below, give an example of an expansion that the LI might produce to enhance the child's awareness of an adjective.

1. Child: *her got one*
   LI: _____
2. Child: *give me that*
   LI: _____
3. Child: *Bobby give me that*
   LI: _____
4. Child: *that book*
   LI: _____
5. Child: *Pooh go toot-toot*
   LI: _____
6. Child: *Pooh don't wanna go*
   LI: _____
7. Child: *Pooh said that*
   LI: _____
8. Child: *go to Pooh's party*
   LI: _____

Exercise 4G

Read the following transcript, in which a language interventionist and children are engaged in an activity centered on adjectives. Underline the adjectives the children produced.

LI: What was the description word, T?

T: He has itchy hands!

LI: Yeah, go ahead and pick your next card.

T: The blonde-haired girl who was wearing a blue shirt is kicking the soccer ball toward the net.

K: Three people are camping next to a fire with marshmallows.

LI: Very good.

T: Sometimes at night when people go camping, they marsh marshmallows.

LI: They marsh marshmallows? It starts with a /r/.

T: They melt them.

K: Roast them.

E: The little family is roasting marshmallows on the big, hot fire.

J: People who like to camp eat marshmallows.

LI: A good sentence, but where's your description word?

J: I don't know.

LI: What do they look like?

J: Happy marshmallows.

LI: Happy marshmallows? No.

T: We can roast marshmallows.

LI: Roasted.

ANSWER KEY

Exercise 4A

1. <u>Missy's</u> story was <u>a fascinating</u> account of <u>her father's</u> life.
2. Plan to find <u>a well-paying</u> job after you graduate.
3. Please call <u>Jeffrey's</u> mom about <u>the used</u> clothing.
4. <u>The</u> story was told by <u>a</u> very <u>well-known folk</u> singer.
5. Rabbits always look after <u>their</u> young.
6. Please clean <u>your</u> room.
7. I study for <u>this</u> class.
8. She is applying for <u>the modeling</u> position.
9. You can go to <u>the new</u> exhibition; however, I will not pay.
10. <u>The preschool</u> children were excited about <u>the substitute</u> teacher.

Exercise 4B

Positive	Comparative	Superlative
1. *good*	better	best
2. *bad*	worse	worst
3. *new*	newer	newest
4. *scared*	more scared	most scared
5. *shiny*	shinier	shiniest
6. *far*	farther	farthest
7. *concerned*	more concerned	most concerned
8. *few*	fewer	fewest
9. *prestigious*	more prestigious	most prestigious
10. *ugly*	uglier	ugliest

Exercise 4C

Well, the boy's dog got the jar on his head. The <u>little</u> boy's looking for the <u>little green</u> froggie. The dog being mean to that <u>little</u> boy. The dog fell out the window. He's looking in that <u>deep</u>, <u>deep</u> hole. It's <u>dark</u>. Dog's trying to climb that <u>big</u> tree. The boy falls out the tree. The dog runs. The <u>little</u> boy climbs that <u>big tall</u> rock. And he howls. And that <u>big</u> moose knocks them off. He's in the <u>cold</u> water. That water is <u>cold</u>. He climbs on that <u>broken</u> log. He sees a lot of <u>baby</u> frogs. He sees them sitting on the log. The end.

Exercise 4D

1. Once there was a <u>beautiful</u> girl and she had a <u>rich</u>, <u>mean</u> father. Her <u>mean</u> father wouldn't let the <u>beautiful</u> girl get married. Then there was a <u>handsome young</u> prince and he said, "Will you marry me?" The girl said she couldn't because of her <u>mean</u> dad. The prince went very fast to talk to her dad. It took a <u>long</u> time, but the dad finally said yes. The prince and the <u>pretty</u> lady got married in a <u>big</u>, <u>white</u> castle. And they went far away to a <u>new</u> country, where they lived in a <u>big</u> house the prince's dad gave them.

2. $14 \div 102 = .14 \times 100 = 14\%$ Adjectives

3. Typically, adjectives comprise about 20% of the total words used by school-age children (Davis, 1938), so this 7-year-old's production of adjectives is less than what you'd expect.

Exercise 4G

LI: What was the description word, T?

T: He has <u>itchy</u> hands!

LI: Yeah, go ahead and pick your next card.

T: <u>The blonde-haired</u> girl who was wearing <u>a blue</u> shirt is kicking <u>the soccer</u> ball toward <u>the</u> net.

K: <u>Three</u> people are camping next to <u>a</u> fire with marshmallows.

LI: Very good.

T: Sometimes at night when people go camping, they marsh marshmallows.

LI: They marsh marshmallows? It starts with a /r/.

T: They melt them.

K: Roast them.

E: <u>The little</u> family is roasting marshmallows on <u>the big, hot</u> fire.

J: People who like to camp eat marshmallows.

LI: A good sentence, but where's your description word?

J: I don't know.

LI: What do they look like?

J: <u>Happy</u> marshmallows.

LI: Happy marshmallows? No.

T: We can roast marshmallows.

LI: Roasted.

CHAPTER FIVE

Adverbs

Chapter at a Glance

What Is an Adverb?

Simple and Compound Adverbs

Positive, Comparative, and Superlative Forms

Adverb Types

- Manner
- Place
- Time
- Degree
- Number
- Reason
- Affirmation
- Negation

Conjunctive Adverbs

Developmental Notes

Chapter Exercises

Answer Key

What Is an Adverb?

Adverbs, like adjectives, serve to modify elements in a sentence and so are also considered *modifiers*. Whereas adjectives modify nouns and pronouns, adverbs modify verbs, adjectives, and other adverbs, as seen in these three examples:

> She thought **quickly**. (*quickly* modifies the verb *thought*)
>
> The coat is **too** ugly. (*too* modifies the adjective *ugly*)
>
> We are **almost** there. (*almost* modifies the adverb *there*)

Generally speaking, adverbs provide information about manner, place, time, degree, number, and reason. In addition, adverbs are often used to affirm and to negate. Let's look at some examples of adverbs providing this sort of information:

> We **laboriously** placed the mice back in their cages. (manner)
>
> Please put the boxes **here** until they all arrive. (place)
>
> We went **early** to the party so that we could help. (time)
>
> I was **pretty** tired after the race. (degree)
>
> Sally will **first** explain how she got that answer. (number)
>
> **Because** she hit the dog, Jill is in time-out. (reason)
>
> **Indeed**, we have been waiting on you. (affirmation)
>
> Tommy has **never** been to the Grand Canyon. (negation)

In some cases, adverbs (particularly adverbs of degree) may be confused with adjectives. This confusion most often occurs when adverbs modify adjectives, as in *Jennifer is really tired*. In such situations, you might make the common mistake of characterizing both *really* and *tired* as adjectives, when, in fact, *really* is an adverb that is modifying the predicate adjective *tired*. Common degree adverbs (and those for which such confusion often occurs) include *very, quite, rather, really, so, somewhat, too, often, much,* and *terribly* (Master, 1995).

Adverbs are more flexible than adjectives in terms of placement within a sentence since adverbs can occur in any position. Regardless of positioning, however, adverbs are always linked most significantly to a single word in the sentence, referred to as the **head word** (Williams, 1999). A head word is the word (usually a verb) modified by the adverb. Generally, adverbs are positioned as close to the head word as possible, although this is not always the case, as with the following examples, in which the adverbs occur in various places. Can you identify the head word in these three sentences?

> **Effortlessly**, she completed the exercise.
>
> She **effortlessly** completed the exercise.
>
> She completed the exercise **effortlessly**.

The head word is *she*, right? Wrong. (Sorry!) The verb *completed* is the head word for each of these sentences. The adverb *effortlessly*, regardless of its positioning, is describing how (in what manner) the action (*completed*) was performed.

Adverbs are one of the more difficult word classes to describe. Many words are classified as adverbs because they do not seem to fit neatly into any other category (Master, 1995). A number of adverbs can easily be identified by the appearance of the suffix *-ly*. (There was an example of this in that last sentence; can you spot it? Yep! It's . . . Wait a minute. Did you really look back to find it, or are you just reading this to get the answer? Just for that, we're not going to tell you the answer.) A number of other common adverbs do not use the handy *-ly* suffix, such as *fast* and *well*, making them more difficult to spot. (Okay, okay, you wore us down. The answer was *easily*.)

Simple and Compound Adverbs

Simple adverbs are single words. The majority of simple adverbs are formed by adding the suffix *-ly* to a word stem, as in these two examples:

The letter was written so **courteously** that I couldn't believe it was from John.

I suppose *syntax moron* is not a **politically** correct term.

Adverbs may also be formed by adding three other adverbial suffixes (Stageberg, 1981). You could add *-wise* to a noun, as with these two sentences:

Play continues **clockwise**.

The report met the requirements **wordwise**, but it was lousy.

You could add the suffix *-ward* to a noun, as these examples illustrate:

He looked **skyward** for an answer.

We finally steered the boat **shoreward**.

And you could add *-s* to a noun, as shown here:

I have class only **Tuesdays** and **Thursdays** this semester.

Mornings I'm busy, but **afternoons** I'm free.

We know what you're thinking . . . Those highlighted words in the examples above look like plural nouns. But they are actually adverbs that answer the questions of when you have class and when you are busy or free.

Compound adverbs are constructed from two words, joined either by combining two words or by hyphenating two words or a prefix and a word. There are not too many of these, and some examples include *counterclockwise, counterintuitively,* and *contralaterally.* Can you think of some more examples of compound adverbs?

Some adverbs commonly occur as groups of words, such as *over there, very early,* and *too much*. One way of looking at such constituents is that the first adverb is modifying the second adverb in the pair. Such groupings may be more accurately referred to as *adverb phrases* and are described more thoroughly in Chapter 10.

Positive, Comparative, and Superlative Forms

Like adjectives, adverbs can vary their form so as to reference one entity (the positive form), to compare two entities (the comparative degree), or to compare three or more entities (the superlative degree).

The **positive form** of adverbs usually is one of three varieties (Leech, 1991):

- The adverbial form is made by adding a suffix to an adjectival form.
- The adverbial form is the same as its adjectival counterpart.
- The adverbial form is the only form in which it occurs.

The first variety was alluded to earlier, in which the suffix *-ly* is added to an adjective. These adverbs are the easiest to recognize and include such words as *easily, happily,* and *completely*. Here are two examples of *-ly* adverbs used in sentences:

She **slowly** bowed as the crowd began clapping.

My father always tells me to drive **carefully**.

It is important to note, though, that not all words ending in *-ly* are adverbs. Words like *silly* and *lovely* are actually adjectives that just happen to end in *-ly*. Therefore, in the following sentence, there is only one adverb, even though there are two words that end in the *-ly* suffix:

The silly girl jumped through the hoop **sillily**.

The second variety of adverbs are those that use the same form as their adjectival counterparts, meaning that the same word can be used as both an adjective and an adverb. Common words in this group include *early, late, pretty, north, west, left, right, forward,* and *backward*. Examples of their use in sentences follow:

Early risers always get the worm! (adjective)

She wants to get there **early**. (adverb)

She didn't think it would turn out so **pretty**! (adjective)

I feel **pretty** good about what we have accomplished. (adverb)

The third variety of adverbs is a set of words that simply needs to be recognized as adverbs. These include such words as *so, too, there, here,* and *very.* Here are a few examples:

I will play the song **too**.

He drives **so very** slowly.

Now consider the positive, comparative, and superlative degrees of the adverb *furiously* in the following examples:

Lee pedaled **furiously**.

Lee pedaled **more furiously** than Allen.

Ginger pedaled **most furiously** of all.

The positive form is *furiously.* The **comparative degree** is formed by adding either *more* or *less* in front of the positive form of the adverb (*more furiously*). The **superlative degree** is formed by adding either *most* or *least* in front of the positive form of the adverb (*most furiously*). Some common exceptions to these formation rules are adverbs that have the same form as their adjective counterparts, which instead form the comparative and superlative degree by adding *-er* and *-est* (e.g., *Lin arrived earliest to the party*) and adverbs such as *badly,* which form the comparative and superlative degree irregularly like their adjective counterparts (e.g., *I did badly on the syntax quiz, but Dora did worse*).

Adverb Types

The following provides an overview of the major categories of adverbs, based on work by Opdycke (1965). These categories include adverbs of manner, place, time, degree, number, reason, affirmation, and negation. Table 5.1 lists examples of each type of adverb.

TABLE 5.1
Examples of Major Adverb Types

ADVERB TYPES	EXAMPLES
Manner	*quickly, particularly, well*
Place	*here, near, outside*
Time	*before, immediately, once*
Degree	*more, nearly, very*
Number	*first, secondly, seventh*
Reason	*because, consequently, since*
Affirmation	*absolutely, indeed, yes*
Negation	*never, no, not*

Manner

Adverbs of manner answer the questions *How?* and *In what way?* and also indicate aspects of quality. Manner adverbs include many of the *-ly* adverbs (e.g., *lazily, slowly,* and *particularly*) as well as *anyway, how, however, somehow,* and *well*; here are two examples of sentences containing adverbs of manner:

> The way she drives so **slowly** drives me crazy.
>
> The cost was divided **evenly** amongst us all.

Place

Adverbs of place answer the question *Where?* These adverbs include words like *about, anywhere, around, behind, here, nowhere, near, on, outside, there, upon, where, within,* and *without*. A subclass of place adverbs, sometimes referred to as *adverbs of direction*, also answer the question *Where?* and are typically used when preparing directions. These include *above, back, below, forward, onward,* and *out*. Here are two sentence examples depicting use of adverbs of place:

> Put that **there**.
>
> They hid **below** during the storm.

Time

Adverbs of time are used to provide information related to duration and frequency of events. In general, adverbs of time answer the questions *How long? When?* and *How often?* Such adverbs include *after, again, already, always, before, immediately, instantly, lately, now, once, presently, rarely, today, weekly,* and *while*. Here are examples of sentences containing adverbs of time:

> She is late **again**.
>
> I see him **weekly** for advice.

Degree

Adverbs of degree are used to answer the question *How much?* Such adverbs include *all, almost, barely, besides, equally, even, evenly, little, much, more, most, nearly, only, quite, really, some, surely,* and *very,* as seen in these examples:

> The coffee here is **really quite** strong.
>
> The dress **almost** fit.

Number

Adverbs of number provide information about the order of events and include words like *first*, *second*, and *third*. They may also be formed by adding *-ly* to cardinal numbers, as in *secondly* and *thirdly*. The two sentences here illustrate use of adverbs of number:

First, she will need to fill out a time sheet.

Secondly, I will ask that you all close your books.

Reason

Adverbs of reason are used to answer the questions *Why?* and *What was the cause?* The adverbs of reason include words like *consequently, therefore, thus, because,* and *hence*, as shown here in these examples:

Sales have been strong this year; **consequently**, many of you will receive a bonus.

Because it rained, the trip was canceled.

Affirmation

Adverbs of affirmation express agreement, approval, or assent. Examples include *absolutely, certainly, definitely, indeed, really, surely,* and *truly*. *Yes* also falls into this category, as seen here in these examples:

I will **certainly** help you with that!

Yes, the results were sent home to the parents.

Negation

Adverbs of negation are used to indicate denial. These include *no, not,* and *never*, as seen here:

He **never** drinks two cups of coffee at home!

That is simply **not** true.

Conjunctive Adverbs

Adverbs may also serve as conjunctions (covered in Chapter 7), which are then known as **conjunctive adverbs** or **adverbial conjuncts**. Conjunctions join two or more sentence elements, and many adverbs serve such a role. Conjunctive adverbs include words like *accordingly, also,* and *however.* Additional examples are provided in Table 5.2.

Conjunctive adverbs are easy to spot because they are often preceded by a semicolon and followed by a comma, as in the following examples:

I was broke; **still**, I felt I needed to buy a new car.

We were broke; **consequently**, we were not able to buy a new car.

It is important to recognize the conjunctive role often played by adverbs. However, note that not all conjunctions are adverbs. (Conjunctions are more thoroughly described in Chapter 7. Feel free to go there now if you just can't wait to learn more!)

Developmental Notes

Adverbs rarely occur in the speech of very young children. As noted in Chapter 4, modifiers (including both adjectives and adverbs) comprise only about 10% of the first 50 words in children's vocabulary, and the majority of these are best classified as adjectival forms (Nelson, 1973). The earliest adverbial modifiers to be observed usually include *here* and *there,* which are deictic terms that specify information about place. (Deictic terms rely on the position of the speaker to the listener for both use and interpretation.) This developmental trend of early preferences for simple adverbs that denote place has similarly been observed in young children's beginning use of adverb phrases, such as *on top* or *in here* (deVilliers & deVilliers, 1978).

Early two-word combinations may reflect the use of these early adverbial place modifiers in such constructions as *baby there* or *here Mommy.* These are sometimes called *protoadverbials* (the precursors to true adverbial use). Although children may use these items in early sentences, they often experience difficulties with use due to listener perspective; that is, the child may use the term *here* but mean *there* (Clark & Sengul,

TABLE 5.2
Common Conjunctive Adverbs

accordingly	*further*	*likewise*	*so that*
additionally	*furthermore*	*moreover*	*still*
also	*hence*	*nevertheless*	*that is*
alternatively	*however*	*notwithstanding*	*then*
besides	*in addition*	*on the contrary*	*therefore*
consequently	*in contrast*	*otherwise*	*thus*
even so	*in fact*	*rather*	
for example	*indeed*	*similarly*	

1978). This may be because young children have difficulties with perspective taking (i.e., taking the perspective of another individual).

Within the fourth year of life, many children begin to use time markers more frequently and specifically. The earliest adverbial markers to designate time of action typically include *tomorrow* and *yesterday* (see Owens, 2012). Subsequently, children begin to use other adverbial terms, such as *before, later,* and *after*. The use of these adverbial markers seems to correspond to increasing understanding, in general, of terms used to mark the temporal order of things, whether they are adverbs or other syntactic forms, such as conjunctions (we'll discuss these in Chapter 7). For instance, between 3 and 7 years of age, children are improving their understanding of the terms *after* and *before* when used as connectives in sentences (e.g., *Janet hit him before she ran away*) (Feagans, 1980).

There has been limited examination of adverbial comprehension and production in older children, although Nippold (2007) notes that children's understanding of adverbs continues to mature throughout the school years. By about 10 years of age, many children master adverbs of likelihood, such as *possibly* versus *definitely* and *possibly* versus *probably*. Children's comprehension of adverbs of magnitude, such as *slight, quite,* and *decidedly,* also gradually improves during adolescence. These findings suggest that expressive and receptive knowledge of adverbial form and function may not be complete until late adolescence.

CHAPTER EXERCISES

Exercise 5A

Consider the following story produced by a 5-year-old child. Underline all the adverbs.

That's a frog there. And the kid's looking in it to see if stuff was there. He's now trying to jump up here. He's going faster. This one already on. He's going faster and faster. He's very fast now! He's trying to go there. Now that's a frog in his hand. That boy's really happy now. But he'll never do that again.

Exercise 5B

Identify each underlined adverb as one of the following: Manner (M), Place (P), Time (T), Degree (D), Number (N), Reason (R), Affirmation (A), or Negation (NG).

_____ 1. Since I was sick, I went to bed <u>early</u>.
_____ 2. <u>Yes</u>, I never saw him.
_____ 3. She feels <u>absolutely</u> ready for this.
_____ 4. I <u>never</u> had to take the GRE.
_____ 5. We <u>carefully</u> climbed down the cliff to reach the water.
_____ 6. They were a good deal; <u>consequently</u>, we bought them.
_____ 7. <u>As soon as</u> a James Taylor concert is announced, he'll be in line.
_____ 8. She <u>really</u> knows what she's talking about!
_____ 9. I have been looking <u>all over</u> for this!
_____ 10. This is the <u>first</u> opportunity I've had to relax.

Exercise 5C

Identify each underlined word as either an Adverb (A) or an Adverbial Conjunct (AC).

_____ 1. <u>Suddenly</u>, she realized what she needed to do.
_____ 2. <u>Before</u> joining the circus, she was an accountant.
_____ 3. We will have more guests than we expected; <u>accordingly</u>, we need to order more food.
_____ 4. I run into him everywhere I go; <u>in fact</u>, I ran into him at Subway.
_____ 5. Cayden is <u>truly</u> one of the sweetest children I know.
_____ 6. This torte is absolutely wonderful; <u>likewise</u>, the cake is delicious.

_____ 7. The power went out; <u>consequently</u>, I missed my morning class.
_____ 8. The assets of the will were <u>equally</u> divided among the heirs.
_____ 9. I'm not a proponent; <u>rather</u>, I'm an opponent.
_____ 10. I am <u>really</u> looking forward to Friday.

Exercise 5D

Write a sentence using an adverbial conjunct that joins the two sentences in each pair.

1. I want to go to Columbia. The political situation is unstable.
   _____
   _____

2. I adore wine and cheese. We are having it at the gala tomorrow night.
   _____
   _____

3. Every year we vacation in Florida. This year we're going to Mexico.
   _____
   _____

4. Brady has been diagnosed with apraxia of speech. Unfamiliar listeners have no trouble understanding him.
   _____
   _____

5. I need to get some gas. I'll be walking to the lab.
   _____
   _____

6. Sarah is strikingly gorgeous. She always has plenty of admirers.
   _____
   _____

7. Stewart thought Melissa didn't like him. She liked him very much.
   _____
   _____

8. John likes sports. He plays baseball, football, and golf.
   _____
   _____

9. The movie was not very good. It was the worst movie I've ever seen.
   _____
   _____

10. There are fewer and fewer wolves in Wisconsin. They are becoming extinct.
    _____
    _____

Exercise 5E

1. Examine the following story told by a 4-year-old child. Underline all the adverbs.

   That's his house there. They had a doggie too. Then the dog fell down. He's crying. He very angry. Now he go outside. The dog left now. The dog can't get out. He's pulling fast. Now he's pulling hard. Oops! He fell. The boy is in the boat now. The dog got in the water. And he did too.

2. Determine the proportion of words that are adverbs in comparison to all the other types of words produced in the above story.

   - Count the total number of adverbs used and write it in the blank below.
   - Count the total number of words produced and write it in the blank below.
   - Divide the total number of adverbs used by the total number of words produced.
   - Multiply this total by 100 to obtain the percent of adverbs used.

   Calculating the Proportion of Adverbs

   _____ ÷ _____ = _____ × 100 = _____ % Adverbs
   Total number   Total number
   of adverbs   of words

3. What proportion of adverbs would you expect for a 4-year-old child?

   _____

ANSWER KEY

Exercise 5A

That's a frog <u>there</u>. And the kid's looking in it to see if stuff was <u>there</u>. He's <u>now</u> trying to jump up <u>here</u>. He's going <u>faster</u>. This one <u>already</u> on. He's going <u>faster</u> and <u>faster</u>. He's <u>very</u> fast <u>now</u>! He's trying to go <u>there</u>. <u>Now</u> that's a frog in his hand. That boy's <u>really</u> happy <u>now</u>. But he'll <u>never</u> do that <u>again</u>.

Exercise 5B

1. T
2. A
3. D
4. NG
5. M
6. R
7. T
8. D
9. P
10. N

Exercise 5C

1. A
2. A
3. AC
4. AC
5. A
6. AC
7. AC
8. A
9. AC
10. A

Exercise 5E

1. That's his house <u>there</u>. They had a doggie <u>too</u>. Then the dog fell <u>down</u>. He's crying. He <u>very</u> angry. <u>Now</u> he go <u>outside</u>. The dog left <u>now</u>. The dog can't get <u>out</u>. He's pulling <u>fast</u>. <u>Now</u> he's pulling <u>hard</u>. Oops! He fell. The boy is in the boat <u>now</u>. The dog got in the water. And he did <u>too</u>.

2. $13 \div 62 = .21 \times 100 = 21\%$ Adverbs

3. At least 7%

CHAPTER SIX

Determiners

Chapter at a Glance

What Is a Determiner?

Articles

Possessives

Demonstratives

Quantifiers

Wh- Words

Developmental Notes

Chapter Exercises

Answer Key

What Is a Determiner?

Many nouns, when occurring in phrases and sentences, have not only adjectives serving to provide additional information about them, but also determiners to do this job as well. Nouns occurring within noun phrases are often preceded by at least one determiner, which serves to clarify aspects of the noun. In fact, noun phrases can contain several determiners. The major categories of determiners are articles (definite and indefinite articles), possessives (possessive nouns and possessive pronouns), demonstratives, quantifiers, and *wh-* words. See Table 6.1 for examples.

    The role of the **determiner** is important since it "determines the grammatical reality of the noun to which it is attached" (Master, 1995, p. 213). For example, the noun *cat* has only limited meaning until we attach determiners to it, allowing us to specify exactly which cat we are discussing: <u>that</u> *cat,* <u>the one</u> *cat,* and so on.

TABLE 6.1
Determiner Categories

CATEGORY	EXAMPLES
Articles	*a, an, the*
Possessives	*my, his, their, man's, Janet's*
Demonstratives	*this, that, those*
Quantifiers	*every, nine, another*
Wh- Words	*what, whatever, whichever*

Determiners are akin to limiting adjectives in that they modify nouns; however, determiners are limited in the modifications they can make. Determiners can also look suspiciously like pronouns at times, with an important exception: Determiners, by nature, cannot exist outside a noun phrase; pronouns can.

It's likely you'll get confused as you try to classify a given word into the category of determiner, adjective, or pronoun. Suffice it to say that your confusion is warranted. And to make matters worse, there is often overlap between these three categories. For example, several possessives (some of which may also be considered limiting adjectives, such as *his*) are able to serve as both pronouns and determiners, with categorization dependent on their place within a sentence, as in the following examples:

The coat is **his**. (possessive pronoun)

His coat is on the hanger. (possessive as a determiner/limiting adjective)

Some scholars (e.g., Opdycke, 1965) would characterize *his* in the second example sentence as a limiting adjective; others would consider it a determiner (e.g., Hoff-Ginsberg, 1997; Retherford, 2000). Both sides could be argued well, but ultimately, neither side would win, because *his* is being used as an adjective to modify the noun *coat*, but *his* is, in fact, also a determiner. (Can't we all just agree to disagree?)

Articles

The most commonly used determiners are the articles *a* and *the*. A third article is *an*, which occurs less frequently. These three articles are divided into two categories: definite and indefinite. The **definite article** *the* is used in reference to a specific entity. In contrast, the **indefinite articles** *a* and *an* are used to refer to nonspecific entities. The use of *a* and *an* are based on the phonetic contexts in which they appear. That is, use *a* before words that begin with a consonant sound (e.g., *bird*, *tie*, and *monkey*); use *an* before words that begin with a vowel sound (e.g., *apple, hour,* and *itch*). Consider the difference in the use of the three articles highlighted in the following examples:

> **A** cat is stalking the birds by the fountain.
>
> **An** orange cat is stalking the birds by the fountain.
>
> **The** cat is stalking the birds by the fountain.

In the first and second examples, the cat is a nonspecific entity. It could refer to any cat—your cat, my cat, the neighbor's cat, the Cat in the Hat. In contrast, the cat in the third example is a known and specific entity. We know this because the speaker's use of the word *the* implies that the listener knows exactly which cat is doing the stalking. (Perhaps because earlier in the conversation, the speaker identified the cat.) What it boils down to is this: Indicate that information is new by using the indefinite articles *a* or *an*. Then, after the information is no longer new, switch to the definite article *the,* as in the following example:

> I have to tell you about **a** party I went to. At **the** party, there was this strange man who . . .

Possessives

Possessives can be divided into two types: possessive nouns and possessive pronouns. Both common and proper **possessive nouns** can serve as determiners. Here are a few examples:

> **Students'** syntactic analysis skills can improve if they read this book. (possessive common noun as a determiner)
>
> **John's** green apple is in the bag. (possessive proper noun as a determiner)

The **possessive pronouns** *my, your, his, her, its, our,* and *their* may serve as determiners. The remaining possessive pronouns (*mine, yours, hers, ours,* and *theirs*) cannot serve as determiners. (You wouldn't say *Mine pen just ran out ink,* would you?)

Remember from Chapter 2 that when possessive pronouns stand alone, they are not determiners (which modify nouns), as in both of the following:

> That apple is **his**. (possessive as a pronoun)
>
> You need to give it to **her**. (possessive as a pronoun)

In the following examples, however, the possessives are acting as determiners, modifying the subsequent nouns (*apple* and *purse*):

> **His** green apple is in the bag. (possessive as a determiner)
>
> **Her** little purse was stolen. (possessive as a determiner)

Demonstratives

Demonstratives also can serve as determiners. Recall from Chapter 2 that these include *this, that, these,* and *those*. The demonstrative determiners *this* and *these* refer to entities that are close to the speaker, whereas the demonstrative determiners *that* and *those* refer to entities that are farther away from the speaker. Similar to possessives, demonstratives can stand alone to take the place of nouns; in such cases, they are not serving as determiners, but as demonstrative pronouns. This is the case with the following examples:

> You need to put **those** in the water. (demonstrative as a pronoun)
>
> Give me **that**. (demonstrative as a pronoun)

In the following examples, however, the demonstratives are serving in the role of determiner. Recall that in Chapter 4, we referred to these as *demonstrative adjectives,* but you will more commonly come to know demonstratives used in this way as *determiners*:

> **Those** little blue ones are the ones that she wanted. (demonstrative as a determiner)
>
> It was **that** boy who was crying. (demonstrative as a determiner)

Quantifiers

There is an array of words that serve as determiners to provide additional information regarding quantity. A number of these words can also serve as pronouns, adverbs, and adjectives. Thus, it is important to understand when a particular form is serving as a determiner. Again, determiners always introduce and elaborate on a noun phrase. Quantifiers include words like *all, any, both, every, first, each, either, few, less, neither, three, another, no, some, more, most,* and *never*. Here are a few examples of quantifiers as used in sentences:

> I need **more** coffee before the day begins. (quantifier as a determiner)
>
> Jen needs **another** green piece to finish the puzzle. (quantifier as a determiner)
>
> **Every** Wednesday I buy **two** lottery tickets. (quantifier as a determiner)

Note that determiners precede not only nouns, but adjectives as well, as in the second example sentence. Remember also that many quantifiers can serve other roles. In the following examples, two of the quantifiers used in the previous examples are used in the role of pronoun, not determiner:

> **More** is never better. (quantifier as a pronoun)
>
> May I have **another**? (quantifier as a pronoun)

Wh- Words

A number of *wh-* words can serve in the role of determiner. This means that these words can modify a noun or a pronoun. In other situations, however, *wh-* words are not serving such a role (e.g., *What is your name?*). The *wh-* words that are often seen in a determiner role include *what, which, whose, whatever,* and *whichever.* In the following examples, these words are serving the role of determiner:

Which one do you want?

What flavor are you having?

I'll have **whichever** kind of coffee you have.

Developmental Notes

Children's acquisition of several types of determiners has already been described in earlier chapters. For example, it was noted in Chapter 2 that children often acquire the pronoun *my* in Brown's (1973) Stage II (27–30 months of age). When this form is used to introduce a noun, it would be considered an early use of a determiner. Likewise, children typically begin to use the articles *the* and *a* in Brown's Stage II. In fact, these two articles are included in Brown's definitive chronology of young children's acquisition of the 14 major grammatical morphemes.

Research conducted by deVilliers and deVilliers (1973) further substantiated Brown's observations. These researchers showed that as children's chronological age and mean length of utterance (MLU) increased over the second and third year of life, children increased their obligatory use of these two articles. For example, at age 2 years, the children studied by deVilliers and deVilliers used *a* and *the* in only about 6% of obligatory contexts. By age 4, however, children used these articles in about 90% of obligatory contexts. Their data suggest that children master use of these determiners by about 4 years of age.

In very early language development, children's use of the indefinite article *a* tends to predominate over use of *the*. Children at these early ages don't seem to choose between these articles on the basis of rules; rather, their use seems to be somewhat indiscriminate. By 3 years of age, most children are able to discriminate between the appropriate usage of the two articles as determiners, but there is a tendency to overuse the article *the* (Emslie & Stevenson, 1981).

When a child begins to use determiners, he or she is elaborating on the use of nouns by creating noun phrases. Until that time, or until he or she begins using determiners, the child's speech will sound incomplete, with a telegraphic quality. Elaborated noun phrases typically become more prevalent in the latter half of the second year, in Brown's Stage III. By this time, determiners of various categories often begin to be observed, including articles (*a, the*), possessive pronouns (*my, your*), demonstratives (*this, that, these, those*), and quantifiers (*more, some, two*) (see Brown, 1973). Determiners continue to be acquired as lexical items, although by 3 years of age, children have a fairly sophisticated understanding of the placement of determiners in a grammatical sense. After 3 years of age, children may begin to use more lexically complex determiners, such as *another, other,* and *something* (Wells, 1985), as well as the *wh-* words, particularly *what*. The proportion of determiner use in children's speech, as compared to other forms (such as nouns and pronouns), remains low throughout the developmental period. For the period from 5 to nearly 10 years, determiners comprise only about 6% of children's spoken words (Davis, 1938). However, children's accurate comprehension and expression of these terms continues to grow over the school-age years.

An interesting line of research (e.g., Curenton & Justice, 2004; Westby, 1994) has studied how children use determiners to promote the specificity of their written and oral language. As children develop, their language—both spoken and written—shows increased sophistication in terms of decontextualization, that is, their ability to refer to events out of context. Decontextualized language needs to be highly specific, given that supportive cues are not available in the immediate environment to promote the accuracy of the message. For instance, in detailing a recent event (for which listeners were not present), a child needs to use specific syntactic structures to encourage accurate comprehension of his or her meaning: *We went over a very, very long bridge, and then came upon what looked like a huge rescue mission of some sort. . . .* What is it in the child's syntax that most effectively creates the picture of the event in the mind of the listener? Key syntactic elements for doing so include the frequent use of adverbs, adjectives, determiners, and so forth. Some authors (e.g., Curenton & Justice, 2004) refer to children's use of particular syntactic structures to promote specificity as *literate language features.*

An important literate language feature is the use of elaborated noun phrases, in which noun specificity is enhanced by elaborate use of determiners, such as articles, demonstratives, quantifiers, and *wh-* words. School-age children show gradual increases in their use of elaborated noun phrases, as do young preschool-age children. However, this is a relatively new area of research, and consequently our understanding of children's use of determiners as a primary literate language feature is currently incomplete. For instance, there is very little known about children's emergent use of *wh-* words as determiners, which is presumably an important way in which noun specificity is enhanced. What we do know is that school-age children need to learn to use determiners in their speech and writing to enhance the specificity of their language, and that misunderstanding of demonstratives and quantifiers may result in problems with academic subjects.

CHAPTER EXERCISES

Exercise 6A

In the following sentences, identify the category of each underlined determiner as one of the following: Article (A), Possessive (P), Demonstrative (D), Quantifier (Q), or *Wh-* Word (W).

_____ 1. <u>Those</u> shoes look ridiculous.

_____ 2. We must ensure that <u>every</u> child reads by third grade.

_____ 3. You didn't tell her <u>which</u> test you'd be using.

_____ 4. <u>Whose</u> purse is that?

_____ 5. Jennifer didn't like <u>either</u> option.

_____ 6. It was <u>his</u> idea.

_____ 7. Tell <u>her</u> sister you won't be going.

_____ 8. <u>President Obama's</u> address was quite unexpected.

_____ 9. It is definitely not <u>an</u> option.

_____ 10. Tell her it was <u>your</u> concept in the first place.

_____ 11. The program will not enroll more than <u>nine</u> children.

_____ 12. It is all in <u>your</u> head!

Exercise 6B

1. Take a look at this brief story produced by a 6-year-old child. Underline all the determiners.

    Once upon a time there was a little boy. His name was Bobby. Bobby told his friends to come over for a party. The kids came. Jamie, Scott, Annie, and some other kids too. They had a cake and some ice cream. And then Bobby's dad helped them with some fireworks. Like firecrackers and those snakes in the grass. Then they opened the presents. Bobby didn't know what present to open first. So he picked the biggest one. It was Jamie's present. And it was another truck! Like the one his grandma gave him. So now he had two trucks! He loved this one. Then after the presents the kids went outside for more fireworks.

2. Categorize the determiners you underlined in Step 1 by writing each word in the appropriate column below.

ARTICLE	POSSESSIVE	DEMONSTRATIVE	QUANTIFIER	WH- WORD

3. Use the chart above to characterize this child's use of determiners. Write a brief descriptive sentence.

   _____

   _____

Exercise 6C

1. A child client (4 years of age) never uses determiners and speaks with a telegraphic quality, saying things like *give me ball, want car,* and *horse crying.* Give three examples of other utterances the child might produce during conversational speech.

   - _____
   - _____
   - _____

2. Provide three examples of utterances a language interventionist might produce to model production of the above utterances with an emphasis on determiner use.

   - _____
   - _____
   - _____

Chapter Six: Determiners

Exercise 6D

Examine each of the following child utterances. Determiners are obviously missing in this child's speech. Develop a grammatical expansion (i.e., embellish the child's production by adding the target syntactical structure) that includes use of a particular type of determiner, and identify the category of the determiner being targeted.

1. *you got more*
   Expansion: _____ Category: _____
2. *me got kitty*
   Expansion: _____ Category: _____
3. *that sister's house*
   Expansion: _____ Category: _____
4. *I want bubbles*
   Expansion: _____ Category: _____
5. *she needs piece*
   Expansion: _____ Category: _____
6. *that his*
   Expansion: _____ Category: _____
7. *put in here*
   Expansion: _____ Category: _____
8. *Momma got blue*
   Expansion: _____ Category: _____
9. *me got cookie*
   Expansion: _____ Category: _____
10. *blow bubbles*
    Expansion: _____ Category: _____

Exercise 6E

1. Read the following transcript that represents an interaction between a language interventionist (LI) and a 5-year-old child (K). Underline each determiner.

   LI: You wanna read another book?

   K: Yeah.

   K: Read that one.

   K: No, read that one.

   LI: Look at that. What's that? Tell me.

K: That's hooking together and flying over park.

K: And she got mail to him.

LI: And what about that page?

K: That's Riley.

K: That his bumblebee.

K: That his froggie.

K: That boy's hat.

K: That the fishy.

K: That the alligator.

K: That some froggies.

K: That a bumblebee.

LI: What's he doing?

K: He trying to get up there.

LI: What's this boy doing?

K: He trying to get up there.

LI: What's she doing?

K: She swimming in the water.

K: And say "Help, help."

K: But he not scary.

K: He's a nice boy.

2. Look closely at K's utterances to examine his use of determiners. Look for examples of determiners of the following types: articles, possessives, demonstratives, quantifiers, and *wh-* words. Using the chart provided, provide examples of determiners that occur in each category. If no examples occur for a particular category, leave the column blank.

ARTICLE	POSSESSIVE	DEMONSTRATIVE	QUANTIFIER	WH- WORD

3. Determine the proportion of words that are determiners in comparison to all the other types of words that K produced in the previous transcript.

- Count the total number of determiners used and write it in the blank below.
- Count the total number of words produced and write it in the blank below.
- Divide the total number of determiners used by the total number of words produced.
- Multiply this total by 100 to obtain the percent of determiners used.

Calculating the Proportion of Determiners

_____ ÷ _____ = _____ × 100 = _____ % Determiners

Total number of determiners   Total number of words

4. What proportion of determiners would you expect of a typical 5-year-old child?

_____

ANSWER KEY

Exercise 6A

1. D   2. Q   3. W   4. W   5. Q   6. P
7. P   8. P   9. A   10. P   11. Q   12. P

Exercise 6B

1. Once upon <u>a</u> time there was <u>a</u> little boy. <u>His</u> name was Bobby. Bobby told <u>his</u> friends to come over for <u>a</u> party. <u>The</u> kids came. Jamie, Scott, Annie, and <u>some other</u> kids too. They had <u>a</u> cake and <u>some</u> ice cream. And then <u>Bobby's</u> dad helped them with <u>some</u> fireworks. Like firecrackers and <u>those</u> snakes in <u>the</u> grass. Then they opened <u>the</u> presents. Bobby didn't know <u>what</u> present to open first. So he picked <u>the</u> biggest one. It was <u>Jamie's</u> present. And it was <u>another</u> truck! Like <u>the</u> one <u>his</u> grandma gave him. So now he had <u>two</u> trucks! He loved <u>this</u> one. Then after <u>the</u> presents <u>the</u> kids went outside for <u>more</u> fireworks.

2.

ARTICLE	POSSESSIVE	DEMONSTRATIVE	QUANTIFIER	WH- WORD
a (4x) the (7x)	his (3x) Bobby's Jamie's	those this	some (3x) other another two more	what

3. Approximately 23% of this child's productions consist of determiners. The majority of determiners are articles followed by quantifiers and possessives. (Note that in this calculation, *ice cream* is counted as one word since it is a compound noun.)

Exercise 6E

1.
LI: You wanna read another book?
K: Yeah.
K: Read that one.
K: No, read that one.
LI: Look at that. What's that? Tell me.
K: That's hooking together and flying over park.
K: And she got mail to him.
LI: And what about that page?
K: That's Riley.
K: That his bumblebee.
K: That his froggie.
K: That boy's hat.
K: That the fishy.
K: That the alligator.
K: That some froggies.
K: That a bumblebee.
LI: What's he doing?
K: He trying to get up there.
LI: What's this boy doing?
K: He trying to get up there.
LI: What's she doing?
K: She swimming in the water.
K: And say "Help, help."
K: But he not scary.
K: He's a nice boy.

2.

ARTICLE	POSSESSIVE	DEMONSTRATIVE	QUANTIFIER	WH- WORD
the (3x) *a* (2x)	*his* (2x) *boy's*	*that** (2x)	*some*	

* The child's use of *that* in the utterances *That his bumblebee* through *That a bumblebee* is probably not as a determiner; rather, the child appears to be omitting the copula *is*, in which case *that* becomes a demonstrative pronoun.

3. $11 \div 73 = .15 \times 100 = 15\%$ Determiners

4. 6%

CHAPTER SEVEN

Conjunctions

Chapter at a Glance

What Is a Conjunction?

Simple, Compound, and Phrasal Conjunctions

Conjunction Types

- Coordinating Conjunctions and Conjunctive Adverbs
- Correlative Conjunctions
- Subordinating Conjunctions

Developmental Notes

Chapter Exercises

Answer Key

What Is a Conjunction?

Conjunctions comprise a relatively small set of words that serve to join words with words, phrases with phrases, and clauses with clauses. You could think of conjunctions as the glue that connects words, phrases, and clauses together. Conjunctions are what allow the 6-year-old child in the example below to continue on so breathlessly (the conjunctions are underlined).

> We went to the store <u>and then</u> we got some popcorn <u>and after</u> that we stopped to see Daddy at his work <u>and then</u> my mom said I needed new shoes <u>so</u> we went to the shoe store <u>and</u> I tried on some new shoes <u>but</u> none of them fit <u>so</u> . . .

The most common conjunction (in general and in the example above) is *and*. Other common conjunctions used to connect words include *or* and *but*, as seen in the following examples:

> The horse **and** carriage are in the backyard.

> They got in the car **and** drove to town.

> You can have chocolate **or** vanilla ice cream.

> I'll do anything **but** that.

Conjunctions also join phrases, as seen in these examples:

> The new dog **and** the old dog do not get along.

> Please pass me the Kleenex tissues **or** one of those handkerchiefs.

The conjoining of clauses is also an important role of conjunctions, as seen here:

> She told me to come, **but** she did not invite my father.

> You should have a party this Friday, **unless** John has one then.

Even though conjunctions are a closed class of words, there are many of them. They include words like *after, although, and, unless,* and *until,* to name only a few. In addition, some conjunctions are groups of words, such as *as soon as, rather than,* and *in case*.

A number of adverbs can also serve as conjunctions when they connect two or more independent clauses; they are known as **conjunctive adverbs** or **adverbial conjuncts**. These include, for example, *besides, hence,* and *indeed*.

Simple, Compound, and Phrasal Conjunctions

Many conjunctions are just one word, such as *and, but, so,* and *either*. These are **simple conjunctions**. Other conjunctions are **compound conjunctions**, so called because they consist of two or more words combined to form one word, such as *nevertheless, therefore, thereafter, wherever, however,* and *whenever*. A third category of conjunctions, **phrasal conjunctions**, occur as complete phrases; they include *in other words, that is, even if, as such,* and *to this end*. Notice the use of all three of these types of conjunctions in the following examples:

> I am going, **so** you will too. (simple)

> I am going; **therefore**, you will too. (compound)

> I am going; **as such**, you will too. (phrasal)

Conjunction Types

There are three major types of conjunctions: coordinating, correlative, and subordinating. These types of conjunctions are considered in the following sections.

Coordinating Conjunctions and Conjunctive Adverbs

Coordination means that the information on both sides of either a coordinating conjunction or a conjunctive adverb has equal weight and importance (Master, 1995). The **coordinating conjunctions** are *for, and, nor, but, or, yet,* and *so*. A handy way to remember these is with the mnemonic FANBOYS (*f* stands for *for, a* stands for *and,* and so on). Note that *and then* is also often included in this group when analyzing narratives (Hughes, McGillivray, & Schmidek, 1997). Coordinating conjunctions are used to join words, phrases, or clauses (as seen in the examples below), each of which has equal weight:

Hello, boys **and** girls.

John was told to vacuum his room **or** clean the garage.

Don't tell anyone, **but** that movie won't be playing in this town.

Adverbs that connect two or more independent clauses (don't worry, you'll learn about clauses in Chapter 11) are **conjunctive adverbs**, also known as *adverbial conjuncts*. Examples of conjunctive adverbs used in coordination are depicted in Table 5.2 in Chapter 5. Examples of their use in sentences include the following. Note that conjunctive adverbs are often preceded by a semicolon and followed by a comma:

Share the cookies; **otherwise**, share the brownies.

The play is tonight; **however**, we don't have tickets.

Opdycke (1965) classified coordinating conjunctions and conjunctive adverbs into four categories, as seen in Table 7.1.

TABLE 7.1
Coordinating Conjunction and Conjunctive Adverb Categories

CATEGORY	EXAMPLES
Additive	*also, and, besides, likewise, moreover, then*
Contrasting	*but, however, nevertheless, notwithstanding, still, yet*
Separative	*or, otherwise*
Final	*consequently, for, hence, so, so that, therefore, thus*

Correlative Conjunctions

There are several sets of words that go together in pairs to form correlative conjunctions. Examples include *both/and, either/or, neither/nor, whether/or, as/as,* and *if/then*. In general, if the first word in one of these pairs occurs in a sentence, then the second word in the pair must follow. For example, you wouldn't say *Either Stephen is going.* See how that leaves you hanging? Notice how the pairs are used in the examples below:

Both Jason **and** Stuart will be at the match.

Either you take a bath **or** you are not going.

If you meet me at the bus, **then** we can go together.

Whether we pass **or** fail, we've certainly learned a lot!

Subordinating Conjunctions

Subordinating conjunctions are the most frequently used conjunctions. They serve to join ideas together in a sentence. In contrast to coordinating conjunctions, **subordinating conjunctions** are used to connect one clause (a main or independent clause) to another clause (a subordinate or dependent clause) that has less weight and importance (Master, 1995). (Skip ahead to Chapter 11 if you need clarification on independent and dependent clauses.) Some common subordinating conjunctions are depicted in Table 7.2, and some examples of their use connecting clauses follow. Note that the dependent clauses are bracketed and begin with a subordinating conjunction:

Tell him [**why** you won't be going.]

[**Although** Mya won't be going,] she thinks we should still go.

Don't touch it [**while** it's cooking.]

Developmental Notes

An excellent description of children's acquisition of coordinating terms (conjunctions) is provided in Berko Gleason (1993), from which many of the following developmental

TABLE 7.2
Common Subordinating Conjunctions

after	*since*	*where*
although	*that*	*whereas*
as	*though*	*wherever*
as well as	*unless*	*whether*
because	*until*	*while*
if	*when*	*why*

notes have been drawn. At approximately 2 years of age, many children with typical development begin to use the coordinating conjunction *and*. Young children's particularly liberal use of the conjunction *and* to conjoin clauses has given it the important label of "discourse glue" by some researchers (e.g., Peterson & McCabe, 1988).

There are several patterns to children's early use of conjunctions. As noted at the beginning of this chapter, children tend to rely on *and* as a coordinating conjunction. Phrasal coordination, in which two noun or verb phrases are conjoined (e.g., *The dog and cat are here* or *The baby is screaming and yelling*) generally appears prior to clausal coordination (e.g., *He's doing the laundry and I'm washing the dishes* or *We're going on vacation and we're visiting Grandpa*). At this stage, the use of *because* also emerges as a conjunction used to coordinate clausal structures. Tyack and Gottsleben (1986) found a substantial increase in children's use of *and* as a coordinating conjunction during the period in which children's mean length of utterance (MLU) increased from 2.0 to 5.0. Owens (2012) wrote that Brown's (1973) Stage V (41–46 months) represents the time in which children begin to conjoin clauses using *if*; this is followed by the appearance of conjoining using *when, but,* and *so* after approximately 4 years of age. In general, children's gradual growth of more sophisticated conjunctive terms follows the pattern of temporal conjunctions (e.g., *when* and *then*), followed by causal conjunctions (e.g., *because* and *so*) (Hoff-Ginsberg, 1997). An example of this developmental transition is offered by Hoff-Ginsberg through two examples, both by 5-year-old children, as shown below.

CHILD 1: And then he goes up there. And then an owl comes out and he falls.

CHILD 2: And the boy was looking through the window when a owl came out and bammed him on the ground. (p. 273)

One particularly interesting aspect of study is children's acquisition of *because* (Owens, 2012). *Because* is often used to link a subordinate clause and a head word (usually a verb, although not necessarily) to detail cause and effect. Children at ages 3 and 4 years are often observed using *because,* but demonstrate difficulty coordinating its use to demonstrate true cause-and-effect relations. For instance, a child might say *I fell off my bike because I hurt my leg.*

From 4 to 6 years of age, conjunctions comprise only a small portion of children's expressive speech—about 3% of total words spoken (Davis, 1938). This figure increases only slightly, to about 5%, as children move into adolescence. However, the types of conjunctions used may show a shift, with older children using and understanding more sophisticated connectors, such as *furthermore* and *however*. Certain types of conjunctions, such as conjunctive adverbs, are used rarely by children and adolescents. As would be expected, children continually show greater comprehension of more common conjunctive adverbs, such as *then* and *so,* as compared to more esoteric terms, such as *nevertheless* and *moreover* (Scott & Rush, 1985).

Children's use of conjunctions serves an important role in that it allows children to link ideas as they learn to form more complex sentence structures (Nippold, 2007). Children's acquisition of coordinating terms is gradual. Certain terms (e.g., *but, and,* and *because*) are mastered at earlier ages (Grade 6) compared to other terms (e.g., be-

fore and *so that*) (Nippold). Investigations of the relative difficulty of comprehending various conjunctions have suggested that *because* and *although* are easier to understand than the conjunctions *if* and *unless* (Wing & Scholnick, 1981).

An interesting study of the development of coordination in adolescents and young adults—particularly their use of conjunctive adverbs—was reported in 1992 by Nippold, Schwarz, and Undlin. Evidence from administration of a reading task indicated the following order of difficulty for adolescent and young adults' (aged 11–29 years) understanding of conjunctive adverbs:

> Therefore → However → Consequently → Rather → Nevertheless → Furthermore → Moreover → Conversely → Contrastively → Similarly

Nippold et al. (1992) reported that "use and understanding of adverbial conjuncts in the written mode improve steadily during the adolescent years" (p. 113). Moreover, mastery with respect to comprehension of adverbial conjuncts was demonstrated by most young adults, although mastery in terms of production (or use) had not yet been reached.

CHAPTER EXERCISES

Exercise 7A

Combine each pair of sentences into one sentence using a conjunction.

1. Call Jillian. Ask to speak to Francis.
   _____

2. Lend her the money. I'll sign the check over to you.
   _____

3. It is probably going to rain. We should cancel.
   _____

4. The child's evaluation is on Thursday. It might be on Friday.
   _____

5. The song is about peace. It is not about freedom.
   _____

6. One of the kittens is called Lexie. The other kitten is called Harold.
   _____

7. She will not visit. I will visit.
   _____

8. The president will give the address. He will not be at the reception.
   _____

Exercise 7B

In the following sentences, identify each underlined conjunction as either Coordinating (C) or Subordinating (S).

_____ 1. The child made a mess with the blocks <u>and</u> refused to clean them up.

_____ 2. Evolution is somewhat controversial, <u>although</u> it is still taught in many schools.

_____ 3. She received her certification; <u>then</u>, she began to pursue her Ph.D.

_____ 4. Autism has long been considered a functional disorder, <u>but</u> it likely has an organic cause.

_____ 5. He was told to prepare dinner <u>while</u> she finished the floral arrangements.

_____ 6. Jason was subtle, <u>but</u> it was clear to everyone why he was visiting.

_____ 7. <u>Why</u> he declined the invitation, Derick did not say.

_____ 8. The plan was to meet for dessert <u>after</u> the play was over.

_____ 9. Hayley did not win first place, <u>yet</u> she still felt the victor.

_____ 10. The clinician did not complete the evaluation; <u>however</u>, she felt it was imperative that treatment commence immediately.

Exercise 7C

1. Underline each conjunction in the following story told by a 5-year-old child.

   That's his house and they had a doggie. The doggie fell down and that's the boy holding him. He's crying because he angry. The boy and the dog so mad. He ask where my doggie? Then he get up there but the dog left them. The dog can't get them out, so he pulled him. Look at him because that's him. He hid him but he don't know that. He fall down then the dog fell in the water too. He see the turtle gone and the dog see the turtle but the boy don't see the dog. The dog got in the water then he did too.

2. Place each of the conjunctions you underlined in the passage in the appropriate column below.

COORDINATING	CORRELATIVE	SUBORDINATING

ANSWER KEY

Exercise 7B

1. C
2. S
3. C
4. C
5. S
6. C
7. S
8. S
9. C
10. C

Exercise 7C

1. That's his house <u>and</u> they had a doggie. The doggie fell down <u>and</u> that's the boy holding him. He's crying <u>because</u> he angry. The boy <u>and</u> the dog so mad. He ask <u>where</u> my doggie? Then he get up there <u>but</u> the dog left them. The dog can't get them out, <u>so</u> he pulled him. Look at him <u>because</u> that's him. He hid him <u>but</u> he don't know that. He fall down <u>then</u> the dog fell in the water too. He see the turtle gone <u>and</u> the dog see the turtle <u>but</u> the boy don't see the dog. The dog got in the water <u>then</u> he did too.

COORDINATING	CORRELATIVE	SUBORDINATING
and (4x) so but (3x) then (2x)		because (2x) where

CHAPTER EIGHT

Prepositions

Chapter at a Glance

What Is a Preposition?
Prepositional Function
Preposition Types
Prepositional Verbs
Developmental Notes
Chapter Exercises
Answer Key

What Is a Preposition?

Prepositions comprise a relatively small, and therefore finite, class of words that serve to connect nouns and pronouns to other nouns, pronouns, and verbs. Prepositions depict a precise relationship between two sentence units; more specifically, between two or more nouns or pronouns (Master, 1995). According to Opdycke (1965), "a preposition is a word or a term that shows a relationship between a word that follows it, called its *object*, and a word before it [called its *antecedent*] to which it pertains or relates" (p. 184).

Prepositions usually serve as the first word in a particular type of phrase (a prepositional phrase, described in Chapter 10). The role of the preposition is to create a relationship between its antecedent and its object. For example, in *Put the butter <u>on</u> the table*, the preposition *on* connects the object *table* to the antecedent *butter*, indicating where the butter should be put.

Prepositions may modify both nouns and verbs; thus, they can function in both adjectival and adverbial roles. Consider the following sentences, in which the preposition is in all capital letters, the object of the preposition is in red, the antecedent is circled, and the entire prepositional phrase is bracketed:

Please put the (milk)[IN the **refrigerator**].

The (man)[WITH the **shovel**] helped us.

Jacob (drove)[OFF the **road**].

The ball (fell)[BETWEEN the **cracks**].

In the first two examples, the prepositions and their phrases modify the preceding nouns (*milk* and *man*). In both cases, the preposition links a noun phrase (*the milk* and *the man*) to another noun phrase (*the refrigerator* and *the shovel*). In the last two examples, the prepositions and their phrases modify the verbs in the sentences (*drove* and *fell*); consequently, these prepositions serve an adverbial function. In both of these latter cases, the preposition links a verb (*drove* and *fell*) to a noun phrase (*the road* and *the cracks*).

Typically, prepositions occur before nouns and noun phrases, as in the previous examples. Occasionally, and most commonly in informal speaking situations, prepositions occur at the ends of sentences, as in the following examples:

What did you tell him **for**?

I don't think she wrote that part **in**.

Although this arrangement is acceptable in casual speaking situations, most of us remember being chastised in school for ending a sentence with a preposition. (What do you mean *No*? I suppose your teacher let you dangle your modifiers any way you saw fit too, huh?) At least in formal writing situations, you should instead link prepositions to the object of the preposition. For example, the two sentences above might be better stated (at least in formal or written language) as follows:

[**For** what reason] did you tell him?

I don't think she wrote that part [**in** the manuscript].

Sometimes it may be tricky for you to identify a preposition. For example, verb particles look a lot like prepositions, as in *I ran into my old teacher*, in which *into* is a verb particle (not a preposition). It would be a common error to mistake this particle as a preposition. The distinction between particles and prepositions is explained in more detail later in this chapter (see "Prepositional Verbs").

Prepositional Function

Prepositions serve a variety of functions, including providing information about time, place, accompaniment, destination/purpose, means, possession, and relation (Master, 1995). Examples of prepositions within each of these categories are depicted in Table 8.1.

TABLE 8.1
Prepositional Functions

FUNCTION	EXAMPLE(S)
Time	at, between, during, for, since, through, until, within
Place	against, among, around, beside, between, by, in, near, on
Accompaniment	with, without
Destination/Purpose	for, to
Means	by, with, without
Possession	of
Relation	of

Examples of these various functions within sentences are as follows:

Tom will not arrive **until** Friday. (time)

Use the umbrella that is **next to** my dresser. (place)

I never jog **without** my dog. (accompaniment)

Do not leave **for** the party until I arrive. (destination)

We arrived **by** bus and then took a cab to the inn. (means)

He is the author **of** the book. (possession)

Nancy is the sister **of** my cousin. (relation)

Preposition Types

There are three types of prepositions: simple, compound, and phrasal. **Simple prepositions** are single words. They represent a fairly large group of closed-class words, many of which appear in Table 8.2. Examples of simple prepositions within sentences are as follows:

You need to get that thing **off** the table.

He has called every hour **on** the hour.

Recall that one important function of prepositions is to provide information about place. To this end, there is a relatively large group of simple prepositions, including such words as *about, across, below,* and *through,* that are referred to as **prepositional adverbs** (Leech, 1991). These prepositions provide additional information about verbs in a sentence. This characterization of some prepositions as prepositional adverbs is subtle;

however, it is important to recognize that this is just a fine distinction made among the fairly large set of simple prepositions when put to use. Some of the more common prepositional adverbs appear in Table 8.3. Some examples of these prepositional adverbs as used in sentences are as follows:

We walked **across** the bridge.

Let's look **within** ourselves.

Some prepositions are compound words, so they are known as **compound prepositions**. Examples of these are shown in Table 8.4. Here are some examples of their use in sentences:

Julie will try to go **without** a reservation.

Meet us **alongside** the store.

TABLE 8.2
Common Simple Prepositions

about	behind	like	to
above	below	near	toward
across	between	off	under
against	beyond	on	until
around	by	out	up
before	down	over	with

TABLE 8.3
Common Prepositional Adverbs

about	below	under
above	beyond	up
across	by	within
after	past	
along	through	
around	throughout	

TABLE 8.4
Common Compound Prepositions

alongside	outside	within
inside	throughout	without
nearby	underneath	

In English there are a number of prepositions that consist of a group of two or more words: **phrasal prepositions** (also known as *complex prepositions*). Commonly, the form of these phrasal prepositions is "Adverb + Preposition" (Turner, 1966). These should not be confused with prepositional verbs, which are explained in the next section. Some common phrasal prepositions are depicted in Table 8.5. Examples of phrasal prepositions used in sentences appear below:

Don't go **along with** the plan if you don't like it.

I'll have that **instead of** this.

Prepositional Verbs

There are a number of prepositions that can occur in tandem with a verb, as in the verb phrases *drop in* or *pick on*. These idiomatic phrases are called **prepositional verbs** (and sometimes *phrasal verbs* or *two-part verbs*) and are formed by combining a verb with a preposition. In such cases, the preposition is not actually considered a preposition, but rather is referred to as a *particle* or, more specifically, a **verb particle**. Some common prepositional verbs appear in Table 8.6.

Strictly speaking, particles are not prepositions at all; they are part of the verb. (They just look like prepositions to make your job tougher!) Thus, when seeking to identify prepositions, you must consider what the word is modifying. Words may look like prepositions, but be meaningfully connected to verbs, thus making them particles.

TABLE 8.5
Common Phrasal Prepositions

according to	because of	instead of
across from	for the sake of	outside of
along with	in comparison with	over to
as for	in spite of	prior to
as to	inside of	up for

TABLE 8.6
Common Prepositional Verbs

allow for	look at	run into
attend to	look for	stand up
believe in	object to	wish for
drop in	pick on	

Such forms should be identified as prepositional verbs. Consider the difference in meaning between the verbs in each pair of the examples presented here:

> Krista **ran into** a snag.
>
> Krista ran **into** the burning building.
>
> Jason **waited on** a customer.
>
> Jason **waited** on the white line.

The first sentence in each pair contains a prepositional verb (*ran into* and *waited on*) with one or more direct objects (*snag* and *customer*) following it. The second sentence in each pair takes the form of "Verb + Prepositional Phrase" (*ran* and *waited* + *into the burning building* and *on the white line*). Note that in the first example, *ran into* is used together in a figurative sense to mean that Krista encountered a problem. In the second example, however, Krista physically ran inside of a building. Skillin and Gay's (1974) *Words Into Type* may prove helpful if you have trouble identifying prepositional verbs.

Verb particles often appear immediately after the verb. Unlike prepositions, verb particles can often be separated from the verb and still retain their meaning, as the following examples illustrate:

> Jennifer **handed off** the bill to her friend.
>
> Jennifer **handed** the bill **off** to her friend.
>
> I'd like to **check out** these books.
>
> I'd like to **check** these books **out**.

Note that occasionally, it would be awkward to separate a particle from the verb to which it is linked, as in the following examples:

> Jackie **called out** to Taylor to bring her another bathing suit.
>
> The items have not yet been **paid for**.

The distinction between prepositional verbs and prepositions is an important one for the language interventionist, both when analyzing language and when remediating it. If the terms are confused in analyzing language, assessment outcomes may be tainted. If a targeted structure in intervention is prepositions, you would want to be careful not to use prepositional verbs in the intervention context, as this could be confusing for the child.

Developmental Notes

Two important prepositions are acquired relatively early, typically within Brown's Stage II (27–30 months): *in* and *on* (Brown, 1973). These early prepositions are often seen in the speech of young children who are beginning to use three-word sentences, depicted in such utterances as *baby in bed* and *puppy on chair*.

In Brown's Stage III, fully formed prepositional phrases like *in the cup* and *on a sofa* begin to be observed. Lois Bloom's daughter, Allison, spontaneously used the following prepositions at 22 months (Bloom, 1973): *in, on, out, down, up, away,* and *around*. Although it is quite possible that Allison was especially precocious, given her status as the child of an eminent language researcher, these particular prepositions do represent those typically seen in the speech of young children. Radford (1990) argued that children's use of such prepositions in these early stages of language development (in the period when one-, two-, and three-word utterances predominate) is indicative of their attaining a lexical system that is beginning to represent prepositional constituents. Radford provided several examples produced by very young children:

Paula, 18 months: *in there, Mummy; put in there, go in there*

Hayley, 20 months: *in water, in bag, mouse in window*

Jem, 23 months: *pee with potty, peep in keyhole*

As noted by Owens (2012), children's receptive understanding of such prepositional terms typically precedes their ability to accurately express them. This suggests that Allison, Paula, Hayley, and Jem were likely comprehending the meaning of prepositions and prepositional phrases early in their second year of life.

By approximately 36 months of age, most children have a fairly firm grasp of not only the prepositions *in* and *on*, but also the preposition *under* (see Owens, 2012, for an overview). Other prepositions acquired during this period, from about 30–36 months of age, include *off* and *toward* and the phrasal prepositions *away from* and *out of*. In this period, children are more apt to understand locational prepositions (e.g., *in, on,* and *under*) in contrast to prepositions representing spatial relations (e.g., *behind, beside, in front of,* and *between*) (Johnston, 1984). Children's use of prepositional phrases to enhance the complexity of sentences begins to emerge at approximately 3 years of age. During this period, sentences with four or more elements may include prepositional phrases of the following scheme: "Noun + Preposition + Noun" (e.g., *dog in the garden* or *the girl with the blue shirt*) (Crystal, Fletcher, & Garman 1974).

Between the ages of 42 and 60 months of age, most children accurately comprehend the meaning of the simple and phrasal prepositions *in front of, in back of, next to, around, beside,* and *down* (Kent, 1994). In general, comprehension of simple prepositions occurs prior to comprehension of more syntactically complex prepositions (e.g., <u>on</u> the table before <u>across from</u> the table). Children's accurate use of these locational and spatial prepositions as noun modifiers within sentences continues to emerge in the years that follow, as does children's increasing use of elaborated noun phrases. Over one's life span, prepositions—while certainly important—constitute only a small portion of total words used. Data from Davis (1938) indicate that during the preschool period, prepositions account for about 10% of total words spoken, a figure that remains relatively constant into adolescence.

CHAPTER EXERCISES

Exercise 8A

Underline each preposition that occurs in the following parent–child shared book-reading interaction, using the book *Top Cat,* by Lois Ehlert.

CHILD: Look, he's pecking on that red thing.

MOTHER: Yeah, what do you think that red thing is?

CHILD: A chair.

MOTHER: Looks like the cat's going to stay.

CHILD: Grey cat. He's going in the basket.

MOTHER: He is. What other color do we have in here?

CHILD: Black. It looks like he has a little bit of brown blended into him. They both have black on them. He's not supposed to be on that.

MOTHER: So do you think they're supposed to eat leaves off from the plant?

CHILD: We shouldn't ever eat things off from plants in the house.

MOTHER: But sometimes kitties eat things we don't want them to eat.

CHILD: Remember when Smokie brought that mouse inside the house? And you made Dad take it outside? He put it by the rocks, I mean he put it by the fence in back.

Exercise 8B

In each of the following prepositional phrases, identify the preposition and the object of the preposition and write each on the corresponding line.

	Preposition	Object
1. *on the winding road*	_____	_____
2. *during our vacation*	_____	_____
3. *with Jane and Susan*	_____	_____
4. *for the money*	_____	_____
5. *by any means*	_____	_____
6. *without further ado*	_____	_____
7. *inside the dark cabin*	_____	_____
8. *since last month*	_____	_____
9. *within the boundaries*	_____	_____
10. *near the blue robin*	_____	_____

Exercise 8C

Underline the prepositional verb in each of the following sentences.

1. The professor picks on students who don't come to class.
2. Xander has been scolded for always shouting out the answer.
3. You will need to look that word up in the dictionary.
4. Juan can find out the answer on the internet.
5. Tell the children to put on their coats before we leave.
6. Carly told the teacher she is planning to drop out of school.
7. It is important to look out for deer on the highway.
8. Please look after my mother while I am gone.
9. Crystal said that she would point out the man.
10. Please do not give away the saucers that my grandmother left me.

Exercise 8D

Read the following poem created by a group of kindergarten children studying rhyme. Underline each simple preposition, and circle each object of the preposition.

It is time to clean our room.
Everything has a place.
I help my friends and my friends help me.
I have a smile on my face.
Crayons go in the bucket.
The train goes in the box.
The chairs go under the table.
My shoes go on my socks.
The books go on the shelf.
Our coats go by the door.
We keep on working in our room.
Until there is no more!

Exercise 8E

1. Consider the following story about the highlight of a child's vacation. Underline each prepositional phrase.

   We were driving in our car. My mom was driving. We went into a big underground tunnel. My mom said it was two miles long. People turned on their lights in the tunnel. We were going to the beach in Virginia. When we were at the middle of the tunnel, there was an accident just ahead. I guess a van had run out of gas, and this semi truck ran into it. Anyway, we sat there for three hours, and my dad told us stories about his childhood. It was really boring, but I liked hearing about my dad.

2. Review each prepositional phrase in the above narrative, and complete the following chart.

SIMPLE PREPOSITION	ARTICLE(S)/ADJECTIVE(S)	OBJECT OF PREPOSITION

Exercise 8F

Preschool children with language disorders may demonstrate delayed attainment in their comprehension and use of prepositions and prepositional phrases. For such a child, a clinical goal might read like this (Cole & Cole, 1989): (Child) will accurately respond to phrases illustrating "Preposition + Article + Object" constructions (e.g., *on the table*).

A language interventionist, within naturalistic and functional activities, wants to determine the child's ability to comprehend constructions of this type. Provide examples of a series of tasks (or phrases) that the clinician might present to the child.

1. _____
2. _____
3. _____
4. _____
5. _____

Exercise 8G

1. Read the following interaction between a mother and child during a shared-reading session. T is 6 years old.

    Mom: Do you know where they are?

    T: **They're at school.**

    Mom: Right. And are these people in a restaurant?

    T: **They at a restaurant.**

    Mom: And what's he doing?

    T: **He's been shopping.**

    T: **He has lots of things in his basket.**

    Mom: What is this rhinoceros doing?

    T: **He's getting on a bus.**

    T: **He's getting a ride.**

    Mom: And what's the little boy doing?

    T: **He got a ride.**

    Mom: What's the crocodile doing?

    T: **He's sad.**

    T: **That's his body.**

    T: **There my body and my arm.**

    Mom: What's this here?

    T: **That's my arm.**

    Mom: Where's your foot?

    T: **In my shoe.**

    T: **In my shoes.**

    T: **In my boots.**

    Mom: Those are your new boots.

2. Find at least four different prepositions in T's utterances and complete the following chart.

T's Prepositional Use	
PREPOSITION	EXAMPLE PREPOSITIONAL PHRASE

ANSWER KEY

Exercise 8A

CHILD: Look, he's pecking <u>on</u> that red thing.

MOTHER: Yeah, what do you think that red thing is?

CHILD: A chair.

MOTHER: Looks like the cat's going to stay.

CHILD: Grey cat. He's going <u>in</u> the basket.

MOTHER: He is. What other color do we have in here?

CHILD: Black. It looks like he has a little bit <u>of</u> brown blended <u>into</u> him. They both have black <u>on</u> them. He's not supposed to be <u>on</u> that.

MOTHER: So do you think they're supposed to eat leaves off* <u>from</u> the plant?

CHILD: We shouldn't ever eat things off* <u>from</u> plants <u>in</u> the house.

MOTHER: But sometimes kitties eat things we don't want them to eat.

CHILD: Remember when Smokie brought that mouse <u>inside</u> the house? And you made Dad take it outside**? He put it <u>by</u> the rocks, I mean he put it <u>by</u> the fence <u>in</u> back.

*Note that *off* is a verb particle, and is part of the verb phrase *eat off*.
**Note that *outside* is an adverb in this sentence.

Exercise 8B

	Preposition	Object
1.	on	road
2.	during	vacation
3.	with	Jane/Susan
4.	for	money
5.	by	means
6.	without	ado
7.	inside	cabin
8.	since	month
9.	within	boundaries
10.	near	robin

Exercise 8C

1. The professor <u>picks on</u> students who don't come to class.
2. Xander has been scolded for always <u>shouting out</u> the answer.
3. You will need to <u>look</u> that word <u>up</u> in the dictionary.
4. Juan can <u>find out</u> the answer on the internet.
5. Tell the children to <u>put on</u> their coats before we leave.

6. Carly told the teacher she is planning to <u>drop out</u> of school.
7. It is important to <u>look out</u> for deer on the highway.
8. Please <u>look after</u> my mother while I am gone.
9. Crystal said that she would <u>point out</u> the man.
10. Please do not <u>give away</u> the saucers that my grandmother left me.

Exercise 8D

It is time to clean our room.

Everything has a place.

I help my friends and my friends help me.

I have a smile <u>on</u> my (face).

Crayons go <u>in</u> the (bucket).

The train goes <u>in</u> the (box).

The chairs go <u>under</u> the (table).

My shoes go <u>on</u> my (socks).

The books go <u>on</u> the (shelf).

Our coats go <u>by</u> the (door).

We keep on working <u>in</u> our (room).

Until there is no more!

Exercise 8E

We were driving <u>in our car</u>. My mom was driving. We went <u>into a big underground tunnel</u>. My mom said it was two miles long. People turned on their lights <u>in the tunnel</u>. We were going <u>to the beach in Virginia</u>. When we were <u>at the middle of the tunnel</u>, there was an accident just ahead. I guess a van had run out <u>of gas</u>, and this semi truck ran into it. Anyway, we sat there <u>for three hours</u>, and my dad told us stories <u>about his childhood</u>. It was really boring, but I liked hearing <u>about my dad</u>.

SIMPLE PREPOSITION	ARTICLE(S)/ADJECTIVE(S)	OBJECT OF PREPOSITION
in	our	car
into	a big underground	tunnel
in	the	tunnel
to	the	beach
in	—	Virginia
at	the	middle
of	the	tunnel
of	—	gas
for	three	hours
about	his	childhood
about	my	dad

Exercise 8G

T's Prepositional Use	
PREPOSITION	EXAMPLE PREPOSITIONAL PHRASE
at	at school, at a restaurant
of	of things
in	in his basket, in my shoe, in my shoes, in my boots
on	on a bus

PART II

Syntactic Function

NINE:	**Sentence Structure**
TEN:	**Phrases**
ELEVEN:	**Clauses**
TWELVE:	**Sentence Types**
THIRTEEN:	**Complex Syntax**

CHAPTER NINE

Sentence Structure

Chapter at a Glance

What Is Sentence Structure?
- The Subject
- The Object
- The Subject Complement
- The Predicate

Developmental Notes

Chapter Exercises

Answer Key

What Is Sentence Structure?

One way of thinking about sentence structure is by viewing a sentence as comprising several slots. These slots will decidedly be filled by nouns, adjectives, adverbs, and so on. The relationship between the sentence slots is based on the different roles that words may take (that is, their functions) more than it is based on their part of speech (that is, their form). Recall that there are several word forms (e.g., nouns) that can function in different roles (e.g., as adjectives). Part of what makes language generative is our ability to use words in different ways. It is just this flexibility that children work toward as they learn to be mature language users.

Sentences are typically characterized using one of two systems. The first (and the simplest) identifies two basic sentence slots:

Subject + Predicate

In this system, the subject occurs first in the sentence and reflects the action or state of the verb; the predicate is everything else, including the verb (Palmer, 1939). In the following examples, the subject is set off from the predicate with brackets:

[I] am not going to the party.

[My back] aches.

[The diagnosis] is specific language impairment.

[Those two girls] were admitted to the hospital.

In the examples above, the subject information is relatively straightforward. For one thing, the subject slots are dominated by nouns and pronouns (*I, back, diagnosis,* and *girls*) as well as determiners providing further details about these nouns and pronouns (*my, the, those,* and *two*).

The fact that the predicate is everything except the subject makes it less straightforward. The predicates in the previous examples include *am not going to the party, aches, is specific language impairment,* and *were admitted to the hospital.* What do the predicates in these examples have in common? For starters, they all contain verbs (*am [not] going, aches, is,* and *were admitted*). To this end, one definition of predicate is "the grammatical unit made up of the verb plus other constituents following it" (Jacobs, 1995, p. 14). This is helpful for characterizing the commonalities of the above four examples of predicates.

It is important to recognize that many scholars use a different system for characterizing sentences. This second system identifies three basic sentence slots:

Subject + Verb + Object

Simply put, in many sentences, such as *Cats stalk birds,* the subject is that which performs the action (*cats*), the verb reflects or describes the action (*stalk*), and the object is the recipient of the action (*birds*). This common arrangement of sentence elements can be represented as "S + V + O." The verb and object are both elements of the predicate structure. Not all sentences contain these three elements, however. That is, one of the three major elements in this sentence structure is not obligatory. Can you tell which one? Use the following examples to help you.

I ache.

Ian studies.

The peanut fell.

Colorless green ideas sleep furiously.

The latter example (attributed to the great linguist, Noam Chomsky) demonstrates the point that whereas a subject (*colorless green ideas*) and a verb (*sleep*) are always obligatory, the object is not. In this particular example, the word *furiously,* although immediately following the verb, is not an object. Rather, as you may know having already read

Chapter 5, it's an . . . C'mon. Do we really have to tell you? All right, all right. Just in case you missed that chapter—It's an adverb. *Furiously* serves the function of providing additional information about the verb (*sleep*), and thus is part of the predicate phrase. It is not, however, an object. Sentences like those in the previous examples do not follow the S + V + O pattern, and rather may be characterized as S + V + A. Suffice it to say that, at least in English, the S + V + O sentence pattern is quite common. We'll tell you about yet another sentence pattern (S + V + C) later in the chapter after we've explained what a subject complement is, so you'll have to be patient until then.

The Subject

In the English language, the **subject** usually appears at the beginning of a sentence before the verb (or the predicate, which you'll learn more about later in this chapter). The subject defines who or what is the instigator of the action or state reflected by the verb. Of course, sometimes the subject of a sentence is an abstract entity that cannot instigate action (e.g., <u>Syntax</u> *is quite interesting!*). In such cases, consider the subject as depicting who or what the rest of the sentence is providing additional information about.

Subjects can be simple, complete, or compound. **Simple subjects** are typically nouns and pronouns (e.g., <u>Curiosity</u> *killed the cat* and <u>Tommy</u> *is crying*). **Complete subjects** are simple subjects and their modifiers (e.g., <u>Intense curiosity</u> *drives that cat* and <u>The little boy named Tommy</u> *is crying*). **Compound subjects** are subjects that are conjoined via a conjunction (e.g., <u>Intense curiosity and sheer bravery</u> *drive that cat* and <u>The little boy named Tommy or the little girl next to him</u> *is crying*). Regardless of which of these three types it is, the subject of a sentence is typically one of the following:

- A noun
- A pronoun
- A noun phrase
- A clause

Subjects are most often nouns or pronouns, which can comprise the entire subject slot, as in the following sentences:

Pennies are becoming obsolete. (common noun as a subject)

Alaska is a beautiful state. (proper noun as a subject)

She has never had an evaluation. (pronoun as a subject)

Recall from Chapter 2 that when pronouns fill the subject slot, they must be in the nominative (sometimes called *subjective*) case. These include *I, you, he, she, it, we,* and *they*.

A third form that can fill the subject slot is a noun phrase. A noun phrase is formed by adding modifiers (i.e., determiners, adjectives, and adverbs) to nouns and pronouns. (Don't worry if you don't fully understand what a noun phrase is yet; you'll learn more about them in Chapter 10.) Look at the noun phrases that fill the subject slots in the following examples:

>**New pennies** are less likely to be discarded than old pennies.

>**Wild and beautiful Alaska** is home to numerous species of mammals.

The subject slots in sentences can also be filled by more complex structures, such as clauses. (More information on clauses is presented in Chapter 11.)

>**What I'd like** is a sunny day.

>**That they will attend the party** is uncertain.

Although clauses are more complex than simple subjects like *pennies* and *Alaska*, you can readily recognize the subjects in the example sentences if you remember that the subject tends to fill the slot directly preceding the verb. That is, the subject defines who or what is instigating or being referred to by the verb. So, for the previous examples, you can easily spot the subjects by asking yourself "Who or what is it you'd like?" and "Who or what is uncertain?"

Occasionally, you'll see sentences in which the subject slot is filled by an adjective, an infinitive, or a gerund, as in the following examples:

>**The meek** shall inherit the earth. (adjective as subject)

>**To err** is human; **to forgive**, divine. (infinitives as subjects)

>**Seeing** is believing. (gerund as subject)

On some occasions, the subject may be left unstated altogether, as in *Get the door* and *Call me*. These omitted subjects are sometimes called *covert subjects*, because their reference points are difficult to interpret or identify without some context. These are also sometimes referred to as *you-understood subjects*, meaning that the subjects are simply understood to be "you" (e.g., *[You] get the door* and *[You] call me*).

Regardless of how complex or beguiling the content of the subject slot may appear, the task of identifying the subject in a sentence need not be intimidating. The important thing to remember is that the subject slot—whether a simple noun or a clause—identifies the instigator of the action or state reflected by the verb.

The Object

Many, but not all, sentences include an object. Recall from Chapter 3 that verbs may be classified as intransitive or transitive. Sentences that contain intransitive verbs as main verbs often do not contain an object (e.g., *The tree fell* or *The tree fell loudly*) and therefore better fit one of the following sentence structures:

Subject + (Intransitive) Verb

Subject + (Intransitive) Verb + Adverb

Many other sentences contain transitive verbs and thus include an object (e.g., *Jackie hammered the nail*). Technically, the object is viewed as part of the predicate (which we describe in detail later in this chapter), or a constituent of the verb. The object in a sentence defines who or what receives the action reflected by the verb.

In terms of function, the object is very different from the subject. In terms of form, however, the object and the subject are similar in that they both typically consist of a noun or a pronoun, as in the following examples:

Janie breeds **dogs**.

Billy paid **her**.

Often, the object fills the third slot in a sentence, as in:

Subject + (Transitive) Verb + Object

The object slot may be followed by additional modification (adverbial or other) that provides further information about the action, as in the following examples:

Janie breeds dogs **annually**.

Billie paid her **yesterday**.

Earlier, we simplified the definition of an object by defining it as the recipient of the action in a sentence. Now we'd like to broaden that definition to include two types of objects—direct objects and indirect objects—each of which takes a different role in a sentence.

The **direct object** coincides with the previous discussion of the object slot in a sentence. That is, the recipient of the action is the direct object. As noted by Master (1995), direct objects often answer the question of "What?" or "Who/Whom?" with respect to the verb, as in the following examples:

Tyrone wrote WHAT? Tyrone wrote **the letter**.

Tyrone drove WHAT? Tyrone drove **the red corvette**.

Tyrone picked WHOM? Tyrone picked **him**.

Note that in the third example, the direct object is a pronoun. When pronouns are in the object slot, the pronouns must be in the objective, rather than subjective, case. Remember from Chapter 2 that pronouns in the objective case include *me, you, him, her, it, us,* and *them*.

While direct objects are the firsthand recipients of a verb's action, **indirect objects** are the recipients of the direct objects. They answer the questions "To whom was the action done?" and "For whom was the action done?" as in the following examples:

Pete gave the letter TO WHOM? Pete gave the letter to **Ming**.

The girl made the card FOR WHOM? The girl made the card for **Jennifer**.

So while there are actually two objects in each of the above sentences: *letter/Ming* and *card/Jennifer, letter* and *card* are the direct objects (the recipients of the verbs' actions) and *Ming* and *Jennifer* are the indirect objects (the recipients of the direct objects).

As if that wasn't confusing enough, not all sentences contain indirect objects, and not all verbs allow for indirect objects. Examples of verbs that commonly co-occur with indirect objects include *bring, buy, cook, get, give, make, promise, read, save, tell, throw,* and *write*. In such situations, the direct object tends to be the immediate receiver of the action in a sentence and the indirect object tells who or what is the beneficiary of that action. But this can result in some difficulty when you try to decipher who or what is the receiver versus who or what is the beneficiary of a particular action or state, as the following examples illustrate:

Malia gave the test to the child.

Malia gave the child the test.

Who (or what) is the direct object in the first example? And in the second? (Hint: *Malia* is the subject and *gave* is the verb in both sentences). Now ask yourself the *what* and *who/whom* questions for each sentence: What did Malia give? She gave *the test*. So *the test* is the direct object in both sentences. (Here when we say that the test was given by Malia, we mean that it was opened, manipulated, scored, and so on.) To whom or for whom did Malia give the test? Well, it would appear that in both sentences Malia gave the test to *the child*. Since the child is the beneficiary of the action in both sentences, it is the indirect object (though it is certainly much easier to spot in the first sentence!).

The above examples illustrate how confusing it can be to tell if an object is direct or indirect when both appear in a single sentence. So here's a tip: The indirect object typically precedes the direct object. Both of the following examples place the indirect object prior to the direct objects. Can you find them?

Dean gave her the papers.

Dean gave Tessa the papers.

The indirect objects in these sentences are *her* and *Tessa*, whereas *the papers* serves as the direct object in both cases. Because it is often possible to transform a sentence so that the direct and indirect objects are reversed in order (e.g., *Dean gave her the papers* → *Dean gave the papers to her*), a useful technique for identifying the indirect object is by checking if the word *to* or *for* may logically be inserted before one of the objects in the sentence. Going back to our previous example, *Malia gave the child the test*, if you were unsure whether *the child* or *the test* was the indirect object, you could use this strategy. Add the word *to* in front of each object to see which could be used to help you transform the sentence so that the objects are reversed in order. As you will see, *to* can only be inserted in front of *the child*, as in *Malia gave the test <u>to the child</u>*, since *Malia gave the child <u>to the test</u>* does not make sense. *The child* must, then, be the indirect object.

The Subject Complement

Some sentences have subjects and verbs but no direct or indirect objects. Despite their apparent shortcomings (they have no objects!), such sentences can appear complex, at least in terms of analyzing their structure. For example, each of the sentences below contains a subject, a verb, and additional information about the subject:

The famous linguist was **Noam Chomsky**.

It is **I**.

Ginger will be **famous**.

Notice that the additional information doesn't include a direct object or an indirect object. Instead, it includes a predicate nominative (a noun or a pronoun) or a predicate adjective—collectively known as *subject complements*.

Subject complements provide further information about a subject and follow *copular* (also known as *linking*) verbs. (See, there really was a reason you had to learn about these in Chapter 3! But just in case you forgot: Copular verbs include the *be* verbs [e.g., *is, am,* and *are*] as well as a handful of intransitive verbs like *seem, feel,* and *become*.) Sentences that contain a predicate nominative or a predicate adjective following a copular verb have the following sentence structure:

Subject + (Copular) Verb + Subject Complement

While a subject and an object (which follows a transitive verb) refer to different entities, a subject and a subject complement (which follows a copular verb) refer to the same entity (Williamson, 2001). That is, the copular verb links the subject to the complement much like an equal sign (=). For example, in the sentence *Hiroshi is becoming sleepy, sleepy* refers back to *Hiroshi*. Some scholars (e.g., Gordon, 1993) might also describe object complements, but since this is our book, we're going to focus only on subject complements, since they're more important to language interventionists.

The Predicate

If the subject is the instigator of the action or state reflected in the verb in a sentence, then the **predicate** may be viewed as the action or state that is "stated, asked, ordered, or exclaimed by the use of a finite verb" (Opdycke, 1965, p. 224). Opdycke's definition suggests, though, that the predicate is synonymous with the verb in a sentence, which is, in fact, not so. The predicate is actually everything in a sentence that is not the subject; that is, the verb and its constituents. (Note that this can include subject complements as well.) This being the case, it's not very difficult to identify the predicate of a sentence once you identify the subject:

I **always jog with my dog**.

Clearly, she **is in this for the prestige**.

He **was hit with the baseball bat**.

We **arrived by bus, but then took a cab to the inn**.

Cora **is the author of the book**.

The predicate needs to agree with the subject in terms of tense and number. The subject slots in the next examples are filled by a noun (*Grandpa*), a more complex noun phrase (*my sister Nancy*), and pronoun (*they*). In the first two examples, the subject is singular and thus the verbs that follow (*was* and *is*) are also singular in form. In the last example, the subject is plural (*they*) and therefore the verb that follows (*are*) is plural too:

Grandpa was jumping.

My sister Nancy is attending Humboldt State University.

They both **are** attending Humboldt State University.

One way to characterize the information comprising the predicate slot is by the following distinction: simple predicate, complete predicate, and compound predicate. The **simple predicate**, also referred to as the *essential predicate,* is usually the main verb in the sentence or clause (e.g., *descended* in *The mist descended slowly*). As the simple predicate, *descended* provides the principle information contained in the entire predicate. The rest is detail. The simple predicate plus all the modifiers that provide additional information about the simple predicate form the **complete predicate** (e.g., *descended slowly* in *The mist descended slowly*). **Compound predicates** consist of two or more simple predicates (e.g., *descended* and *evaporated* in *The mist descended and evaporated*).

There are many systems of classification (beyond simple, complete, and compound) for making sense of the myriad of predicate types. The system we use in this handbook is that prescribed by Palmer (1939) in his text on the grammar of English. According to Palmer, predicates (whether simple, complete, or compound) may best be classified into two main categories: nominal predicates and verbal predicates.

Nominal Predicates

Nominal predicates occur when the verb in a sentence is copular. Generally speaking, the copular function is seen primarily with the *be* verbs (e.g., *is, am, are*), but also with such linking verbs as *get, seem, look,* and *keep.* Recall from Chapter 3 that these particular types of verbs do not require an object of the action and are referred to as **intransitive verbs**. When the predicate slot is filled by a nominal predicate, it includes primarily the copular verb followed by a noun, a pronoun, a prepositional phrase, an adjective, or an adverb:

It **is** a **fungus**. (copula + noun)

You **are** the **one**! (copula + pronoun)

The hat **is in the closet**. (copula + prepositional phrase)

The cake **looks horrible**! (copula + adjective)

It **is over**. (copula + adverb)

These types of predicate structures were described in the previous section as *subject complements*, and the terms are more or less synonymous. Differentiation is subtle and really a matter of terminology: *subject complement* vs. *nominal predicate*. Some scholars use the term *predicate* to refer to information following transitive verbs, and use the term *complement* to refer to information following copular verbs. The following details on the various categories of nominal predicates are provided for students and practitioners involved or interested in more specific levels of syntactic analysis.

Given the infinite number of sentences that can be generated by the individual mind, there is seemingly an endless classification of nominal predicates. A number of the more commonly seen types of nominal predicates may be categorized along four primary dimensions: (1) prepositional noun predicates, (2) prepositionless noun predicates, (3) qualificative predicates, and (4) adverbial predicates.

The first category of nominal predicates is the **prepositional noun predicate**. This refers to sentences in which a prepositional phrase follows a copular verb:

The bananas **are in the basket**.

The diagnosis **seems by the book**.

The second category of nominal predicates is that of the **prepositionless noun predicate**. As with all nominal predicates, the main verb is copular. But, in this case, the information following the verb is a noun (or a pronoun) with no prepositional information included:

Those **are not your black gloves**.

Money **isn't everything**.

The third category of nominal predicates is that of the **qualificative predicate**. In these cases, the subject is followed by a copular verb and the predicate provides qualitative information about the subject:

The fish **is absolutely delicious**.

She **seems a little shy**.

The final category is the **adverbial predicate**. In these cases, the copular verb is followed by an adverb:

It **is not here**.

The airplane **appears far away**.

Verbal Predicates

Verbal predicates occur when the verb in a sentence is transitive (i.e., not a copula or a linking verb). Examples of transitive verbs, while seemingly endless, include *think, pull, know, give, understand, hit,* and *take*. Verbal predicates may be categorized along five dimensions: (1) verb standing alone, (2) prepositional object, (3) prepositionless object, (4) adverb, and (5) adverb clause.

The first category, **verb standing alone**, is seen with a free-standing verb; that is, a subject is followed by a verb that stands alone. However, verbs may be modified by tense with auxiliaries:

> I **understand**.
>
> She **does understand**.

The second category of verbal predicates is that of the **prepositional object**. Again, the verb must be transitive. The prepositional object is seen in cases in which the predicate contains indirect objects or modifying information about manner, place, or time:

> She called **with his calling card**. (manner)
>
> Carlos called **from Alaska**. (place)
>
> Luke will come **on Wednesday**. (time)

The third category of verbal predicates is that of the **prepositionless object**. In these cases, the verb is followed by a direct or an indirect object with no modification by prepositional information. This category also includes those predicates (with full-meaning transitive verbs) that contain information about manner, place, or time:

> The pan **hit the table**. (direct object)
>
> You **give her the money**. (indirect and direct objects)
>
> She **called using his calling card**. (manner)
>
> Carlos **called Alaska**. (place)
>
> Luke **will come Wednesday**. (time)

The fourth category of verbal predicates is the **adverb**. In such instances, the verb is followed by an adverb (sometimes with an intervening direct object):

> We **teach here**.
>
> The clinician **conducted** the screening **hastily**.

The fifth category of verbal predicates is that of the **adverb clause**. These are similar to the previous example with the exception that the adverbial information is presented in the form of a clause:

> She **addressed** them **before the microphone was on**.
>
> I **will go when I am ready**.

Table 9.1 provides an overview of Palmer's (1939) predicate classification system. While to readers today this must seem ancient, our syntactic system (including the classification of predicates) is not something that changes; thus, it is safe to rely on classical resources, as we do in much of this book. Remember, nominal predicates often contain copulas or intransitive verbs, whereas verbal predicates often contain transitive verbs.

Developmental Notes

When very young children begin to produce sentences (two- and three-word combinations), they are generally not described in terms of their syntactic structure, but rather by the semantic relations expressed among the sentence constituents. In other words, sentences such as *kitty eat* and *Mommy up* are referred to by the semantic (or semantic-syntactic) relations among words, not their sentence structure. Both the examples given above fall within a semantic relations category described as "Agent + Action." It is not typically until about Brown's (1973) Stage III, when the child's mean length of utterance (MLU) is within the boundaries of 2.5 to 2.99, that terms relating to syntactic structure are generally used to describe young children's sentences. It is within this period, beginning at about 31 months, that we begin to see true development of sentence structure emerge. For example, at about 31 months, young children demonstrate mastery of several basic forms of sentences, such as "Subject + Verb + Object" and "Subject + Copula + Complement" (Crystal, Fletcher, & Garman, 1974). At this point, characterization of children's sentence structure—with respect to analysis of subject and predicate structures—becomes possible.

TABLE 9.1
Palmer's (1939) Predicate Classification System

NOMINAL PREDICATES	EXAMPLE
Prepositional Noun Predicate	The child <u>was with her</u>.
Prepositionless Noun Predicate	The child <u>is my friend</u>.
Qualificative Predicate	The child <u>is so fussy</u>!
Adverbial Predicate	The child <u>is back</u>.
VERBAL PREDICATES	
Verb Standing Alone	That child <u>is yelling</u>.
Prepositional Object Prepositionless	The child <u>is calling to her mother</u>.
Object	The child <u>is holding something</u>.
Adverb	The child <u>fell yesterday</u>.
Adverbial Clause	The child <u>panicked when mom came</u>.

In the subsequent chapters, we discuss children's development of phrases and clauses and their acquisition of various sentence types. In this second edition, we've included a new chapter (Chapter 13), which provides a useful overview of complex syntax, pulling together content addressed in Chapters 1–12. For readers who desire more depth, we refer them to Turnbull and Justice (2011) and Retherford (1996, 2000). To preface these upcoming discussions, a brief explanation of the young child's developmental progression in syntactic acquisition is provided here.

Crystal et al. (1974), in a classic text, characterize children's acquisition of syntax as a seven-stage process, with the sixth stage representing completion of the syntactic system. Specifically, these authors hypothesize that there is a distinct set of syntactic stages through which children progress towards adult language. We find Crystal et al.'s stage descriptions of particular interest due to their interpretation of very young children's utterances in syntactic, rather than only semantic, terms. Hence we include a synopsis of their stages here. Of primary interest to the current discussion are those stages during which it appears that true sentence structure emerges.

Stage One, in which one-element sentences predominate, typically transcends the period from about 9–18 months. "Sentences" at this stage consist of one word, which we may liberally refer to as nouns (*Daddy*), verbs (*up!*), or questions (*Mommy?*).

Stage Two, in which two-element sentences predominate, transcends the period from about 18–24 months. Within this time frame, children with typical development use sentence patterns that consist of two structural (syntactic) elements. In other words, "given a possible S-V-O-A type sentence [Subject + Verb + Object + Adverbial], e.g., *Daddy will kick the ball into the car*, typical sentences emerge as having any two out of a maximum four elements, viz, *Daddy kick, Daddy ball, Daddy car, kick ball, kick car,* or *ball car*" (Crystal et al., 1974, p. 67). In these productions (given enough context to judge the child's intent), *Daddy car* could be classified as "Subject + Adverb," whereas *ball car* could be characterized as a complement consisting of "Object + Adverb." Conventional sentence patterns that are used within this time frame include "Subject + Verb": *Daddy kick*, "Subject + Object/Complement": *Daddy ball* or *me baby*, and "Verb + Object/Complement": *want kitty* or *be baby*.

Stage Three, the period in which three-element sentences predominate, occurs from about 24–30 months. Many syntactic advances occur during this pivotal period of linguistic growth. It is within this time frame that "true" sentence structure emerges. In other words, such classic sentence constructions as "Subject + Verb + Object" (S + V + O) become prevalent. Several important trends that warrant mention are the development of subject, object, and complement expansions. Children begin to combine adjectives with nouns to expand the subject slot (e.g., <u>red hat</u> on or <u>big baby</u> eat), determiners with nouns to expand the object slot (e.g., see <u>that kitty</u> or want <u>this one</u>), and adjectives or determiners with nouns to expand the complement slot (e.g., are <u>mean boys</u> or is <u>this dress</u>). Sentence patterns, at this time, clearly depict true subject and predicate structures, in particular those three-element sentences neatly comprising the S + V + O pattern, such as *Tommy kick me, me want cookie,* and *baby drink milk*.

At Stage Four, four-element sentences predominate. This period occurs typically from about 30–36 months. As with the third stage, major syntactic developments occur during this very important, and surprisingly brief, period. S + V + O sentences become even more complex and syntactically specific: *The puppy ate the peanut, Daddy gave it to me,* and so on. Both direct and indirect objects begin to be used with precision in this period. Also, most varieties of nominal and verbal predicates are seen to emerge within this time frame: *That is my coat!* (prepositionless noun predicate), *Baby's in the bed* (prepositional noun predicate), *I'm eating* (verb standing alone predicate), and *Mommy's going outside* (adverb predicate).

By Stage Five (36–42 months), children have more or less mastered clause and phrase structure rules. This means that fully realized sentence structure has occurred. Within Stages Five and Six, subtle nuances in syntactic acquisition occur, such as development of the recursive system (learning those connective devices, such as subordinating conjunctions, that allow them to interrelate clauses).

Stage Six, which is reached at about 42 months, characterizes what Crystal et al. (1974) call "system completion," meaning that the major elements of syntactic acquisition are in place. In other words, "stable patterns of word order, along with a wide range of sentence structures and types, are at the root of this impression, and make the speech highly intelligible, so that one often fails to notice the many 'local' errors of syntax which remain to be sorted out, or the new ways in which syntactic processes already present come to be extended" (p. 78). Once the basic variety of syntactic forms and functions are achieved, the child learns to incorporate and refine pragmatic influences, thus enriching and enhancing language function into a rich, complex system.

CHAPTER EXERCISES

Exercise 9A

Place brackets around the subject of each sentence below.

1. Language development is a fascinating area of research.
2. I expect the leaves will start turning in October.
3. Accurate pronoun usage tends to be particularly difficult for children with a language impairment.
4. The car wreck was on the news last night.
5. Keeping people happy is my main objective.
6. The man with the tattoo will probably be our waiter.
7. The well water tested out all right.
8. I don't know where she keeps the coupons.
9. We will probably go to the sale on Thursday.
10. Joe Alamo, the guest speaker, always runs late.

Exercise 9B

Identify the underlined item in each sentence as the Direct Object (DO) or the Indirect Object (IDO).

_____ 1. Have your mother sign <u>the form</u>.
_____ 2. Give <u>her</u> the note you wanted me to read.
_____ 3. You need to tell <u>her</u> that.
_____ 4. Give <u>the officer</u> the registration.
_____ 5. The student asked <u>the principal</u> about the new rules.
_____ 6. The dog brought <u>the ball</u> back to the owner.
_____ 7. We paid <u>the bill</u> right on time.
_____ 8. Please give <u>the children</u> their lunch.
_____ 9. The car hit <u>the side rail</u>.
_____ 10. Give <u>Allison</u> the message that I won't be going.

Exercise 9C

Categorize each of the underlined predicate structures as either a Nominal Predicate (NPr) or a Verbal Predicate (VPr).

_____ 1. Nancy <u>will call tomorrow</u>.

_____ 2. Those flowers <u>are gorgeous</u>!

_____ 3. The wheelbarrow <u>is around back</u>.

_____ 4. Johnny <u>seems really tired</u>.

_____ 5. The manager <u>will be here tomorrow</u>.

_____ 6. The group <u>is meeting on Friday</u>.

_____ 7. Please <u>eat</u>!

_____ 8. He <u>feels warm</u>.

_____ 9. It <u>is up there</u>.

_____ 10. The class <u>is going on Friday</u>.

Exercise 9D

Read the following excerpt of a language interventionist (LI) conversing with J, her 7-year-old client. Place a slash (/) between the subject and the predicate in each of J's utterances.

LI: Can you tell me what the story was about?

J: Um, a man and his wife got a turnip.

LI: And then what happened?

**J: They wanted to pull it out of the ground.
But it was stuck.
It was too big.**

LI: And . . .

J: They got the farm animals to help.

LI: What kind of farm animals?

**J: They got their cats and dogs to help.
And the goats and cows helped too.
The animals pulled on the turnip.
And then the turnip came out.**

LI: And what happened to the turnip?

J: They cut it up for dinner.

Exercise 9E

Classify the nominal predicates in the following sentences as one of the following four major categories: Prepositional Noun Predicate (P), Prepositionless Noun Predicate (PL), Qualificative Predicate (Q), or Adverbial Predicate (A).

_____ 1. The milk is in the refrigerator.
_____ 2. She looked a little tired.
_____ 3. The goal seems attainable.
_____ 4. Those are your muddy footprints.
_____ 5. The lawn is a luscious green color.
_____ 6. The tent looks usable.
_____ 7. The message seemed unclear.
_____ 8. Your check is inside your wallet.
_____ 9. This dog is a champion.
_____ 10. Beef jerky keeps well.

ANSWER KEY

Exercise 9A

1. [Language development] is a fascinating area of research.
2. [I] expect the leaves will start turning in October.
3. [Accurate pronoun usage] tends to be particularly difficult for children with a language impairment.
4. [The car wreck] was on the news last night.
5. [Keeping people happy] is my main objective.
6. [The man with the tattoo] will probably be our waiter.
7. [The well water] tested out all right.
8. [I] don't know where she keeps the coupons.
9. [We] will probably go to the sale on Thursday.
10. [Joe Alamo, the guest speaker,] always runs late.

Exercise 9B

1. DO
2. IDO
3. IDO
4. IDO
5. DO
6. DO
7. DO
8. IDO
9. DO
10. IDO

Exercise 9C

1. VPr
2. NPr
3. NPr
4. NPr
5. NPr
6. VPr
7. VPr
8. NPr
9. NPr
10. VPr

Exercise 9D

LI: Can you tell me what the story was about?

J: Um, a man and his wife/ got a turnip.

LI: And then what happened?

J: They/ wanted to pull it out of the ground.
But it/ was stuck.
It/ was too big.

LI: And . . .

J: They/ got the farm animals to help.

LI: What kind of farm animals?

J: They/ got their cats and dogs to help.
And the goats and cows/ helped too.
The animals/ pulled on the turnip.
And then the turnip/ came out.

LI: And what happened to the turnip?

J: They/ cut it up for dinner.

Exercise 9E

1. P
2. Q
3. A
4. PL
5. Q
6. A
7. A
8. P
9. PL
10. A

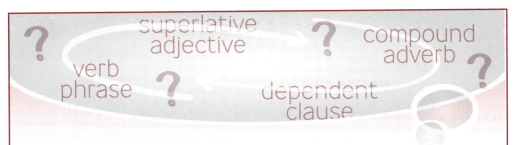

CHAPTER TEN

Phrases

Chapter at a Glance

What Is a Phrase?

Heads of Phrases

Types of Phrases
- Noun Phrases
- Verb Phrases
- Prepositional Phrases
- Adjective Phrases
- Adverb Phrases
- Infinitive Phrases
- Participle Phrases
- Gerund Phrases

Developmental Notes

Chapter Exercises

Answer Key

What Is a Phrase?

Chapter 9 described two ways to classify the major slots in a sentence: "Subject + Predicate" and "Subject + Verb + Object." An additional way to classify sentences, "Subject + Verb + Subject Complement," was also referred to in the previous chapter. Regardless of how you label the sentence elements, the slots are rarely filled by single words. That is, there are few sentences as simple as the following:

Jack ate.

Mother agreed.

Kitty jumped.

Leslie is.

In the above examples, the subject and predicate slots (or subject and verb slots) are filled with single words. More typically, though, these slots are filled by more elaborate structures that provide additional information:

My brother Jack ate the leftovers after the party.

Mother agreed with the neurologist regarding the diagnosis.

Harry's new kitty jumped when the ball rolled by her.

Leslie is not coming to the party.

These examples are composed of a series of phrases that fill the major sentence slots. A **phrase** is a syntactic structure that includes one main word and usually one or more closely associated words grouped around it. By some contentions, a phrase can consist of just one word. It could also be argued that a phrase must comprise at least two or more words. In this text, we refer to phrases as structures that contain one or more words.

A phrase, in and of itself, does not have its own subject or predicate; phrases can, however, serve the role of subject or predicate within a sentence. For example, the first sentence in the previous set of examples contains four phrases, one of which forms the subject and three of which are parts of the predicate:

My brother Jack (subject [noun phrase])

ate (predicate [verb phrase])

the leftovers (predicate [noun phrase])

after the party (predicate [prepositional phrase])

So what we know so far about phases is that:

- Phrases include one or more words.
- Phrases may fill the subject or predicate slot in a sentence.
- Phrases can be combined to form sentences.
- Phrases cannot stand alone. (Phrases in and of themselves do not constitute a meaningful sentence, given that they do not contain both a subject and a predicate.)

The building blocks of phrases are nouns, verbs, adjectives, adverbs, prepositions, and so on—the parts of speech you brushed up on in the first eight chapters of this handbook (since you apparently forgot everything your English teacher taught you years ago!). For example, in the sentence presented earlier, *My brother Jack ate the leftovers after the party,* the noun phrase *My brother Jack* is composed of a determiner (the possessive pronoun *my*), an adjectival modifier (*brother*), and a proper noun (*Jack*). So you could say that the building blocks of a phrase are the parts of speech. Along those same lines, you could say that the building blocks of sentences are phrases and clauses (clauses are covered next, in Chapter 11). Think of the structure of sentences, then, as occurring in a hierarchy:

Word → Phrase → Clause → Sentence

This schema has the word as the basic building block of the phrase, the phrase as the basic building block of the clause, and the clause as the basic building block of the sentence. Another way of looking at this hierarchy is to say that a phrase includes one or more words, a clause includes one or more phrases, and a sentence includes one or more clauses.

Heads of Phrases

A phrase typically has one central element, referred to as the *head* of the phrase. Heads of phrases can be nouns, verbs, adjectives, adverbs, and prepositions, as the following examples illustrate:

Noun as head: The blue **bonnet**

Verb as head: will **drive**

Adjective as head: more **intelligent**

Adverb as head: much too **assertively**

Preposition as head: **in** the cupboard

A noun phrase has a noun (or a pronoun) as its head, a verb phrase has a verb as its head, an adjective phrase has an adjective as its head, an adverb phrase has an adverb as its head, and a prepositional phrase has a preposition as its head. These different types of phrases are considered in the following sections. We also consider three types of phrases that do not have heads and are therefore distinct types of phrases. They are phrases formed with nonfinite verb elements: the infinitive, the participle, and the gerund.

Types of Phrases

Noun Phrases

Noun phrases always contain a noun or a pronoun as the head. Even if a noun or a pronoun occurs alone, it is still the head and is still classified as a noun phrase in terms of its syntactic function. For example, in a sentence like *Stephen checked out the test*, *Stephen* is a single word proper noun, but it is still considered a noun phrase in the sentence. More often, however, noun phrases begin with a determiner. Remember from Chapter 6 that these include articles, possessives, demonstratives, quantifiers, and *wh-* words. Noun phrases also may include adjectives, often following a determiner (e.g., *the pretty flower*). Determiners and adjectives included within a noun phrase are usually called *modifiers,* because they provide additional information about (i.e., they modify) the head noun. Take a look at the following examples of various types of noun phrases (the noun phrases of interest are highlighted):

> Jackie picked up **a penny**. (determiner + common noun)
>
> **Leonard** threw it. (proper noun)
>
> Penny has **an iPad**. (determiner + proper noun)
>
> **That little girl** needs to be seen. (determiner + adjective + common noun)
>
> Give **those two new shoes** to me. (determiner + determiner + adjective + common noun)

Note that when a noun phrase follows a preposition, it is classified as a prepositional phrase (covered later in this chapter), not a noun phrase. For example, in the last example above, the pronoun *me* would get lumped together with the preposition *to* to create the prepositional phrase *to me*.

On occasion, a noun phrase can rename another noun phrase. When one noun phrase adds new information to another noun phrase without modifying it, the two noun phrases are said to be in apposition. In the following examples, *Rick Ashbolt* and *a little black dog* are what we call *appositive phrases* because they refer back to the noun phrases *my teacher* and *Detroit*.

> My teacher, **Rick Ashbolt**, likes cats.
>
> Detroit, **a little black dog**, is adorable.

In terms of function, noun phrases may serve as the subject, object, or complement in a clause or sentence. Noun phrases can also serve an adverbial function, often seen in the predicate structure. See Table 10.1 for examples of noun phrase functions.

Verb Phrases

Every sentence and clause contains a verb phrase. The **verb phrase** serves as the main structure of the predicate and includes the main verb, any auxiliary forms attached, and any modifiers. Just as noun phrases can consist of a single noun, so, too, can verb phrases consist of a single verb, as the first example below indicates:

>The boy **came**.
>
>Sheila **will be leaving** shortly.
>
>He **should have told** her about the results.

Recall from Chapter 3 that verbs are vital to overall sentence structure in that they provide information about time, person, number, mood, and voice. Such details are contained within the verb phrase. There are four basic patterns of "Auxiliary + Main" combinations that can form a verb phrase (Leech, 1991), as illustrated in Table 10.2. Clearly, the verb phrase—in all its simplicity—can provide key information regarding the overall meaning of a sentence.

The key element of a verb phrase is the main verb, which serves as the head of the phrase. For example, in Table 10.2, the main verb in all the verb phrase examples is a form of *help*. Also see Table 3.5 (Chapter 3), which shows 54 verb phrases following the initial pronoun in each sentence. Even though the verb phrases in Table 3.5 take so many different forms, all 54 of them can function as only one thing: a verb phrase.

Prepositional Phrases

In a study of communication disorders graduate students' knowledge of syntactic structures, performance was highest for their ability to recognize prepositional phrases, as compared to other types of phrases, such as verb phrases (Justice & Ezell, 1999). (So

TABLE 10.1
Noun Phrase Functions

FUNCTION	EXAMPLE
Subject	*The child* was very frightened.
Object	Susan shared *some candy* with her.
Complement	This is *the one*!
Adverbial	We visited *last week*.

TABLE 10.2
Common Verb Phrase Patterns

PATTERN	EXAMPLE
Modal (modal + verb)	The children *may help*.
Perfect (*have* + past participle)	The children *have helped*.
Progressive (*be* + *-ing* verb)	The children *are helping*.
Passive (*be* + past participle)	The children *were helped*.

there's hope yet that you'll understand what a phrase is, if you don't already!) Prepositional phrases are generally easy to recognize because they always begin with a preposition. Remember from Chapter 8 that some common prepositions include *about, along, at, before, between, by, for, in, near, of, onto, over, since, through, to, under, with,* and *without*.

A **prepositional phrase** is a group of two or more words that begins with a preposition. The preposition itself is the head of the prepositional phrase, although some would argue that, in fact, the object of the prepositional phrase (the noun to which the preposition is referring) is the head. But as we said in Chapter 2, since this is our book, we're going to give you our opinion on the matter, and we say that the head of the prepositional phrase is the initial preposition.

The prepositional phrase thus consists of the preposition and its object, which typically occurs in the form of a noun phrase. Remember that a noun phrase can be as simple as a single noun or a pronoun. Here are some examples of prepositional phrases used in sentences:

> Put the oranges **in the basket**.
>
> Nathan did not do well **on the comprehension subtest**.
>
> She said she gave it **to her**.
>
> **In January**, we will go **to San Francisco**.

Prepositional phrases generally function either adverbially or adjectivally. In other words, they modify nouns and verbs, as the following examples demonstrate:

> I'll stop by **on Friday**. (adverbial function)
>
> The car has been broken **since last week**. (adverbial function)
>
> The bananas **in the basket** are for you. (adjectival function)
>
> His relationship **with her** is a disaster. (adjectival function)

Adjective Phrases

Recall from Chapter 4 that descriptive adjectives function primarily as modifiers of nouns and pronouns (e.g., the *new* test and *two* more). Well, adjective phrases serve the same purposes. In **adjective phrases**, an adjective serves as the head of the phrase and may at times be the only component in the adjective phrase, as the following examples illustrate:

> She has **outlandish** taste in clothing.
>
> The test is **expensive**.

In the latter example, *expensive* is a predicate adjective phrase as well as a subject complement. If you're feeling confused, remember that language is at once an art and a science (meaning that things can go by many different names and we have to know all of them).

An adjective phrase may also be seen in the grouping of several words used together as a single unit to modify a noun, as in the following:

> Give us the **play-by-play** details.
>
> Your donation is **tax-deductible**.

Unlike modified noun phrases (e.g., *the dark green <u>shirt</u>*, in which shirt is modified by three words), modified adjective phrases usually include only one modifier, as seen in the next examples. Note that in such cases, the premodifier of the adjective phrase is typically an adverb (e.g., *very, quite, much,* and *too*):

> She has **quite outlandish** taste in clothing.
>
> The test is **very expensive**.

On rare occasions, two modifiers can occur in an adjective phrase, as the following example illustrates. Again, these adjectival modifiers tend to be adverbs:

> It was **much too difficult** for her.

In some cases, adjective phrases may be seen with postmodification, also typically appearing in the form of an adverb:

> The tuition was **expensive enough**.
>
> Her voice is **dysphonic indeed**.

Some scholars (e.g., Master, 1995) classify groupings of adverbs and adjectives that precede nouns as adjective phrases, as in the following example:

> It was a **very difficult** test to give.

In this example, *very difficult* could be classified as an adjective phrase, preceded by a determiner (*a*) and followed by a noun (*test*). However, another way of looking at the phrase *a very difficult test* and similar structures (e.g., *the dark, dreary morning*) is to classify the entire structure as a noun phrase that consists of a determiner, adjectival modifiers, and a head noun. What is most important in your work as a language interventionist is that you develop a consistent system for analysis. In other words, if you choose to refer to constructions like *a very difficult test* as a noun phrase, then feel free to do so, but do so consistently. In this book, *a very difficult test* is considered a noun phrase.

On a functional note, most other types of phrases can take on an adjectival role. In such cases, these phrases are best characterized by identifying their form as well as their function. For instance, in the sentence *Give me the pencil on that table*, the phrase *on that table* is a prepositional phrase in form, but functionally is narrowing down the properties of *the pencil,* and thus could be viewed functionally as an adjective phrase. Again, you're free to label such phrases either way, but do so consistently.

Adverb Phrases

Adverb phrases have an adverb at the head. Similar to adjective phrases, adverb phrases may consist of a single word (in this case, an adverb), as in the following:

I read **daily**.

Please put that **here**.

Adverb phrases can also consist of a head adverb pre- or postmodified by additional adverbs or adjectives, as in the following:

Rather quickly, panic set in.

Chyanne has been calling him **much too often**.

She smiled **quite brilliantly** for the camera.

Often, but not always, adverb phrases occur at the beginning or end of a sentence, although the last sentence in the examples above demonstrates an adverb phrase in the middle of a sentence. It's important to note that the function of the adverb phrase is the same as that of the simple adverb (Master, 1995): to provide information about manner, place, time, degree, number, reason, affirmation, and negation. Here are examples for each adverbial function:

The children argued **quite loudly**. (manner)

Put that **right here**. (place)

Do it **right now**. (time)

Aaron works **ever so well**. (degree)

We are **first**. (number)

Consequently, we will stay. (reason)

The teacher was **quite right**. (affirmation)

Arturo has **not ever** called. (negation)

In terms of function, any phrase serving one of these purposes (specifying degree, number, reason, and so forth) is considered an adverb phrase. In such instances, as with the phrase *after lunch* in *Take the test after lunch*, it may be helpful to specify a phrase's form (*after lunch* is a prepositional phrase) as well as its function (functionally, *after lunch* is adverbial, indicating time).

Infinitive Phrases

The **infinitive phrase** is a special type of phrase that uses the infinitive form of a verb to introduce the phrase. (See Chapter 3 for a review of infinitives.) Some view infinitives as a special type of clause (clause structure is discussed in the next chapter), but infinitives really do not fit neatly into the clause category. This is because infinitives contain a verb (a predicate), but they usually do not contain a subject. And as you will learn in Chapter 11, clauses are defined by their nature of containing their own subject and predicate. To this end, we consider infinitives in this chapter on phrases, but recognize that some people may find this a violation of their keen syntactic sense. Our decision to not consider infinitives to be clauses is consistent with procedures used to analyze narrative language described in several classic texts, including those by Loban (1976) and Hunt (1965). Loban's CU (communication unit) and Hunt's T-unit (minimal terminable unit) are both based on a count of independent and dependent clauses in the narrative. However, be aware that various procedures for syntactic analysis (e.g., as described by Retherford, 2000) consider the infinitive phrase a dependent clause that contributes to sentence complexity. The bottom line is that you'll need to know and follow the rules of the procedure you're using.

Infinitive phrases consist of the infinitive (i.e., the bare stem of a verb [e.g., *carry*] preceded by the word *to* [e.g., *to carry*]) plus any objects or modifiers:

> To feel successful in your career, you must be able **to plan long-range goals**.

Infinitive phrases include *nonfinite* verbs, in that the verb contained within does not reflect tense and number. (In contrast, *finite* verbs carry information about tense and number.) Infinitive phrases typically do not contain a subject; on occasion, the subject of the infinitive phrase is the subject of the main clause to which it refers. For example:

> She wants him **to go**.

> She wants **to go**.

In the first example, *she* is the subject of *wants* and *him* is the subject of *go*. In the second example, *she* is the subject of both *want* and *go*.

On the rare occasion that infinitive phrases do have subjects, the subjects are usually preceded by the word *for*:

> Ginger is waiting **for us to come**.

> The pediatrician is waiting **for you to send the report**.

Although the presence of an infinitive form of a verb (e.g., *to come*) can be a useful clue in recognizing the presence of an infinitive phrase, sometimes the word *to* is not present. When this occurs, the phrase is referred to as a *bare infinitive*. The infinitive phrases in the following examples are highlighted and the assumed *to* is bracketed:

> Help them **[to] get the room ready**.

> Nicole wouldn't dare **[to] tell me**.

The following examples each include two infinitive phrases, the first of which includes a traditional *to-infinitive*, the second of which is a *bare infinitive:*

Lucy is not **to leave** until she helps them **prepare the room**.

Susan wants **to share the book** rather than **give it** to them.

You can see that in these sorts of sentences, which include both traditional and bare infinitives, it may be difficult to accurately identify the phrasal structures comprising the sentences. Also, an infinitive phrase could be confused with a prepositional phrase (e.g., *to them,* in the second sentence above), but remember that in a prepositional phrase, *to* is followed by a noun or a pronoun and in an infinitive phrase, *to* is followed by a verb. Your increasingly sophisticated knowledge of syntax will serve you well, and you'll find such identification tasks will become simple. (Really, you will!)

Participle Phrases

Participle phrases are another special type of phrase. Recall from Chapter 3 that the **past participle** is a verb form used to depict past tense. For example, *slept, walked, called,* and *met* are all past participles. In contrast, the **present participle** denotes time occurring in the present tense; it may also be referred to as the *present progressive -ing* form of the verb. Present participles of the above verbs include *sleeping, walking, calling,* and *meeting.*

In a participle phrase, either the past participle or the present participle of a verb is the main word in the phrase. Participle phrases may serve adjectival and adverbial functions, as the following examples illustrate:

Born with severe hearing loss, Lisa was learning to sign. (past participle form, adjectival function)

Being a very moral person, Lisa told her boss the dilemma. (present participle form, adjectival function)

Directed toward the door, Trevor felt put off. (past participle form, adverbial function)

Arriving late, Trevor decided to sneak in the back door. (present participle form, adverbial function)

Participle phrases may also be introduced by subordinating conjunctions. (You remember what those are from Chapter 7, right?) The first word in each of the following participle phrases is a subordinating conjunction:

Before arriving at the lab, I stopped off for a sandwich.

When working in the clinic, you cannot wear open-toed shoes.

Like the infinitive discussed in the previous section, the participle structures described here are sometimes viewed as a type of clause (and specifically, a type of nonfinite clause). We consider them here as a special type of phrase because they do not fit neatly into the clause category. (They don't fit neatly into the phrase category either, but they certainly don't merit their own chapter; therefore, we put them here and nod graciously when other more advanced scholars argue with us.) And as mentioned earlier, our decision is consistent with procedures used by other researchers (e.g., Hunt, 1965; Loban, 1963).

Gerund Phrases

A third controversial structure is that of the gerund phrase. Again, there are some scholars who would view the gerund phrase as a clause, but in keeping with our previous decisions, we discuss gerunds as phrases.

A gerund is formed by adding *-ing* to the verb stem (to form the present participle). A gerund phrase includes a gerund plus any objects or modifiers. A gerund phrase always functions as a noun in the sentence, as shown in the following examples:

We like **playing dominoes**.

Hunting little mice is my cat's passion.

Cooking helps me relax.

Developmental Notes

In Chapter 9 we pointed out that by about 31 months of age—during Brown's (1973) Stage III—children are fairly adept at using the basic sentence structure of "Subject + Verb + Object" (e.g., *Kitty wants milk*). Elaboration of subjects and verbs—clearly recognizable as noun phrases and verb phrases—within sentences begins to occur at about this period. Prior to this period, however, elaborated nouns (which we may assert marks the period of the first use of noun phrases) may be seen as early as 19 months. Noun phrases, occurring not yet in true sentences at 27 months, but rather in two-element utterances, typically include indefinite articles or demonstratives in addition to the head word (e.g., *a baby, that cookie,* and *big hat*). About this same time (27 months), children elaborate simple verbs by adding present progressive inflections to verbs (e.g., *eating* and *going*) and by using semi-infinitives, referred to as *catenatives* (e.g., *gonna* and *hafta*).

By Brown's Stage III (31–44 months), however, declarative sentences (S + V + O) are a natural part of a child's speech. True noun phrases and verb phrases become a regular part of the child's syntax. Noun phrases, which fill the subject and object slots of these early declaratives, include formats such as "Demonstrative + Noun" (e.g., *this baby* sleeping), "Article + Noun" (e.g., *the kitty* ran), and "Adjective + Noun" (e.g., Give me *big cookie*). At the same time, true verb phrases are also evident, commensurate with the child's attainment of many of the grammatical or inflectional morphemes, such as uncontractible copula, regular past tense *-ed,* and the regular third person *-s*. Auxiliary verbs are frequently used in coordination with main verbs in Brown's Stage III (e.g., Sally *is going*, baby *was sleeping*, and I *can go*) (Brown, 1973). By Brown's Stage IV (35–42 months), children are further embellishing their use of verb phrases by including modal auxiliaries (e.g., *could*, *would*, and *might*) to assert intention. Also at this time, infinitive phrases appear, often occurring at the ends of sentences (e.g., I want *to go* and Mommy said *to stay*).

Crystal, Fletcher, and Garman (1974), a key reference on children's syntactic stages that was introduced in "Developmental Notes" in Chapter 9, provide a chronology of children's development of phrase structures. Table 10.3 provides an overview of Crystal et al.'s abbreviations for describing syntactic advances. These abbreviations are also used in Table 10.4, which provides an overview of phrase structure attainments adapted from their work. You may find these abbreviations useful in your own work.

TABLE 10.3
Abbreviations Used in the Study of Syntax
(Crystal, Fletcher, & Garman, 1974)

ABBREVIATION	SYNTACTIC STRUCTURE
ADJ	Adjective
ADV	Adverb
AUX	Auxiliary
CONJ	Conjunction
COORD CONJ	Coordinating Conjunction
DET	Determiner
N	Noun
NEG	Negative
NP	Noun Phrase
O	Object
O_d	Direct Object
O_i	Indirect Object
P	Preposition
PART	Particle
PP	Prepositional Phrase
POSS	Possessive
SUB CONJ	Subordinating Conjunction
V	Verb
VP	Verb Phrase

TABLE 10.4
Developments in Phrase Structure (Crystal, Fletcher, & Garman, 1974)

STAGE	AGE RANGE (IN MONTHS)	DEVELOPMENTS IN PHRASE STRUCTURE
I	9–18	**single-word sentences predominate** nouns and verbs not inflected or elaborated
II	18–24	**two-element sentences predominate** NP: ADJ + N (*big kitty*) DET + N (*that ball*) VP: V + PART (*get out*) PP: P + N (*on chair*)
III	24–30	**three-element sentences predominate** NP: POSS + ADJ + N (*baby big hat*) ADJ + ADJ + N (*big red house*) DET + ADJ + N (*that red box*) VP: AUX + V (*is eating*) PP: P + DET + N (*in the house*)
IV	30–36	**four-element sentences predominate** NP: N + PP (*man in blue shoes*) VP: AUX + AUX + V (*has been eating*) NEG + V (*not eating*) PP: P + DET + ADJ + N (*in the scary room*)
V	36–42	**recursive elements predominate** NP: NP + CONJ + NP (*the man and the little girl*) VP: VP + VP (*was scratching and biting*) PP: PP + PP (*in the car by the window*)
VI	42–54	**syntactic system completion** NP: coordination within NP common (e.g., appositives) NP includes adjectival sequences VP: complex verb phrases mirror adultlike forms (e.g., *I should have been able to*)

CHAPTER EXERCISES

Exercise 10A

In the blank to the left of each sentence, write whether the underlined noun phrase is the Subject (S), Object (O), Complement (C), or an Adverbial (ADV) in the sentence.

_____ 1. I am <u>the speech-language pathologist</u>.

_____ 2. <u>You</u> are not going out like that, are you?

_____ 3. Do that <u>Thursday</u>.

_____ 4. <u>The little green hat</u> will be perfect with that!

_____ 5. Don't hit <u>the counter</u> with that.

_____ 6. I am <u>an overworked mother</u>.

_____ 7. <u>That old couch</u> is hardly worth anything.

_____ 8. We can always visit <u>next month</u>.

_____ 9. Don't touch <u>the hot wax</u>!

_____ 10. He is <u>my friend</u>.

Exercise 10B

Circle the head of each underlined phrase in the following paragraph (from Lonigan, Burgess, Anthony, & Barker, 1998, p. 308).

Because individual differences <u>in phonological sensitivity</u> appear to be relatively stable <u>from an early age</u>, efforts to identify <u>the origins</u> of phonological sensitivity and screening of children for phonological sensitivity deficits are likely to be most productive <u>during the preschool years</u>. . . . Whereas phonemic sensitivity may be <u>the penultimate skill</u> required for translation of the alphabetic code, <u>lower levels</u> of phonological sensitivity <u>are both related</u> to phonemic sensitivity and <u>are measurable</u> in preschool-age children.

Exercise 10C

In the blank to the left of each sentence, write whether the underlined phrase is a Noun Phrase (NP), Verb Phrase (VP), Prepositional Phrase (PP), Adjective Phrase (ADJ-P), or Adverb Phrase (ADV-P).

_____ 1. Please drive <u>carefully</u>.

_____ 2. Jennifer will go <u>with her</u>.

_____ 3. She is <u>just gorgeous</u>.

_____ 4. It's going to be <u>a nice day</u>.

_____ 5. She <u>is driving</u> me there.

_____ 6. I just need <u>more</u>.

_____ 7. <u>That old car</u> will never make it.

_____ 8. You need <u>hot tea</u>.

_____ 9. <u>His ideas</u> are not practical.

_____ 10. That dress is <u>so pretty</u>.

_____ 11. <u>We will be calling</u> on Friday.

_____ 12. Sid walked <u>around the corner</u>.

_____ 13. Take the basket that is <u>on the fridge</u>.

_____ 14. I swear I put it <u>right there</u>.

_____ 15. The sun sets <u>in the west</u>.

Exercise 10D

Underline the infinitive phrase that occurs in each sentence.

1. Tell Juanita to call her now.
2. Don't invite them to go.
3. Help Mother choose the menu.
4. To win, we must persevere.
5. We wanted to visit, but had no time.
6. Tell Sierra to interview the parents.
7. Help them call the parents.
8. No one wants to attend the convention.
9. You need to send the report.
10. Help Ruby prepare the ingredients.

Exercise 10E

In the space to the left of each sentence, write whether the underlined verb phrase's "Auxiliary Verb + Main Verb" pattern is Modal (M), Perfect (PF), Progressive (PG), or Passive (PS).

_____ 1. We <u>have driven</u> by there four times.

_____ 2. The window <u>was fixed</u>.

_____ 3. Candy <u>has tested</u> her already.

_____ 4. The matter <u>was investigated</u> by the committee.

_____ 5. We <u>have addressed</u> the seriousness of the situation.

_____ 6. My mother and father <u>may call</u> this evening.

_____ 7. Please inform them what you <u>are doing</u>.

_____ 8. The doorknob <u>was replaced</u> already this year.

_____ 9. We <u>are planning</u> on having the dinner at our house.

_____ 10. The director <u>has talked</u> to her staff about it.

Exercise 10F

1. Read the following transcript, which represents a series of successive utterances produced by J, a 3-year-old child, during an interaction with his mother. As you read, identify all the multiword phrases and write them in the appropriate columns of the chart on the next page.

This piece don't go in there.

Mommy, does this piece go in here?

Ouch, my finger got bit.

That tiger bit it.

That tiger real mean.

That tiger a bad cat.

Mommy, do you like that tiger?

Here goes the race car?

My race car goes so fast.

My race car goes so far.

Two cars sit on garage.

That black one going first.

Mommy, look my black race car!

That man is real mad.

NP	VP	ADJ-P	ADV-P	PP

2. What types of phrases predominate? _____

Exercise 10G

Consider the following utterances created by a 2-year-old child. Fill in the language interventionist's (LI's) line with an expansion (an embellishment) of the child's utterance that includes an adjective phrase. The first one is done for you.

1. Child: *that a ball*
   LI: **That is a green ball.**

2. Child: *a baby*
   LI: _____

3. Child: *truck*
   LI: _____

4. Child: *Mommy dress*
   LI: _____

5. Child: *cookie is hot*
   LI: _____

6. Child: *my cookie*
   LI: _____

7. Child: *put car on*
   LI: _____

8. Child: *that Pooh*
   LI: _____

9. Child: *me eat*
   LI: _____

10. Child: *that my dress*
    LI: _____

Exercise 10H

1. Consider the following series of successive utterances produced by a 5-year-old child. Underline each multiword noun phrase that occurs.

   - you drive it
   - with gas
   - from Burger King
   - you cut it
   - scissors
   - apple pies
   - they make honey
   - Winnie the Pooh like honey
   - the baby make pie
   - make big pie

2. Now characterize this child's use of noun phrases, based on the phrases you underlined above.

   _____

   _____

ANSWER KEY

Exercise 10A

1. C
2. S
3. ADV
4. S
5. O
6. C
7. S
8. ADV
9. O
10. C

Exercise 10B

in phonological (sensitivity)
from an early (age)
the (origins)
during the preschool (years)

the penultimate (skill)

lower (levels)

are both (related) to

are (measurable)

Exercise 10C

1. ADVP
2. PP
3. ADJP
4. NP
5. VP
6. ADVP
7. NP
8. NP
9. NP
10. ADJP
11. VP
12. PP
13. PP
14. ADVP
15. PP

Exercise 10D

1. Tell Juanita <u>to call her now</u>.
2. Don't invite them <u>to go</u>.
3. *Help Mother <u>choose the menu</u>.
4. <u>To win</u>, we must persevere.
5. We wanted <u>to visit</u>, but had no time.
6. Tell Sierra <u>to interview the parents</u>.
7. *Help them <u>call the parents</u>.
8. No one wants <u>to attend the convention</u>.
9. You need <u>to send the report</u>.
10. *Help Ruby <u>prepare the ingredients</u>.

*This sentence contains an example of a bare infinitive.

Exercise 10E

1. PF
2. PS
3. PF
4. PS
5. PF
6. M
7. PG
8. PS
9. PG
10. PF

Exercise 10F

1.

NP	VP	ADJ-P	ADV-P	PP
this piece	don't go	real mean	so fast	in there
this piece	does go	real mad	so far	in here
my finger	got bit			on garage
that tiger	do like			
that tiger				
that tiger				
a bad cat				
that tiger				
the race car				
my race car				
my race car				
two cars				
that black one				
my black race car				
that man				

2. Noun phrases comprise almost 50% of all the multiword phrases that occur in this transcript.

Exercise 10H

1. • you drive it
   • with gas
   • from <u>Burger King</u>
   • you cut it
   • scissors
   • <u>apple pies</u>
   • they make honey
   • <u>Winnie the Pooh</u> like honey
   • <u>the baby</u> make pie
   • make <u>big pie</u>

2. Fifty percent of the utterances contained multiword noun phrases. Two were proper nouns, two included nouns modified by adjectives (*apple* and *big*), and one was modified by a determiner (a definite article).

CHAPTER ELEVEN

Clauses

Chapter at a Glance

What Is a Clause?

Clause Elements

Independent Clauses

Dependent Clauses

- Noun Clauses
- Adjective (Relative) Clauses
- Adverb Clauses
- Comparative Clauses

Developmental Notes

Chapter Exercises

Answer Key

What Is a Clause?

In Chapter 10, we pointed out that the structure of sentences can be conceived as occurring in a hierarchy:

Word → Phrase → Clause → Sentence

In this chapter, we turn our discussion to describing and defining clause structures, the basic foundation for the sentence.

An understanding of clause structure is critical for language interventionists. Many tools that we use for analyzing language transcripts use clause structure as a key for documenting linguistic skill. For example, two frequently used procedures for assessment of children's narrative skills is analysis of Hunt's (1965) T-unit (minimal terminable unit) and Loban's (1976) CU (communication unit) (see Hughes, McGillivray, & Schmidek, 1997, for an overview of these procedures). A T-unit consists of an independent (or main) clause and any attached dependent (or subordinate) clauses. A CU consists of an independent clause with its modifiers. To use these procedures effectively, language interventionists must be able to differentiate independent clauses from dependent clauses, as well as clauses from phrases. Since clause structure mirrors the complexity of the English language, clausal analysis can tell us much about the complexity contained in an individual's language skills and can tell us how much complexity an individual can handle before errors occur.

A clause is a central syntactic structure, which, like phrases, consists of a group of words that are unified by meaning. Clauses are more complex than phrases because clauses have their own subject and predicate. In this way, clauses appear similar to sentences, since sentences, too, must contain both a subject and a predicate. (Recall from Chapter 9 that the subject in a sentence may be covert, as in *[You] stay here.*) In fact, sometimes a clause may sit alone and act as a sentence; that is, a sentence may be made up of a single clause, in which case the clause is the same thing as the sentence. For instance, *Tommy basted the turkey* is a sentence consisting of a single clause, and so the clause and the sentence are viewed as synonymous. Clauses that may sit alone are referred to as **independent clauses** or **main clauses**. The simple sentences below consist of a single independent clause:

> Ken called me.
>
> Juaquin buys the cat food.

Other clauses, known as **dependent clauses** or **subordinate clauses**, do not form a complete sentence on their own, so they must be combined with another clause to form a sentence. So you see, sentences always include an independent (a main) clause, but they can also include one or more dependent (or subordinate) clauses, as shown in the examples that follow, in which the dependent clauses are in bold:

> Ken, **that boy I like**, called me.
>
> **When you go to the store**, please buy some cat food.
>
> I'll go back to work tomorrow **if I feel better** or **if they can't find someone to replace me**.

The key to understanding sentences that consist of more than one clause is recognizing that they include more than one verb (or predicate). For example, the first example above contains two verbs: *like* and *called*. This suggests the presence of two clauses. Remember that by the nature of its definition, every clause must have its own predicate, and predicates are defined by the presence of a verb.

Clause Elements

The structure of clauses is similar to the structure of sentences. Clauses, like sentences, have slots that must be filled. The two slots that must be filled in clauses are the subject and the predicate. (Remember, though, that sometimes the subject is covert, as discussed in Chapter 9.) Consider the following dependent clause:

Ken, **that boy I like**, called me.

The dependent clause *that boy I like* contains both a subject and a predicate. The subject is *that boy* and the predicate is *I like*. There is another clause in this sentence as well, an independent clause: *Ken called me*. This clause also has its own subject and predicate, in which *Ken* comprises the subject slot and *called me* comprises the predicate slot. Thus, one way to classify clause elements is "Subject + Predicate." The elements of clauses can be more finely classified, as shown in Table 11.1. The subject and verb are always obligatory, but the object, complement, and adverbial slots are not always filled.

TABLE 11.1
Key Clause Elements

CLAUSE ELEMENT	DESCRIPTION
Subject (S)	Most clauses contain one or more subjects. The subject usually sits in the first slot of the clause. The subject is nearly always a single noun, a pronoun, or a noun phrase. The subject is what is reflected in the action or state of the verb. Sometimes the subject is assumed, or covert.
Verb (V)	All clauses must contain a verb. The verb usually sits in the second slot in the clause and may be seen as the key element of the predicate structure.
Object (O)	The object slot is not obligatory in clause structure. Clauses that contain transitive verbs are obliged to include an object. The object closely reflects the verb in that it tells who or what is affected by the action or state of the verb. The object may be direct or indirect; some clauses may contain both a direct and an indirect object.
Complement (C)	The complement slot is not obligatory in clause structure. Complements are often seen after copular *be* verbs and intransitive verbs. The complement typically provides further characterization of the subject or the object.
Adverbial (A)	The adverbial slot is not obligatory in clause structure. Adverbials provide additional information about time, location, and manner.

(If this sounds familiar to you, it's because we covered sentence structure in Chapter 9.) So a clause will always have at least two slots filled (the subject and verb) and may have as many as four slots filled at a time (Leech, Deuchar, & Hoogenraad, 1984), as seen in Table 11.2. (Note it is not possible to have all five slots filled in a single clause.)

Independent Clauses

All sentences must have at least one independent (main) clause. As you learned at the beginning of this chapter, independent clauses can sit alone and are not dependent on any other clause for full meaning. Table 11.3 presents some common patterns of active and passive independent clauses, based on Leech et al. (1984).

When two (or more) independent clauses are conjoined with a coordinating conjunction, the two clauses are referred to as **coordinate clauses**. In such cases, the clause that appears on one side of the coordinating conjunction carries equal weight with the clause that appears on the other side. Recall from Chapter 7 that the coordinating conjunctions include *for, and, nor, but, or, yet,* and *so* (remember FANBOYS?). Note that *so then* and *and then* are added to the group when analyzing narratives. In the following example, two independent clauses (highlighted below) are combined into a single sentence with the use of a coordinating conjunction:

Nancy left Mike a message, and **he returned her call**.

Nancy left Mike a message and then **she left**.

TABLE 11.2
Examples of Independent Clauses with Two, Three, and Four Slots

NUMBER OF SLOTS	INDEPENDENT CLAUSE SLOTS				
	S	V	O	C	A
Two	The child	is crying			
Three	The child	wants	her mother		
	The child	is		unhappy	
	The child	is			over there
Four	The child	wants	her mother		now
	The child	seemed		ill	all week
	The child	called	the teacher	"mommy"	

TABLE 11.3
Common Clause Patterns

	PATTERN	EXAMPLE
Active Voice	Subject + Verb	*Jenny sleeps.*
	Subject + Verb + Indirect Object	*Jenny told him.*
	Subject + Verb + Complement	*Jenny is happy.*
	Subject + Verb + Adverbial	*Jenny was here.*
	Subject + Verb + Direct Object	*Jenny took the test.*
	Subject + Verb + Indirect Object + Direct Object	*Jenny gave him the bag.*
	Subject + Verb + Direct Object + Complement	*Jenny thought him a nuisance.*
	Subject + Verb + Direct Object + Adverbial	*Jenny put the hat over there.*
Passive Voice	Subject + Verb	*The bracelet was stolen.*
	Subject + Verb + Indirect Object	*The test was given to her.*
	Subject + Verb + Adverbial	*The vehicle was stolen yesterday.*

Independent clauses can also be joined together with a conjunctive adverb (e.g., *consequently, however, nevertheless,* and *therefore*). Recall that Chapter 5 included a list of common conjunctive adverbs. In the following example, two independent clauses are combined into a single sentence with a conjunctive adverb:

We were tired; **nevertheless**, we plodded on.

Dependent Clauses

Like their independent (main) clause counterparts, dependent (subordinate) clauses also must contain both a subject and a predicate. But dependent clauses differ in that they are unable to stand alone; they must be attached to an independent clause, because they begin with either a subordinating conjunction (words like *although, since, unless, because, if, when, until,* and *whereas*) or a relative pronoun (words like *that, whose, which,* and *whatever*). The attachment of a subordinating conjunction or a relative pronoun to a clause causes it to be dependent. See Chapter 7 for a list of common subordinating conjunctions and Chapter 2 for a list of common relative pronouns. Dependent clauses add information, but they can be deleted without changing the meaning of the independent clause to which they are attached, as seen in the examples below:

>**I can go out** because **I don't have any homework**.

>**Chad bought me roses**, which **I thought was sweet**.

Similar to independent clauses, two (or more) dependent clauses can also be conjoined with a coordinating conjunction. Again, the two clauses on either side of the conjunction are referred to as *coordinate clauses* because each clause carries equal weight. Recall from Chapter 7 that the coordinating conjunctions include *for, and, nor, but, or, yet,* and *so* and on occasion *and then* and *so then*. In the following example, two dependent clauses are combined with the use of a coordinating conjunction:

>**Until you tell me what he did** or **until he confesses**, I don't want to see you.

The following sections provide an overview of some of the more common structures that may be seen in the analysis of language transcripts. They include four types of dependent clauses: noun, adjective (relative), adverb, and comparative.

Noun Clauses

Noun clauses are sometimes referred to as **nominal clauses** (Hughes et al., 1997) or **finite clauses** (Silva, 1996). Noun clauses always contain a subject and, as a dependent clause, are always connected to an independent clause. Noun clauses function as nouns and thus may serve in the roles of subject, object (direct or indirect), or complement. Oftentimes, noun clauses are introduced by a relative pronoun (e.g., *what, that,* and *who*), but be aware that the connective word *that* can be deleted, making it difficult to identify the noun clause:

>**What I believe** is not important. (noun clause as subject)

>I don't believe **[that] he told her**. (noun clause as object)

>This is **who I am**. (noun clause as complement)

Adjective (Relative) Clauses

Adjective clauses immediately follow the noun or pronoun that they modify in an independent clause. They are typically introduced by relative pronouns (e.g., *what, that,* and *who*), which is why they are often called **relative clauses.** Check out the adjective clauses in the following examples, in which the first adjective clause is in the subject position and the second is in the object position:

>The boy **who keeps calling** is driving me crazy.

>Here's the book **that I told you about**.

On occasion, the relative pronoun may be omitted, making it tricky for you to identify the presence of an adjective clause. In the example that follows, the relative pronoun *that* is omitted:

> Here's the book **I told you about**.

Adjective clauses are not always introduced by a relative pronoun. In some instances, they are introduced by a preposition (see the lists in Chapter 8) and then would not fall into the category of relative clause:

> The tests **with which we demonstrated** are in the clinic.

Of course, in more casual situations, it's appropriate for you to move the preposition to the end of the clause:

> The tests **which we demonstrated with** are in the clinic.

Adjective clauses can be characterized as being either restrictive or nonrestrictive. **Restrictive clauses** provide further information about the noun phrases they are modifying, and this information serves to narrow down the reference and is necessary for clarification. For instance, in the example that follows, the restrictive adjective clause *who you called* modifies the noun phrase *the boy* and helps you understand which, of all the boys in the world, is the one who won't speak to us:

> The boy **who you called** won't speak to us.

In contrast, **nonrestrictive clauses** provide additional information about a particular referent, but this information is not necessary for recognizing the referent. In other words, nonrestrictive clauses can be omitted without changing the meaning of the independent clause. (Remember that omitting a restrictive clause would change the meaning of the independent clause.) Consider the following examples:

> Johnny called the lady, **who invited him to dinner**. (nonrestrictive adjective clause)
>
> Johnny called the lady **who had invited him to dinner**. (restrictive adjective clause)

The information in the nonrestrictive clause above doesn't provide further clarification regarding *the lady*; it simply provides further information regarding events. In contrast, the information in the restrictive clause is crucial for accurate identification of the referent; that is, it tells which lady Johnny called.

Adverb Clauses

Adverb clauses serve an adverbial function in that they provide information about time, place, manner, condition, and reason. In other words, adverb clauses answer questions about when, where, how, and why and begin with a subordinating conjunction (see the list of subordinating conjunctions in Table 7.2 in Chapter 7). Adverb clauses that answer *when* questions often begin with subordinating conjunctions like *after, before, since, when,* and *while.* Adverb clauses that answer *where* questions often begin with the subordinating conjunctions *where* or *wherever.* Adverb clauses that answer *how* questions often begin with the subordinating conjunction *if.* Adverb clauses that answer *why* questions often begin with the subordinating conjunctions *because* or *so that.* See the examples that follow:

> I need more coffee **before the day begins**. (time)
>
> **Wherever you go**, there you are! (place)
>
> She sang **as though she were a bird**. (manner)
>
> They won't go **if it's raining**. (condition)
>
> **Because she seems so sad**, we bought her this gift. (reason)

Comparative Clauses

Comparative clauses are a type of dependent (subordinate) clause that serves to compare the information in the dependent clause with information presented in the independent clause. Comparative clauses always begin with the words *than* or *as*:

> John has more experience **than Richard has**.
>
> They bought as many Beanie Babies **as they could afford**.

Developmental Notes

In Brown's Stage IV, which transcends the period from about 35–40 months, children first begin to embed sentence elements and conjoin sentences with *and*. Soon thereafter, Brown's Stage V (from about 41–46 months) characterizes a landmark event in syntactic development: Clauses begin to be expressed as coordinate and subordinate structures within sentences (Brown, 1973). This period of time marks the advent of clausal structure and the developing complexity of language function.

Usually late within Brown's Stage V (43–46 months), children begin to use adjective clauses (relative clauses). These occur primarily in the object position: *He ate the cookies that were mine* and *That's the hat Mommy gave me.* After mean length of utterance (MLU) reaches 4.5, in the period referred to as Brown's Stage V+, children demonstrate growing mastery with clausal coordination and subordination: Relative clauses occur in relation to the subject of sentences, clausal subordination using *because* and *when* occurs, and clausal coordination with *but* and *so* becomes more prevalent.

Tyack and Gottsleben (1986) examined 110 preschool children's use of particular subordinating conjunctions during conversational play. In particular, these researchers looked at the use of particular conjunctive adverbs, including *because, when, if, after, before, until,* and *since*. Results from this work indicated that prior to an MLU of 3.0, use of these conjuncts occurred rarely if at all. From the period of time in which children's MLU increased from 3.0 to 5.0, use of many—but not all—of these conjuncts became more prevalent. The conjunctive adverbs used most frequently were *because* and *when*, which accounted for about 22% and 20% respectively of total conjunctive adverbs used by children with MLUs between 4.0 and 4.99. Many of the other conjunctive adverbs, including *if, after, before, until,* and *since*, occurred quite rarely, comprising only about 1% of conjunctive adverbs used. (In fact, *until* and *since* were not observed in spontaneous speech until MLU surpassed 5.0.)

As we did in "Developmental Notes" in Chapters 9 and 10, let's consider Crystal, Fletcher, and Garman's (1974) classic description of syntactic attainment with respect to clauses, specifically, as they have observed in their data on preschool children. Their data are presented in Table 11.4 (following page), which provides an excellent illustration of young children's major attainments in clause structure.

TABLE 11.4
Developments in Clause Structure (Crystal, Fletcher, & Garman, 1974)

STAGE	AGE RANGE (IN MONTHS)	DEVELOPMENTS IN CLAUSE STRUCTURE
I	9–18	**single-word sentences predominate** nouns and verbs not inflected or elaborated (*mommy; eat*)
II	18–24	**two-element sentences predominate** true clausal structures not evident (*mommy up; eat cookie*)
III	24–30	**three-element sentences predominate** independent clauses (not coordinated or subordinated) emerge S V O: *baby want cookie* S V C: *mommy is pretty* V O ADV: *put hat here* V O_d O_i: *give bite kitty*
IV	30–36	**four-element sentences predominate** new types of independent clauses (not coordinated or subordinated) continue to emerge; internal structures of clauses are completed in this period S V O ADV: *Tommy hit Johnny there* S V C ADV: *I am pretty now* S V O_d O_i: *The teacher gave it to me*
V	36–42	**recursive elements predominate** connecting devices used to coordinate and subordinate clauses emerge rapidly, for example: *and* as COORD CONJ: *I told daddy and I told mommy* *because* as SUB CONJ: *I'm sleepy because I'm tired* N CLAUSE as S, O, or C: *I thought <u>that Carrie left</u>* *I said <u>Jimmy's cheating</u>* COMPARATIVE CLAUSE: *I'm <u>bigger than you</u> are* REL CLAUSE: *Jenny, <u>that girl who is from school</u>, is here*
VI	42–54	**syntactic system completion** more complex patterns of subordination and coordination emerge, for example: CLAUSE AS COMPLEMENT: *She's not <u>feeling good</u>*

CHAPTER EXERCISES

Exercise 11A

Offset the dependent clause in each of the following complex sentences by placing brackets around it.

1. [After Nina gets here,] we will meet you.
2. Don't tell them [that it didn't happen.]
3. The test [she gave] is not valid.
4. It sure is cold, [although it is a nice break from the heat.]
5. Wendy will do [what her doctor says.]
6. [Still waiting for the results,] we cancelled the reservations.
7. [Unless the pediatrician calls,] we'll wait to write the report.
8. The team was late [because the bus broke down.]
9. We are presenting today, [as well as attending some workshops.]
10. The professor will not share his formula, [which is groundbreaking.]

Exercise 11B

A noun clause is presented in brackets in each of the following sentences. Identify whether the noun clause is serving as the Subject (S), Object (O), or Complement (C) in the sentence.

_____ 1. His opinion is [what I expected.]

_____ 2. [Creating extra revenue] is the idea behind the proposal.

_____ 3. [Telling the counselor] might make you feel better.

_____ 4. She won't share [how she feels.]

_____ 5. It is [what he wanted.]

_____ 6. The problem is [generating enough support.]

_____ 7. This is [getting out of control.]

_____ 8. Nancy will tell [what she is experiencing.]

Exercise 11C

Place brackets around the relative clause embedded in each of the following sentences.

1. The child [she is concerned about] was dismissed.
2. The driver [who held the bus for you] got in trouble.
3. I told you [that I can't come.]
4. Jayden doesn't know [which one will be chosen.]
5. Contact the doctor [they recommended.]
6. Complete the sections [that are marked.]
7. The toddler [who was biting] has now stopped.
8. The plans [they shared with us] are being implemented.
9. The gala [they weren't invited to] has been cancelled.
10. The horse [that was so sick] won't be in the race.

Exercise 11D

Spontaneous language samples are often divided into T-units (Hunt, 1965) in the process of syntactic analysis. A T-unit consists of an independent clause along with any dependent clauses. Place a slash (/) between T-units in the following narrative.

The puppy went off on a walk by himself/and he saw a little rabbit/The rabbit ran fast into the woods/and the puppy chased him until he got tired/Then he sat down/and he thought for a minute/He changed his mind/and he decided to eat something/He looked around for stuff/but he couldn't find nothing/Then he saw his best friend, who is Max/And Max said he was having a party at his house/They went to Max's/and all the friends were there.

Exercise 11E

Create a simple sentence (consisting of a single independent clause) that follows each major clause pattern identified.

1. Subject + Verb

   _____

2. Subject + Verb + Indirect Object + Direct Object

   _____

3. Subject + Verb + Direct Object

   _____

4. Subject + Verb + Direct Object + Complement

   _____

5. Subject + Verb + Direct Object + Adverbial

   _____

Exercise 11F

Of the following utterances produced by a 7-year-old child, which ones contain more than one clause? Circle the number preceding those utterances.

1. That's hooking together and flying over the park.
2. That's a fishy.
3. He riding a bicycle.
4. (circled) But he's not scary, he's nice.
5. (circled) He's riding and he's trying to get up there and ride.
6. He has lots of things in his basket.
7. (circled) This is your body and that's his body.
8. There my foot and there my arm.
9. The giraffe on the bike and told him *No*.
10. The giraffe fell onto the little boy.

ANSWER KEY

Exercise 11A

1. [After Nina gets here], we will meet you.
2. Don't tell them [that it didn't happen.]
3. The test [she gave] is not valid.
4. It sure is cold, [although it is a nice break from the heat.]
5. Wendy will do [what her doctor says.]
6. [Still waiting for the results], we cancelled the reservations.
7. [Unless the pediatrician calls], we'll wait to write the report.
8. The team was late [because the bus broke down.]
9. We are presenting today, [as well as attending some workshops.]
10. The professor will not share his formula, [which is groundbreaking.]

Exercise 11B

1. C 5. C
2. S 6. C
3. S 7. C
4. O 8. O

Exercise 11C

1. The child [she is concerned about] was dismissed.
2. The driver [who held the bus for you] got in trouble.
3. I told you [that I can't come.]
4. Jayden doesn't know [which one will be chosen.]
5. Contact the doctor [they recommended.]
6. Complete the sections [that are marked.]
7. The toddler [who was biting] has now stopped.
8. The plans [they shared with us] are being implemented.
9. The gala [they weren't invited to] has been cancelled.
10. The horse [that was so sick] won't be in the race.

Exercise 11D

The puppy went off on a walk by himself/ and he saw a little rabbit./ The rabbit ran fast into the woods/ and the puppy chased him until he got tired./ Then he sat down/ and he thought for a minute./ He changed his mind/ and he decided to eat something./ He looked around for stuff/ but he couldn't find nothing./ Then he saw his best friend, who is Max./ And Max said he was having a party at his house./ They went to Max's/ and all the friends were there.

Exercise 11F

1. That's hooking together and flying over the park.*
2. That's a fishy.
3. He riding a bicycle.
4. But he's not scary, he's nice.
5. He's riding and he's trying to get up there and ride.
6. He has lots of things in his basket.
7. This is your body and that's his body.
8. There my foot and there my arm.**
9. The giraffe on the bike and told him No.
10. The giraffe fell onto the little boy.

*This utterance has one clause with compound verbs.
**This utterance contains no verbs, thus it is neither a sentence nor a clause.

CHAPTER TWELVE

Sentence Types

Chapter at a Glance

What Is a Sentence?

Sentence Classification via Clause Structure
- Simple Sentences
- Compound Sentences
- Complex Sentences
- Compound-Complex Sentences

Sentence Classification via Function
- Declarative Sentences
- Imperative Sentences
- Exclamatory Sentences
- Interrogative Sentences

Developmental Notes

Chapter Exercises

Answer Key

What Is a Sentence?

Taking the perspective that syntactic structures can be viewed along a continuum, or hierarchy, sentences would be viewed as the most complex structural unit (Aarts & Aarts, 1982). Certainly, in human communication, sentences are combined into larger segments, such as paragraphs, narratives, and so on. However, analysis of such larger segments is not so much a matter of syntactic analysis as it is a matter of discourse analysis; that is, analyzing how the linguistic elements of stories, conversations, and similar events come together in a meaningful manner.

Given the overriding importance of the sentence, a formal definition seems in order. Looking at a classic reference, Turner (1966) defines **sentence** as a structure that "consists of one or more clauses capable of presenting a complete thought in a manner which is grammatically acceptable" (p. 87). Key elements of this definition include: (1) sentences must include at least one independent clause (remember that means they must include a subject and a predicate); (2) sentences must present a complete thought; and (3) sentences must be grammatically acceptable. Keeping Turner's definition in mind, would *Come in* be classified as a sentence? (1) It consists of an independent clause; the subject is covert (it's understood to be *you*), and the predicate is *come in*. (2) It appears to present a complete thought. (3) It seems to be grammatically acceptable. Therefore, *Come in* does fit Turner's criteria and can thus be classified as a sentence.

How about *Oh my!* or *Really?* Would these be classified as sentences? No, they would not. These two structures, although looking suspiciously like sentences, especially given that they begin with capital letters and end with punctuation marks, would not be classified as sentences, because neither contains one or more independent clauses. It could be argued that both structures present complete thoughts. It could even be asserted that the two structures are grammatically acceptable (so long as we do not argue that they are grammatically acceptable as *sentences*). It could not, however, be asserted that either of these structures contains a subject, and, clearly, neither contains a predicate. So neither of these utterances could be considered a sentence. In fact, it is not really clear how to define the syntactic structures *Oh my!* and *Really?* (although the function of each would be referred to as *exclamatory,* which we'll cover later in this chapter). What is unequivocal is that neither may be defined as a sentence.

Sentences come in many shapes and sizes. For instance:

> It is?
>
> It is not true.
>
> It is simply not true!
>
> It is simply not true about the kitten Larry bought.
>
> It is simply not true that the kitten Larry bought bit me when I was taking the garbage out for my Aunt Susan, who is visiting from Peoria.

The complexity of the sentences above relates directly to the number of clauses each contains. The first three examples contain only one clause each. The fourth example contains two clauses—one independent clause (*It is simply not true*) and one dependent clause ([*that*] *Larry bought*). (Recall that the relative pronoun *that* can be assumed and not stated.) The fifth example contains one independent clause—*It is simply not true*—and four dependent clauses—*that the kitten bit me,* [*that*] *Larry bought, when*

I was taking the garbage out for my Aunt Susan, and *who is visiting from Peoria.* The classification of sentential complexity as a function of clause structure results in four primary types of sentences: simple sentences, compound sentences, complex sentences, and compound-complex sentences. This classification system will be described in the sections that follow.

Sentences may also be classified based on their overriding function. This classification system frequently occurs in discussions of children's acquisition of four sentence types: declarative, imperative, exclamatory, and interrogative. Classification of sentences by their function will be considered later in this chapter.

Sentence Classification via Clause Structure

The following sections describe ways in which sentences may be classified according to their clause structure. There are four sentence types for such classification: simple sentences, compound sentences, complex sentences, and compound-complex sentences.

Simple Sentences

Simple sentences consist of only one independent clause, with no dependent clauses. In other words, an independent clause is a simple sentence. It would follow, then, that simple sentences contain only one predicate structure—or one verb. They may, however, contain more than one phrase, often making them lengthy and therefore more difficult to identify as a simple sentence. The important point to remember is that simple sentences always contain only one predicate, as shown in the following examples:

The parents **signed the release form**.

The parents of Jordan **signed the release form**.

The parents of Jordan **signed the release form on Thursday**.

The parents of Jordan **signed the release form on Thursday of last week**.

Compound Sentences

Compound sentences contain two simple sentences (that is, two independent clauses) conjoined via (1) a coordinating conjunction (*for, and, nor, but, or, yet,* and *so*); (2) a semicolon; or (3) a conjunctive adverb (note that usually a semicolon precedes the conjunctive adverb and a comma follows it). As such, compound sentences include two predicates: the predicate of the first independent clause and the predicate of the second independent clause. In the following examples, each independent clause is set off with brackets and the manner in which the independent clauses are conjoined is indicated in parentheses:

> [The mother scheduled a consultation,] but [I still don't have a release form.] (coordinating conjunction)
>
> [This test is for preschool children]; [it should not be used for older children.] (semicolon)
>
> [The children didn't enjoy it]; nevertheless, [it was a learning experience.] (conjunctive adverb)

In many cases, conjunctive adverbs and their close allies, the subordinating conjunctions, conjoin independent clauses with one or more dependent clauses. However, when this is the case, the sentence is not compound, but rather is complex or compound-complex, both of which are discussed in the next sections.

Complex Sentences

Complex sentences include one independent clause and one or more dependent clauses. The dependent clause(s) may be embedded within the sentence or may occur at the beginning or end of the sentence and begin with a subordinating conjunction (e.g., *after, when, before*) or a relative pronoun (e.g., *that, which, who*). In the following examples, the dependent clauses are set off with brackets:

> Allan, [the little boy I told you about,] was discharged last week.
>
> [As the group had suspected,] Mary would not help at all.
>
> The house burned [while the crowd stood mesmerized].
>
> She asked me to tell you [when we are leaving].

Note that some scholars also consider sentences that contain an independent clause and a nonfinite verb phrase, such as an infinitive phrase, a gerund, or a participle, as complex.

Compound-Complex Sentences

Compound-complex sentences include elements of both compound sentences and complex sentences. These types of sentences include two or more independent clauses and one or more dependent clauses. The two independent clauses are connected via a coordinating conjunction (e.g., *and, or, but*), a semicolon or a conjunctive adverb (e.g., *then, however, thus*). Often, the dependent clause is conjoined to the independent clause—of which it is a constituent—by a subordinating conjunction (e.g., *after, when, before*) or a relative pronoun (e.g., *that, which, who*). In the following examples, the independent clauses are in bold and the dependent clauses are set off with brackets:

It was true [that the building was elevated above the flood level,] but **the state fined them anyway**.

[Before the week is through,] **the volunteers** [who were here yesterday,] **will fill out the affidavit** and **they will send it to the judge**.

Clean this mess up; also, [when you're finished,] **be sure to turn the stove off**.

An overview of the four types of sentences that can be distinguished based on the relationships between and among their dependent and independent clauses is provided in Table 12.1.

Sentence Classification via Function

The preceding sections described the ways in which various sentences could be classified according to their clause structure. Sentences can also be classified in terms of their function: Declarative sentences make a statement of assertion. Imperative sentences make a request or give an order. Interrogative sentences seek to obtain information. And exclamatory sentences express strong emotion.

Declarative Sentences

Sentences that have the overriding function of making a positive or negative statement or an assertion are **declarative sentences**. Declarative sentences almost always contain a "Subject + Verb" word order, as the following examples illustrate:

TABLE 12.1
Classification of Sentences as a Function of Clause Structure

SENTENCE TYPE	EXAMPLE
Simple	*Syntax is one domain of language.*
Compound	*Syntax refers to the internal structure of sentences, and morphology refers to the internal structure of words.*
Complex	*Syntax, which refers to the internal structure of sentences, is one of several domains of language.*
Compound-Complex	*Syntax, which refers to the internal structure of sentences, is one domain of language; morphology, which is yet another domain of language, refers to the internal structure of words.*

Jason isn't coming.

Jason isn't coming, so I'm not going.

I truly doubt that Jason will be coming.

My mother told me that Jason called, and she said that he won't be coming.

Note from the previous examples that in terms of clause structure, declarative sentences may be simple, compound, complex, or compound-complex. In other words, despite the apparent differences in the above examples in terms of clause structure, all four sentences would be classified as declarative due to their similarities in function.

Imperative Sentences

Imperative sentences are those that have an overall function of making a request or giving an order. When you use an imperative sentence, you are generally asking or demanding that someone act in a particular way. For example:

Drop this shirt off.

You need this shirt, and you need it by 3:00.

You need to drop this off where you bought it.

I don't know why you need to drop this off, but you need to do it by 3:00.

Imperative sentences differ from declarative sentences in one obvious structural way: Imperatives often do not include an explicit subject, as can be seen in the first sentence in the previous example, in which the subject (*you*, or whomever the speaker of the sentence is addressing), goes unstated and is simply implied. The structure of these sentences is still "Subject + Verb," even though the subject is covert. Also note from the examples that imperative sentences can have simple, compound, complex, or compound-complex clause structure.

Exclamatory Sentences

Exclamatory sentences express a strong emotion. For example:

He's a fool!

That's ridiculous!

At least in writing, exclamatory sentences are usually indicated as such by the use of an exclamation point at the end. When speaking, exclamatory sentences are usually indicated by extralinguistic cues, such as pitch changes and increased volume. There tends to not be any specific sentence structure difference for exclamatory sentences; they, too, are typically "Subject + Verb." In terms of clause structure, exclamatory sentences can also be simple, compound, complex, or compound-complex.

Often exclamatory sentences include words like *oh, ouch,* and *well,* which are called *interjections* and denote a "strong or sudden feeling" (Opdycke, 1965). The following are exclamatory sentences including interjections.

Oh my, the bear has the little boy!

Boy, this is a handy book on syntax!

Interrogative Sentences

Sentences with the function of attaining information are **interrogative sentences**. As with the other three sentence types, interrogatives can have various clause structures. There are several sentence patterns that may be used for the purpose of asking questions: (1) *wh-* questions, (2) yes/no questions, and (3) tag questions.

Wh- Questions

Wh- questions begin with either a *wh-* word (*who, what, when, where, why,* or *which*) or *how* (there's always got to be an exception to the rule just to make things tricky for you!) and end with a question mark when presented in written form. When spoken, intonation as well as your syntactic sense helps you know when a question is being asked. The sentence structure of *wh-* questions is different than the "Subject + Verb" pattern typically seen in declaratives and imperatives in that the verb patterns are inverted (e.g., in *What is your name?*, the copula *is* has moved ahead of where it would be located if this were a declarative sentence, which is right behind *name*, as in *your name is . . .*).

The sentence structure for *wh-* word questions also varies with respect to the type of information being sought. For example, the first *wh-* question in the next set of examples seeks information to fill the subject slot and so is referred to as an *s-*form *wh-* question. In contrast, the second example seeks information to fill the predicate slot (e.g., the verb or object) and so is referred to as a *p-*form *wh-* question (Master, 1995):

Who taught the diagnostics class?

What is Dr. Nesbitt teaching?

To clarify, let's look at these two interrogative sentences in their declarative form, with the missing information provided (highlighted):

Dr. Jennings taught the diagnostics class.

Dr. Nesbitt is teaching **Introduction to Communication Disorders**.

The sentence structure of *s-*form and *p-*form *wh-* questions differs. *S-*form interrogative sentences have a structure of "*Wh-* Word + Verb." For example, in *Who taught the diagnostics class?*, the *wh-* word *who* is followed by the verb *taught* (which is followed by the direct object *the diagnostics class*). On the other hand, *p-*form interrogative sentences have a structure of "*Wh-* Word + Auxiliary." For example, in *What is Dr. Nesbitt* *teaching?*, the *wh-* word *what* is followed by the auxiliary verb *is* (which is followed by the subject *Dr. Nesbitt* and the main verb *teaching*). The movement of the auxiliary to precede the subject in *p-*form *wh-* questions is referred to as **subject-auxiliary inversion**.

Yes/No Questions

Yes/no questions, another form of the interrogative sentence, differ from *wh-* questions in that they do not begin with a *wh-* word. Yes/no questions also differ in the type of response that is requested. Whereas *wh-* questions seek information to fill the subject or predicate slot, yes/no questions require only a *yes* or *no* response, as the following examples illustrate:

>Are you going to the farewell party?

>Do you think it will rain?

The sentence structure of yes/no questions differs from that of *wh-* questions. The most obvious difference is that yes/no questions do not begin with *wh-* words; rather, they begin with auxiliary verbs. Like *p-*form *wh-* questions, yes/no questions also use subject-auxiliary inversion. With yes/no questions, however, the auxiliary verb occurs at the beginning of the sentence, followed by the subject and then the rest of the predicate, giving it a sentence structure of "Auxiliary + Subject + Predicate," as can be seen in the examples above.

It should be noted that yes/no questions are not the same as intonation questions. An *intonation question* does not begin with an auxiliary; it is actually a declarative sentence that is presented with a rising intonation (e.g., *Sharon will help me?* or *She's going?*). The confusion in distinguishing these two types of interrogative sentences is likely because both are designed to receive a yes or no response. In terms of structure, however, these two sentence types are quite different:

>Will you help me? (yes/no question)

>You'll help me? (intonation question)

Tag Questions

The third type of interrogative sentence is the tag question. Tag questions are essentially a combination of a declarative sentence and an interrogative sentence. Their structure reflects this combination, as can be seen in the next examples, in which the interrogative tags appear in red:

>He passed the hearing screening, **didn't he**?

>You'll help me with this, **won't you**?

Tag questions are primarily used to ensure feedback or a response from the communication partner. The exact mechanism by which tags are formed is a rather complex process and will not be described here; readers who desire further information are referred to Master (1995).

An overview of the four types of sentences that can be distinguished based on function is provided in Table 12.2.

Developmental Notes

Table 11.4 (located in Chapter 11's "Developmental Notes" section) provided an overview of young children's attainment of clause structures. The information in that table provides a natural precursor to understanding how children's attainment of different types of sentences emerges. It is not clear when we should start using the word *sentence* to describe the speech of very young children. Surely, when children are producing primarily one- and two-word utterances (e.g., *shoe* and *Daddy up*), it seems that *sentence* would not be the best word. This is why language interventionists usually use terms like *one-word utterance* and *two-word utterance* to describe them. However, when children begin to produce three-word utterances with some frequency, as is seen by about 31 months of age (Brown, 1973), the word *sentence* as a means for describing what the child is producing seems appropriate.

Let's first discuss children's acquisition of sentence structures within the framework of clause structure—in other words, their attainment of simple, compound, complex, and compound-complex sentences. Second, we'll discuss children's acquisition of several sentence types as described by function; namely, declarative, imperative, and interrogative (which are the three types language interventionists are most interested in).

Until clause structures become relatively prevalent, which begins to occur at approximately 35–38 months, children's sentences are best described as *simple*. These simple sentences consist primarily of one independent clause: *Daddy go, Grandma is coming, put that here.* However, simple sentences can vary dramatically in their complexity. Consider the following examples of child utterances, both of which may be characterized as simple in complexity:

Me swinging.

They're swinging.

TABLE 12.2
Classification of Sentences Based on Function

SENTENCE TYPE	EXAMPLE
Declarative	*Syntax is one domain of language.*
Imperative	*Tell me about syntax.*
Exclamatory	*It's syntax!*
Interrogative	*What do you think about syntax?*

Clearly, the first example above, *Me swinging*, is not as syntactically complex as the second example, *They're swinging*. The reason for this lies in the grammatical structure represented in the sentences: *Me swinging* demonstrates use of a relatively early-occurring grammatical morpheme (present progressive *-ing*), whereas *I'm playing* includes use of a more advanced, later developing grammatical morpheme (contractible auxiliary *be*). An understanding of children's development of the major inflectional morphemes, also referred to as *Brown's* (1973) *grammatical morphemes*, is critical for assigning complexity values to children's use of simple sentences. An overview of the sequence in which children attain these morphemes is provided in Table 12.3 and in Appendix A.

At about 35 months of age, children typically begin to use the conjunctions *and, but, so,* and *because* with increasing frequency; at the same time, conjoining of independent clauses via these conjunctions also begins to occur. At this time, or roughly between the ages of 34 and 37 months (Paul, 1981), compound sentences such as *I'm going and you're not!* emerge. In fact, many of us have heard young children make liberal use of such devices within this time frame, as in *It's about a cat and it's about a dog and the man comes in and he says "Shoo! . . ."* An example of a typical compound sentence seen at this time is *"Then it broke and we didn't have it anymore"* (Paul, p. 67).

TABLE 12.3
Acquisition of Brown's (1973) 14 Grammatical Morphemes

GRAMMATICAL MORPHEME	AGE (IN MONTHS)	EXAMPLE
Present progressive *-ing*	27–30	*baby crying*
Plural *-s*	27–30	*here puppies*
Preposition *in*	27–30	*cookie in here*
Preposition *on*	31–34	*kitty on chair*
Possessive *-'s*	31–34	*Daddy's cup*
Regular past tense *-ed*	43–46	*we cooked*
Irregular past tense	43–46	*Jacob went*
Regular third person singular *-s*	43–46	*kitty jumps*
Articles *a, the, an*	43–46	*it's a hat*
Contractible copula *be*	43–46	*we're here*
Contractible auxiliary	47–50	*he's coming*
Uncontractible copula *be*	47–50	*we were [we were here]*
Uncontractible auxiliary	47–50	*we were [we were coming]*
Irregular third person	47–50	*Sandy has it*

Work by Paul (1981) demonstrates the growth of complex sentences in preschool children, with analyses conducted during children's spontaneous free play with their mothers. Paul observed complex sentences in the spontaneous speech of 59 children as young as 34 months of age (complex sentences in this age group comprised between 1 and 10% of those produced). Paul's data demonstrated that from 38–42 months, at least 50% of children observed were producing sentences that contained more than one embedded clause. Also emerging in this time frame were compound-complex sentences, containing both a conjoined and an embedded clause. Between the ages of 43 and 46 months of age, true complex sentences were observed more frequently, accounting for 10–20% of sentences produced. More than 50% of the children observed by Paul produced sentences containing relative clauses, such as *"Where are the tracks that belong to us?"* (p. 69). Not until children reached about 47 months of age (with MLU ranging from 4.5 to 5.0) did complex sentences comprise more than 20% of spoken sentences. By about 4 years of age, children were found to be relatively adept at producing all sentence varieties, in terms of clause structure: simple sentences (*I can do it*), compound sentences (*I won't do it and you can't make me*), complex sentences (*She wants the one that you have*), and compound-complex sentences (*This is the year we're going to Disney World, and we'll take Grandpa with us if he wants to go*).

Of interest is also children's development of different types of sentences, in terms of sentence function. In other words, we can also classify sentences by their roles: Do they declare something (declarative)? Request something (imperative)? Ask something (interrogative)? Exclaim something (exclamatory)? Let's now turn to a brief discussion of children's attainments with respect to sentence types of various functions.

Many of the early utterances produced by young children may, in fact, be referred to as *declaratives: man gone, Dada running,* and *eat doggie* (Crystal, Fletcher, & Garman, 1974). When said excitedly, they could be thought of as exclamatory utterances. As discussed in Chapter 9, when true "Subject + Verb + Object" sentences emerge, within the period from roughly 24–30 months, these may be thought of as true declarative-type sentences: *"Daddy kick ball, me get train"* (Crystal et al., 1974, p. 71). Declarative patterns in this period follow one of three primary patterns (Crystal et al.):

S + V + O (e.g., *Mommy eat cookie*)

S + V + C (e.g., *I am tired*)

S + V + ADV (e.g., *Daddy gone bye-bye*)

Declarative patterns that emerge in the following period, from about 30–36 months, include (Crystal et al., 1974; Owens, 2012):

S + V + O + ADV (e.g., *Daddy's hitting the hammer outside*)

S + V + C + ADV (e.g., *Mommy is happy now*)

S + AUX + V + ADV (e.g., *Mommy is working here*)

S + AUX + V + O (e.g., *Timmy is hurting me*)

S + V + O$_d$ + O$_i$ (e.g., *He gave the ball to me*)

As complexities continue to emerge, from about 38 months onward, subsequent patterns of declaratives may include "S + AUX + AUX + V" (e.g., *you won't be coming*) and use of an indirect object preceding a direct object: "S + V + O$_i$ + O$_d$" (e.g., *you give her the bag*).

Imperatives emerge early on also. Some one-word utterances spoken by toddlers (e.g., *up*, *more*, and *want*) clearly act as imperatives, or *proto-imperatives* as they may be called. Between the period of about 24 and 30 months, other, more sophisticated patterns of imperatives begin to emerge, such as "V + O + ADV" (e.g., *put me down*) and "V + ADJ + N" (e.g., *give big hat*). As should be noted, most imperatives spoken by young children are quite direct, with the verb (or "action word") occurring first in the sentence. Only later will children become skilled at making more indirect and subtle imperatives. According to Crystal et al. (1974), imperatives that include true subjects emerge between 30 and 36 months. In this period, imperatives look more like direct commands, in which the subject of the verb is explicitly expressed: "S + V + O" (e.g., *you do it, you tell her*). This coincides with Brown's (1973) Stage III. Owens (2012) points out that is it is difficult to recognize the imperative in English because there are no morphological markers; that is, unlike the interrogative sentences, which will be considered next, there are no obvious or explicit structural-syntactic changes that occur in the formation of imperatives. Rather, it is the intention behind the imperative—or the pragmatic purpose of the utterance—that is of interest when considering the development of imperative forms. A brief discussion of the pragmatic issues involved with the formation of imperatives (including both direct and indirect requests) is provided in deVilliers and deVilliers (1978).

With respect to interrogatives, it is a well-known fact that most children begin to interrogate fairly early on (ask any parent and they'll heartily agree!). The development of interrogatives, at least in the simplest sense, begins with the attainment of question words. *What* and *where* used as single words to express interrogatives are usually seen before 22 months (see Owens, 2012). At the same time, yes/no questions are asked using rising intonation (e.g., *Mommy?*). According to Owens' summary of key syntactic advances, true interrogatives emerge in the latter part of Brown's Stage I (Late/Early Stage II; 23–26 months). In this period, we see children's utterances take the form of "*what* + NP" (e.g., *what Daddy?*) and "*where* + NP" (e.g., *where Daddy?*). From 31 to 34 months, more complex interrogative forms begin to appear, such as "*what* + Subject + Predicate" (e.g., *what Daddy doing?*). Children may use some auxiliaries in their questions (e.g., *where Daddy is?*), but typically the auxiliary is not yet inverted (Crystal et al., 1974). Near Late Stage IV (35–38 months), children begin to invert auxiliaries in their production of such sentences (e.g., *what is Daddy doing?*). Within the same time frame, children begin to invert auxiliaries when asking yes/no questions (e.g., *is that yours?*) By about 40 months of age, children have acquired most of the basic nuances required syntactically for formation of adultlike interrogatives. At the same time, the remaining question words (e.g., *who, when,* and *how*) are being attained. A brief synopsis of children's development of interrogative forms (based on Owens, 2012) is provided in Table 12.4 and Appendix A.

TABLE 12.4
Development of Interrogative Sentences (Owens, 2012)

AGE (IN MONTHS)	INTERROGATIVE	EXAMPLE
12–26	yes/no intonational	*more?*
	what + NP	*what Mommy?*
	where + NP	*where Daddy?*
27–30	*what* + S + Predicate	*what Jenny doing?*
	where + S + Predicate	*where kitty going?*
	what + Copula + S	*what is that?*
	where + Copula + S	*where is baby?*
	why as single word	*why?*
31–34	yes/no AUX inversion	*is that yours?*
35–40	*wh-* question AUX inversion	
	what + AUX + O + V	*what are you doing?*
	where + AUX + O + V	*where can it be?*
	when and *how*	*when are we going?; how is it?*
41–46	tag questions	*you're going, aren't you?*
	modals	*could you do it for me?*
	multiword *why* questions	*why did he do that?*

CHAPTER EXERCISES

Exercise 12A

Identify each of the following sentences as either Simple (S) or Complex (C).

__S__ 1. It is getting really cold in here.
__S__ 2. The cows are grazing by the gate.
__C__ 3. She feels that your reasons are inadequate.
__S__ 4. The director, Ted Simpson, is quite sympathetic.
__S__ 5. We are going to the play this Saturday.
__C__ 6. Connor was concerned about what you said.
__S__ 7. That is not a good excuse.
__S__ 8. Put the files there by the others.
__C__ 9. The child you mentioned is not here.
__S__ 10. Jackie wants to play with Sam.

Exercise 12B

Classify each of the following sentences as either Compound (CP) or Complex (CX).

__CP__ 1. You go and I'll stay.
__CX__ 2. Call me when you get there.
__CX__ 3. The test was cancelled because of the school delay.
__CP__ 4. She went but she had a horrible time.
__CP__ 5. Judy and Jack are coming, but they can't stay.
__CP__ 6. Tom will go, so you don't have to.
__CX__ 7. They'll announce soon that he is the winner.
__CX__ 8. The basket fell when I was cooking.
__CP__ 9. The dogs are inside and the cat is outside.
__CP__ 10. Sheila doesn't want it, but she has already paid.

Exercise 12C

Classify each of the following sentences in terms of their function: Declarative (D), Imperative (IM), Exclamatory (E), or Interrogative (IN).

_____ 1. Give that to me.

_____ 2. You need to tell Randi about your decision.

_____ 3. This test is too hard.

_____ 4. Are you going or not?

_____ 5. That's crazy!

_____ 6. They will be there?

_____ 7. They need to be prompt or we'll cancel.

_____ 8. Oh my, I had no idea!

_____ 9. Martin and Elizabeth are here now.

_____ 10. We cannot be sure of the accuracy of the report.

_____ 11. Fax this for me.

_____ 12. You'll go, right?

Exercise 12D

Provide an example for each of the following clause structures.

1. Simple sentence

    Example: _____

2. Complex sentence

    Example: _____

3. Compound sentence

    Example: _____

4. Compound-complex sentence

    Example: _____

Exercise 12E

Consider the following interaction between a language interventionist (LI) and three students (J, K, and T). Classify each child's sentences in the exchange as either Simple (S), Compound (CP), or Complex (CX).

       LI: Everyone needs to go around and say one sentence about the picture on the card.

_S_   J: Kids are playing soccer.

       LI: Can you put a description word in there?

_S_   J: Kids love to play soccer after school.

_S_   K: In after school sports, the kids play soccer.

       LI: That was an excellent long sentence.

       LI: There are four little girls playing on the soccer field.

       LI: That's my sentence.

_CX_   T: I don't know how to make a sentence.

       LI: Look at the colors in the pictures.

_S_   T: There are two girls with pink shirts.

       LI: That's right.

       LI: There are two girls with pink shirts.

       LI: What are they doing?

_S_   T: They're playing soccer.

       LI: Can you put that in a whole sentence for me?

_CP_   T: There are two girls with pink shirts and they are playing soccer.

       LI: What I want you to do now is to write a sentence about your picture and then read it aloud.

       LI: When you hear a description word, I want you to raise your hand.

Exercise 12F

Examine the following utterances produced by school-age children during speech-language intervention. Classify each sentence in terms of its clause structure: Simple (S), Compound (CP), Complex (CX), or Compound-Complex (CC). Then classify each sentence in terms of its function: Declarative (D), Imperative (I), Exclamatory (E), or Interrogative (I).

Clause Structure	Function		
_____	_____	Richard:	Let's read this one.
_____	_____	Richard:	I want to read this one.
_____	_____	Michelle:	You cut it.
_____	_____	Michelle:	We got French fries and we got hamburgers.
_____	_____	Teddy:	He's not scary but he's not nice.
_____	_____	Sandy:	She swimming in the water.
_____	_____	Sandy:	She swimming in the water and say "Help, help!"
_____	_____	Ricky:	It's not my arm.
_____	_____	Ricky:	There my foot and there my arm.
_____	_____	Eric:	He got a ride.
_____	_____	Eric:	He got lots of things in his basket.
_____	_____	Roger:	That's hooking together and flying over the park.

ANSWER KEY

Exercise 12A

1. S
2. S
3. C
4. S
5. S
6. C
7. S
8. S
9. C
10. S

Exercise 12B

1. CP
2. CX
3. CX
4. CP
5. CP
6. CP
7. CX
8. CX
9. CP
10. CP

Exercise 12C

1. IM	7. D
2. IM	8. E
3. D	9. D
4. IN	10. D
5. E	11. IM
6. D*	12. IN

*This is an intonation question, thus is declarative.

Exercise 12E

S	J:	Kids are playing soccer.
S	J:	Kids love to play soccer after school.
S	K:	In after school sports, the kids play soccer.
CX	T:	I don't know how to make a sentence.
S	T:	There are two girls with pink shirts.
S	T:	They're playing soccer.
CP	T:	There are two girls with pink shirts and they are playing soccer.

Exercise 12F

Clause Structure	Function		
S	D	Richard:	Let's read this one.
S	D	Richard:	I want to read this one.
S	I*	Michelle:	You cut it.
CP	D	Michelle:	We got French fries and we got hamburgers.
CP	D	Teddy:	He's not scary but he's not nice.
S	D	Sandy:	She swimming in the water.
S**	E	Sandy:	She swimming in the water and say "Help, help!"
S	D	Ricky:	It's not my arm.
***	D	Ricky:	There my foot and there my arm.
S	D	Eric:	He got a ride.
S	D	Eric:	He got lots of things in his basket.
S**	D	Roger:	That's hooking together and flying over the park.

*This sentence could also be declarative depending on the context in which it was said.
**This utterance has one clause with compound verbs (conjoined verbs with a second subject omitted).
***This utterance contains no verbs, thus is neither a sentence nor a clause.

CHAPTER THIRTEEN

Complex Syntax

By Mary Beth Schmitt

Chapter at a Glance

What Is Complex Syntax?
Complex Syntax and Complex Sentences
Purpose of Complex Syntax
Literate Language
Measuring Complex Syntax
Developmental Notes
Chapter Exercises
Answer Key

What Is Complex Syntax?

Now we come to the part of this handbook where we consider how the use of certain syntactic forms and functions adds **complexity** to spoken and written language. Consider how both of the following sentences say more or less the same thing, but differ in the complexity with which this is achieved:

> I need some coffee.
>
> I really need some coffee right now, as I'm feeling extremely tired.

While the greatest distinction between the two sentences is that the first is simple and the second is complex (refer back to Chapter 11 if you need a refresher on this), there are other characteristics of the second sentence that make it more complex than the first, such as the use of adverbial phrases (*right now, extremely tired*) and the subordinating conjunction *as*.

Broadly defined, **complex syntax** is the use of advanced syntactic forms and functions so as to allow speakers (children and adults) to precisely communicate abstract thoughts and ideas. As the two examples above show, the second is more precise regarding why coffee is needed, and it is the use of syntax that provides this complexity. Largely, complex syntax relies on the use of finite and nonfinite syntactic functions in both oral and written utterances. Unsure about the terms **finite** and **nonfinite**? Take a second and look back to the discussion of these terms in Chapter 10. (Go ahead—we'll wait for you.) Table 13.1 presents the finite and nonfinite structures that are used to create complexity in spoken and written language.

As important as these syntactic functions are to complex syntax, of additional importance is the use of **advanced morphology**. Advanced morphology refers to the use of derivational morphemes (i.e., prefixes and suffixes) with common root words (Larsen & Nippold, 2007). Derivational morphemes are those that change the grammatical and/or meaning class of the root word. Look at these examples, which show how addition of the morpheme changes the grammatical class of a root word (first three examples) or the meaning of a root word (next three examples):

Learn/Learn*er* (change in class)

Friend/Friend*ly* (change in class)

Irritate/Irrit*able* (change in class)

Welcome/*Un*welcome (change in meaning)

Heat/*Re*heat (change in meaning)

Use/*Mis*use (change in meaning)

It is important to distinguish derivational morphemes from inflectional morphemes identified in Brown's (1973) work, which has been discussed within the "Developmental Notes" section of many prior chapters. Inflectional morphemes (e.g., plural

TABLE 13.1
Syntactic Functions Used in Complex Syntax

FINITE STRUCTURES	NONFINITE STRUCTURES
Independent Clause	Noun Phrase
Dependent Clause	Verb Phrase
Noun Clause	Infinitive Phrase
Relative Clause	Participle Phrase
Adverb Clause	Gerund Phrase
Comparative Clause	

-s, past tense -ed) add information about tense or number to a root word (e.g., apple/apples; Tom/Tom's), but do not change the meaning or the class of the word as do derivational morphemes. The English language has over 100 derivational morphemes (Crystal, 2002), and Table 13.2 identifies the most common derivational morphemes occurring in printed English text (Carroll, Davies, & Richman, 1971).

Complex Syntax and Complex Sentences

There is an important question we should address before going much further: Is complex syntax the same thing as a complex sentence? Glad you asked! You will get different answers depending on who you ask, but since you asked us, we will give you our opinion. Complex syntax certainly includes complex sentences (recall from Chapter 12 that a complex sentence is an independent clause + one or more subordinate or dependent clauses). However, there are other syntactic forms and functions that contribute to

TABLE 13.2
Most Frequently Used Derivational Prefixes and Suffixes (Carroll, Davies, & Richman, 1971)

PREFIXES	SUFFIXES
un-	-s, -es
re-	-ed
in-, im-, ir-, il- (not)	-ing
dis-	-ly
en-, em-	-er, -or
non-	-ion, -tion, -ation, -ition
in-, im- (in or into)	-ible, -able
over-	-al, -ial
mis-	-y
sub-	-ness
pre-	-ity, -ty
inter-	-ment
fore-	-ic
de-	-ous, -eous, -ious
trans-	-en
super-	-er
semi-	-ive, -ative, -itive
anti-	-ful
mid-	-less
under-	-est

complexity, such as the use of adverbial phrases, as shown in our examples previously. In fact, the use of noun phrases, verb phrases, adjectival and adverbial phrases, and verbals all add complexity to our syntax when we write or speak. Advanced morphological markers change the meaning and word classification within the utterance, thereby adding complexity, regardless of the sentence type.

Additionally, we should also point out that the term *sentence* often refers to written constructions and may unnecessarily restrict our definition of complex syntax. Complex syntax can—and should—be used in both oral and written forms, and the rules of spoken communication are often different from written communication (see Arndt & Schuele, 2013). For instance, consider the use of the dependent clause "While my baby sister was sleeping." In written form, this clause is unable to stand alone; use of this clause apart from an independent clause is considered a fragment and not a sentence at all. However, if a teacher asks "When did you and your mom make cupcakes?," the response "While my baby sister was sleeping" is very appropriate. This adverbial clause is not a sentence, per se, but it is complex in its syntax. In sum, use of the term *complex syntax* encompasses all complex structures within oral and written communication, beyond sentence structure alone.

Purpose of Complex Syntax

As children develop language, they shift from using basic syntactic forms (e.g., nouns, verbs) and functions (e.g., simple sentences) for communicating wants and needs to using complex syntactic forms (e.g., noun phases, verbals) and functions (e.g., dependent clauses) for communicating abstract concepts, thoughts, and ideas. Consider the differences between the two examples:

> I want a cookie.
>
> Chocolate-chip cookies with M&Ms are my favorite because they have so much chocolate in them!

In the first example, the purpose of the communication is simple—to get a cookie! And similarly, the syntax is simple (subject = "I", verb = "want", direct object = "more cookies"). No additional syntactic information is needed for this purpose. In the second example, the purpose is more abstract—to describe and convey an opinion about the cookies. And with this abstract purpose, the child uses complex syntax to convey such an opinion. The syntactic forms used to create this complexity include an elaborated noun phrase for the subject (chocolate-chip cookies with M&Ms), an elaborated noun phrase as the complement (my favorite), and an adverbial clause explaining <u>why</u> they are this child's favorite (because they have so much chocolate in them).

Another way to think about complex syntax is to consider how a child utilizes syntactic forms to fulfill obligatory sentence structures to form an utterance (spoken or written). You will recall that in Chapter 9, we identified two obligatory sentence structures. Do you remember what they are? Exactly right—the subject and the predicate! To count as a sentence, one has to include a subject and predicate at minimum. But the child has choices as to how these requirements are fulfilled. For example, the child could use a single noun (and any necessary determiners) as the subject and a single verb as the predicate: *The man sang.*

With this construction, the syntactic obligations of a sentence are met: subject and predicate. Check! Conceptually, in this utterance we know the basic message—the speaker is referring to a man, and this man sang. But this is all we know, and in fact, we are left with many questions: Who is this man? What about his singing? Why is his singing relevant?

Consider, in contrast, the child who uses an elaborated noun phrase as the subject and an elaborated verb phrase as the predicate: *The tall man with the ten-gallon hat sang quite loudly.* Now we know quite a lot. We know the size of the man (tall), we have a mental image of the man's attire (very large hat), we are able to infer meaning about the subject (not only are we talking about a man, but we are talking about a cowboy), and we now know more about the singing (he was not only singing, but doing so quite loudly). The added noun phrase as the subject and verb phrase as the predicate adds complexity to the basic sentence structure and, as a consequence, conveys more detailed information to the listener.

Discussion of complex syntax could quickly become a chicken-or-the-egg conundrum: Do children have complex ideas that then prompt development of complex syntax as a way to express those ideas, or do children develop complex syntax that then allows for comprehension and expression of complex thoughts and ideas? That is a theoretical discussion for another time and place (although if your curiosity is getting the better of you, take a look at Bates, 2003, and Loban, 1976). For our purposes, however, let's consider the importance of context to one's use of complex syntax.

Literate Language

Some researchers and educators refer to complex syntax as a literate language style, because it corresponds to the type of syntax that is more important for literacy, such as comprehending complex academic texts. That is, academic texts do not tend to include simple syntactic constructions, but rather informationally dense and syntactically complex language. In this regard, the understanding and production of complex syntax is an important aspect of being literate and using a literate language style. Experts suggest that children who use a literate language style will show a high level of these syntactic forms and functions in their spoken and written language (see Curenton & Justice, 2004; Westby, 1991):

- Elaborated noun phrases (e.g., *the very tall man*)
- Adverbs and adverbial phases (e.g., *very slowly*)
- Conjunctions (e.g., *for, yet*) when used for coordination and subordination

A literate language style involves use of these forms and functions in both spoken and written communication so as to discuss and understand abstract ideas (Westby, 1991). Literate language is less contextualized than the language we use in everyday conversations with others, meaning the burden of communication lies solely on a person's language abilities without being able rely on intonation, visual supports, or shared experiences. As an example, think about the language differences between writing a research paper for a history class and chatting with a friend over lunch. For the research paper, the burden of communication is solely on you. You have to communicate your knowledge of the subject in a constrained amount of space using only your language—no pictures allowed! The task is very demanding and requires a great deal of precision, and thus requires a high level of complex syntax to adequately convey the necessary information. Visiting with a friend, however, is much more casual and highly contextual. The burden of communication is shared. Both of you are doing the talking and can ask for clarification if something is unclear. Often the topic is about something you can both see or something you have both recently experienced. In this contextual situation, there is less need to use complex syntax to ensure your listener gets all the needed information.

Measuring Complex Syntax

There are two widely accepted ways for measuring syntactic complexity in oral and written utterances: Mean Length of Terminable Units (MLTU) and Subordination Index (SI). To understand these measures, we first need to clarify the term **terminable unit**, which is commonly referred to as a T-unit. A T-unit is defined as one independent clause plus any dependent clauses and embedded phrases. Although T-units are often used to refer to written utterances and C-units (conversational unit) to oral utterances, for ease of interpretation, we will use T-units here to refer to both oral and written samples.

MLTU is the average number of words per T-unit and is calculated by adding the total number of words in a language sample and dividing by the total number of T-units:

$$\text{MLTU} = \frac{\text{Total Number of Words}}{\text{Total Number of T-Units}}$$

So, if a child produces a retelling of a story, and produces 100 words and 10 T-units, her MLTU would be 10. In comparison, a child who produces a retelling of a story and produces 100 words and 20 T-units would have an MLTU of 5. The first child's higher MLTU signifies that she is using more complex syntax, as for her a given T-unit contains more words (10 on average) than the second child, whose T-units contain, on average, 5 words.

Why is length (which is basically what the MLTU tells us) considered a measure of complexity? Great question! Let's revisit our previous example: *The man sang* versus *The man with the ten-gallon hat sang quite loudly.* We already identified the second sentence as having a greater number of complex syntactic structures than the first, including a noun phrase and a verb phrase. But we didn't point out the obvious: the more embedded phrases and clauses a speaker uses, the longer the utterance will be. The MLTU metric captures the differences between T-units with respect to the average number of words contained, and we assume that lengthier T-units correspond to more complexity.

Now, we should add one important caveat here. Although higher values for the MLTU typically signals increased use of complex syntactic forms, increased length does not always equate to more syntactic complexity. In certain literate contexts, a speaker's ability to express ideas using more concise, specific terminology may often be considered more advanced than speakers who require more words and longer utterances to convey a similar message (see Westby, 1991 for discussion of literate style). For instance, consider these two utterances:

> Because many people attended the school board meeting and voiced serious concerns about building a new school, the school board members decided to find other possible solutions to the building proposal.

> After hearing persuasive arguments from the community, the school board reconsidered the building proposition.

Using our formula above, the first example is clearly a lengthier utterance than the second. But, is it the more complex utterance? If we are defining complexity in terms of length, then yes. Yet, in the second example, the speaker conveys the same message using more specific terminology (e.g., persuasive, reconsidered), and in so doing, uses fewer words. The first utterance may be longer, but isn't necessarily more complex in what is being conveyed. MLTU is one way to measure complex syntax in both spoken and written language, but as with all measures, it has limitations, so be aware!

The second measure of complex syntax is the **subordination index**. The subordination index (SI) is a measure of clausal density. The total number of independent and dependent clauses are summed and divided by the total number of T-units.

$$SI = \frac{\text{Independent + Dependent Clauses}}{\text{Total Number of T-Units}}$$

For children who only use independent clauses, the SI will be 1, as the total number of clauses will be the same as the total number of T-units. As the child increases use of dependent clauses, the SI will also increase. For instance, a child who produces 10 T-units and 20 clauses will receive an SI of 2, indicating that, on average, each T-unit contains 2 clauses.

Developmental Notes

A common misconception regarding children's development of complex syntax is that these forms and functions are later developing. In fact, a good deal of evidence suggests that children begin to acquire complex syntactic structures before they have mastered more fundamental forms (Bloom, Tackeff, & Lahey, 1984; Diessel, 2004; Limber, 1973; Paul, 1981). For instance, recall our discussion of work by Paul (1981) in Chapter 12. She reported that complex sentences were observed in children as young as 34 months of age. Likewise, Brown's (1973) work suggests that complex forms begin to emerge as early as 24 months in many children. In fact, Tyack and Gottsleben (1986) suggest that children demonstrate proficiency of adult-like, complex structures as early as kindergarten.

That said, complex syntax is unique from other developmental forms of syntax in that these forms continue to develop through adolescence, specifically as measured by MLTU and SI (Loban, 1976; Scott, 1988; Nippold, 2007). Both indices of complex syntax show steady growth from 3rd grade through 12th grade, as shown in Table 13.3.

In studying these data for MLTU and SI across the grades depicted, we see some interesting patterns of complex syntax development. First, there is a steady, albeit gradual, increase for both metrics as children continue to develop: older adolescents outperform younger children and adolescents in terms of complex syntax use. Second, there is an important transition in adolescence with regard to oral and written samples. For adolescents in 6th and 7th grade, MLTU is higher in oral narratives than in written narratives; in 8th and 9th grade, MLTU in oral and written narratives is equitable; and in 10th to 12th grade, MLTU in written narratives is higher than in oral (Loban, 1976). Third, there is less distinction between SI for oral and written narratives in late adolescence. In late childhood/early adolescence (3rd grade through 6th grade), SI is slightly higher for oral narratives than written. By mid-to-late adolescence (>8th grade) there

TABLE 13.3
MLTU and SI by Age and Context (Oral and Written)
(Loban, 1976; Nippold, 1998; Scott, 1989)

	GRADE				
	3-4	6	8	10	12
Mean-Length T-Unit					
Oral	7.8	9.8	10.7	10.7	11.7
Written	9.5	9.0	10.4	11.8	13.3
Subordination Index					
Oral	1.3	1.4	1.4	1.5	1.6
Written	1.3	1.3	1.5	1.5	1.6

is virtually no distinction in SI between oral and written narratives (Nippold, Hesketh, Duthie, & Mansfield, 2005; Scott, 2005).

Even after adolescence, there is evidence to suggest that complex syntax continues to develop into early adulthood (Nippold et al., 2005), although it is possible that in later adulthood there is a decline in one's comprehension and production of complex syntax. Although Nippold, Cramon, and Hayward-Mayhew (2014) found complex syntax to be fairly similar when comparing 40-year-old adults to 60-year-old adults, Kemper, Kynette, Rash, O'Brien, and Sprott (1989; see also Kemper & Sumner, 2001) found there to be a decline in complex syntax in later adulthood, and attributed this decline to changes in working memory. Future research will help us to understand whether complex syntax is affected by aging and perhaps ways to stave off such effects, such as completing the exercises in this book!

CHAPTER EXERCISES

Exercise 13A

Using Table 13.1 as a reference, underline the phrase or clause in each sentence making it complex, and identify whether it is finite or nonfinite:

The girl with the long red hair is my sister.
They decided that they did not have enough information.
My dog does not always play fetch.
I do not want to memorize the rules.
We like playing card games.

Exercise 13B

Calculate MLTU and SI for the following sample:

This story is about a little girl who lived in a castle/ She was really strong and she was good at playing games/ One day a dragon wanted to play a racing game with her/ She said okay when I am done with breakfast/ They started outside the castle and the king waved the flag when it was time to start/ They ran past the castle, over the bridge, and around a waterfall/ But the princess knew a short cut/ So the princess won the racing game/

[Handwritten notes in margin:]
Total Words: 87
Total T-units: 10
Total Clauses: 13
MLTU: 87/10 = 8.7
SI: 13/10 = 1.3

Exercise 13C

For each of the following words, underline the root word, circle the morpheme, and identify if the morpheme changed the meaning of the root word (M), changed the class of the root word (C), neither (N), or both (B).

_m_	1.	disengage
_C_	2.	likable
_N_	3.	tokens
_m_	4.	unknown
_B_	5.	unimaginable
_C_	6.	teacher
_N_	7.	cleared
_m_	8.	retrace
_C_	9.	carefully
_C_	10.	imagination

Exercise 13D

Using the list of the most frequently occurring prefixes and suffixes, create as many derivations of each of the following root words as you can.

1. *port*: _____

2. *think*: _____

3. *create*: _____

4. *beauty*: _____

5. *logic*: _____

ANSWER KEY

Exercise 13A

1. The girl with the long red hair is my sister. (Nonfinite)
2. They decided that they did not have enough information. (Finite)
3. My dog does not always play fetch. (Nonfinite)
4. Because it is raining, we cannot swim today. (Finite)
5. We like playing card games. (Nonfinite)

Exercise 13B

Total Number of Words: 87
Total T-Units: 10
Total Clauses: 13
MLTU: (87/10) = 8.7
SI: (13/10) = 1.3

Exercise 13C

1. disengage (M)
2. likable (C)
3. tokens (N)
4. unknown (M)
5. unimaginable (B)
6. teacher (C)
7. cleared (N)
8. retrace (M)
9. carefully (C)
10. imagination (C)

Exercise 13D

There are many possibilities, but here are a few answers to get you started:

1. *port*: portable, deport
2. *think*: thinker, unthinkable
3. *create*: creator, creation
4. *beauty*: beautiful, beautification
5. *logic*: logical, illogical

Appendices

APPENDIX A: Major Syntactic Accomplishments in Child Language Acquisition Arranged by Brown's (1973) Stages

APPENDIX B: Examples of Major Syntactic Forms

APPENDIX C: Examples of Major Syntactic Functions

APPENDIX A
Major Syntactic Accomplishments in Child Language Acquisition Arranged by Brown's (1973) Stages

STAGE	MLU	AGE (MONTHS)	GRAMMATICAL MORPHEMES	NEGATION	YES/NO QUESTIONS	WH- QUESTIONS	NOUN PHRASE ELABORATION[d]	VERB PHRASE ELABORATION[d]	COMPLEX SENTENCES
P I Early I	1.01–1.49	19–22[a] 16–26[b]	Occasional use	no as single-word utterance (but not as a negative response to a yes/no question)	Marked with rising intonation	what + this/that	NP → (M) + N[e] Elaborated NPs occur only alone	**Main Verb:** uninflected; occasional use of ing **Auxiliary:** not used **Copula:** not used **Verb + Particles:** occasional use	None used
P I Late I / Early II	1.50–1.99	23–26 18–31	Occasional use	no + noun or verb		what + NP or VP			
P II II	2.00–2.49	27–30 21–35	1. Present progressive tense of verb -ing[c] 2. Regular plural -s 3. Preposition in	not + noun or verb		where + NP or VP	NP same as Stage I Object NP elaboration appears: V + NP	**Main Verb:** occasionally marked **Auxiliary:** 1. Semiauxiliary appears 2. Use of present progressive -ing without auxiliary **Copula:** appears without tense/ number inflection	Semiauxiliary appears: gonna, gotta, wanna, hafta
P II III	2.50–2.99	31–34 24–41	4. Preposition on 5. Possessive -'s	NP + (negative) + VP		Wh- word + sentence why, who, and how questions appear	NP → { (demonstrative) (article) } + (M) + N Subject NP elaboration appears: NP + V	**Main Verb:** 1. Obligatory 2. Overgeneralization of regular past -ed **Auxiliary:** Present tense forms appear: can, will, be, do	Object NP complement; full sentence takes the place of object of the verb
P III Early IV	3.00–3.49	35–38 28–45		NP + auxiliary + (negative) + VP NP + copula + (negative) + VP	Inversion of auxiliary verb and subject noun	Inconsistent auxiliary inversion when questions appear			Simple infinitive phrases appear Simple wh- clauses appear Conjoined sentences with conjunction and

(continues)

211

Appendix A (continued)

STAGE	MLU	AGE (MONTHS)	GRAMMATICAL MORPHEMES	NEGATION	YES/NO QUESTIONS	WH- QUESTIONS	NOUN PHRASE ELABORATION	VERB PHRASE ELABORATION	COMPLEX SENTENCES
Late IV/ Early V	3.50– 3.99	39–42 31–50	No others mastered	No change	No change	No change	NP → (demonstrative) (article) (M) (possessive) + (adjective) + N Subject NP obligatory; noun or pronoun always appears in subject position	**Main Verb:** regular past -ed (double marking of main verb and auxiliary for past in negative sentences) **Auxiliary:** 1. Past modals appear, including *could, would, should, must, might* 2. *be* + present progressive *-ing* appears **Verb Phrase:** semiauxiliary complements take NP	Multiple embeddings Conjoined and embedded clauses in the same sentence
Late V	4.00– 4.49	43–46 37–52	6. Regular past tense of verb *-ed* 7. Irregular past tense of verb 8. Regular third person singular present tense *-s* 9. Definite and indefinite articles 10. Contractible copula	Past tense modals and *be* in contracted and uncontracted form		See Grammatical Morphemes column (6–14)	NP → same as Stage IV Number agreement between subject and predicate verb phrase continues to be a problem beyond Stage V	See Grammatical Morphemes column (6–10)	Relative clauses appear Infinitive phrases with subjects different from that of main sentence Conjunction *if* used
V+	4.50– 4.99	47–50 41–59	11. Contractible auxiliary 12. Uncontractible copula 13. Uncontractible auxiliary 14. Irregular third person singular	No data	No data			See Grammatical Morphemes column (11–14) **Main Verb/Aux.** 1. Past tense *be* appears as main verb and auxiliary 2. Infrequent use of present perfect tense with auxiliary marked	Gerund phrases appear *Wh-* infinitive phrases appear Unmarked infinitive phrases appear Conjunction *because* used
V++	5.00– 5.99	51–67 43–67	No data	No data	No data	No data			Conjunctions *when* and *so* appear

Note. From *Guide to Analysis of Language Transcripts* (3rd ed.) (pp. 111–112), by K. S. Retherford, 2000, Austin, TX: PRO-ED, Inc. © 2000 by PRO-ED, Inc. Reprinted with permission. [a]Predicted age range. [b]Age range within one *SD* of predicted values. [c]Based on 90% use in obligatory contexts, except stages EI–LI/EII. [d]Stages I, II, and III have been used to describe developments within only noun phrase elaboration and verb phrase elaboration based on sources of these data. [e]The following are definitions of sentence notation: → is expanded, or

APPENDIX B
Examples of Major Syntactic Forms

FORM	CATEGORY	EXAMPLE(S)
Noun	Common	state, dessert
	Proper	Alabama, Maria, Jon
	Concrete	brick, elbow
	Abstract	jealousy, heaven
	Count	bow tie, leaf
	Noncount	cement, integrity
	Collective	jury, team
Pronoun	Personal	
	Nominative	I, you, he, they
	Objective	me, you, him, them
	Possessive	my, yours, his, theirs
	Reflexive	yourself, ourselves
	Demonstrative	this, that, these, those
	Indefinite	both, many, some
	Relative	that, who, which
	Interrogative	why, which, what
Verb	Simple	
	Present	Tom <u>calls</u>
	Past	Tom <u>called</u>
	Future	Tom <u>will call</u>
	Progressive	
	Present	Tom <u>is calling</u>
	Past	Tom <u>was calling</u>
	Future	Tom <u>will be calling</u>
	Perfect	
	Present	Tom <u>has called</u>
	Past	Tom <u>had called</u>
	Future	Tom <u>will have called</u>
	Active voice	The dog caught the mole
	Passive voice	The mole was caught by the dog
	Main verb	The ostrich is <u>eating</u>
	Auxiliary verb	The ostrich <u>is</u> eating
	Contractible auxiliary	He <u>is</u> coming → <u>He's</u> coming
	Uncontractible auxiliary	He <u>was</u> coming

(continues)

Appendix B (*continued*)

FORM	CATEGORY	EXAMPLE(S)
Verb, *cont.*	Copula	The man <u>is</u> sad
	Copular verb	arrive, seem, appear
	Contractible copula	We <u>are</u> here → <u>We're</u> here
	Uncontractible copula	We <u>were</u> here
	Modal auxiliary	may, might, shall, should
	Prepositional verb	object to, run for, stand for
	Transitive verb	kick, hit, put
	Intransitive verb	sleep, dream
	Infinitive	I love <u>to run</u>, <u>To draw</u> is divine
	Gerund	<u>Swimming</u> is a fun workout
	Participle	He is <u>running</u>, She was <u>running</u>
Adjective	Simple	<u>ugly</u> dog, <u>dirty</u> mitten
	Compound	<u>ballpoint</u> pen, <u>smashed-up</u> car, <u>health care</u> center
	Positive	pretty, good
	Comparative	prettier, better
	Superlative	prettiest, best
	Descriptive	
	Attributive	a <u>pretty</u> baby, the <u>blue</u> sky
	Predicate	That is <u>cool</u>, She seems <u>nice</u>
	Limiting	
	Proper	<u>English</u> class, <u>Dell</u> computer
	Possessive	the <u>man's</u> coat, <u>Brady's</u> dog
	Demonstrative	<u>This</u> one's red, <u>These</u> boots are cool
	Cardinal	It's only <u>two</u> dollars, I'd like <u>three</u> tickets
	Ordinal	I won <u>first</u> place, It's the <u>fourth</u> edition
	Indefinite	<u>Some</u> cats eat mice, I asked <u>both</u> girls
	Interrogative	<u>Whose</u> house is this?, <u>Which</u> color do you prefer?
Adverb	Simple	here, lastly
	Compound	counterclockwise, contra-laterally
	Positive	slowly, angrily
	Comparative	more slowly, more angrily
	Superlative	most slowly, most angrily
	Conjunctive adverb	thus, additionally, however
	Manner adverb	quickly, particularly, well, slowly
	Place adverb	here, there, near, outside
	Time adverb	before, immediately, now
	Degree adverb	much, more, nearly, only
	Number adverb	first, secondly, lastly
	Reason adverb	because, consequently, since
	Affirmation adverb	absolutely, indeed, surely, yes
	Negation adverb	never, no, not

Appendix B (*continued*)

FORM	CATEGORY	EXAMPLE(S)
Determiner	Article Possessive Demonstrative Quantifier Wh- word	*a, an, the* *my, his, her* *this, that, these, those* *every, each, some, two* *what, which, whichever*
Conjunction	Coordinating Subordinating Correlative Simple Compound Phrasal Conjunctive adverb	*for, and, nor, but, or, yet, so* *after, though, when, because* *either/or, neither/nor, whether/or* *and, after, so, when* *thereafter, however, nevertheless* *that is, even if, as such* *otherwise, however, consequently*
Preposition	Simple Compound Phrasal Prepositional adverb Prepositional verb Time Place Accompaniment Destination Means Possession Relation	*in, on, under, behind* *without, underneath, nearby* *as for, in spite of, according to* *after, below, about, under* *object to, run for, stand for* *at, between, during, for* *against, along, among, on* *with, without* *for, to* *by, with, without* *of* *of*

APPENDIX C
Examples of Major Syntactic Functions

FORM	CATEGORY	EXAMPLE(S)
Subject	Simple Complete Compound	<u>Tommy</u> is crying, <u>Milk</u> is good <u>A little boy</u> is crying, <u>The milk</u> is good <u>A little boy and little girl</u> are crying
Object	Direct Indirect	Jennifer told <u>Helen</u>, He kicked <u>her</u> Jennifer gave <u>Helen</u> the ball, Jennifer gave the ball to <u>Helen</u>
Complement	Following copula *be* Following an intransitive verb	It is <u>cold</u>, They are <u>tired</u> Jack seems <u>aloof</u>, It works <u>well</u>

Predicate	Simple
	Complete
	Compound
	Nominal Predicate
	   Prepositional noun
	   Prepositionless noun
	   Qualificative
	   Adverbial
	Verb Predicate
	   Verb standing alone
	   Prepositional object
	   Prepositionless object
	   Adverb
	   Adverbial clause
		The girl <u>wants</u> a cookie
		The girl <u>wants a cookie</u>
		The boy <u>caught</u> and <u>threw</u> the ball
		
		It <u>is on the stove</u>
		You <u>are my friend</u>
		Gretchen <u>seems scared</u>
		The cat <u>is outside</u>
		
		She <u>called</u>
		Esther <u>called for directions</u>
		Amory <u>caught the ball</u>
		We <u>sit here</u>
		I'll call <u>when he says to</u>

Phrase	Noun Verb Prepositional Adjective Adverb Infinitive Gerund Participle	the boy, a child, a short nap came, has already come in the back, on the refrigerator very expensive, quite outrageous right there, over here, rather quietly The manager needs <u>to tell us</u> <u>Jumping through the hoops</u> was easy <u>Being early</u>, we decided to help
Clause	Independent Dependent (noun) Dependent (adverb) Dependent (adjective) Dependent (comparative)	<u>I am right</u>, aren't I? <u>That you are coming</u> is unbelievable Judy called <u>because I've been so sad</u> The house <u>that caught fire</u> is for sale She is more relaxed <u>than he is</u>

(continues)

Appendix C (*continued*)

FORM	CATEGORY	EXAMPLE(S)
Sentence	Simple	*The cows in the pasture are eating*
	Compound	*The wind is howling and it is raining*
	Complex	*The wind is howling louder than I imagined*
	Compound-complex	*It's Friday and the man whom I love is busy*
	Declarative	*I love the summer*
	Imperative	*Tell me you love the summer*
	Exclamatory	*It's summer!*
	Interrogative	
	Wh- question	*When do you think it will rain?*
	Yes/No question	*Do you think it will rain?*
	Tag question	*It will rain, <u>won't it?</u>*

Glossary

Abstract Noun: A type of noun referring to an intangible, nonphysical entity; describes ideas, emotions, senses, and situations (e.g., *conundrum, excitement*).

Active Voice: A sentence in which the subject is the performer of an action (e.g., "*Mary* opened the letter"); active voice sentences generally follow a "Subject + Verb + Object" or "Subject + Verb + Complement" pattern.

Adjective: A type of modifier that describes a noun or a pronoun (e.g., *The long* and *winding* road is the *famous Deadman's* Drive); can be descriptive or limiting.

Adjective Clause: A dependent clause that elaborates or specifies information about something named (a noun or a pronoun) in the subject or object position; is typically introduced with a relative pronoun. Also referred to as a **relative clause**.

Adjective Phrase: A phrase that has an adjective as its head.

Advanced Morphology: The use of derivational morphemes (i.e., prefixes and suffixes) with common root words.

Adverb: A class of modifiers that provides information about verbs, adjectives, and other adverbs (e.g., *here, really, slowly*); provides information about place, manner, time, degree, reason, number, affirmation, and negation; many are formed by adding *-ly* to a word stem.

Adverb Clause: A dependent clause that provides information about time, place, and motivation for an action or a state.

Adverb Phrase: A phrase that has an adverb as its head.

Adverbial Conjunct: A type of adverb that serves as a conjunction to connect two or more independent clauses (e.g., *accordingly, hence, meanwhile*). Also referred to as a **conjunctive adverb**.

Adverbial Predicate: A type of predicate in which a copular verb is followed by an adverb (e.g., "It is not *here*" or "The book seems *old*"), which is a type of nominal predicate, or in which a transitive verb is followed by an adverb (e.g., "We teach *here*"), which is a type of verbal predicate.

Antecedent: The noun to which a pronoun refers. Also referred to as the **referent**.

Article: One of the determiners *a, an,* or *the*; is either definite (i.e., *the*) or indefinite (i.e., *a, an*).

Attributive Adjective: A type of descriptive adjective that typically precedes the noun it modifies (e.g., "the *blue* sky").

Auxiliary Verb: A verb that is linked to or combined with a main verb to provide additional information about person, tense, or mood (e.g., "Timmy *was* hiding" or "She *will* help you"). Also referred to as a **helping verb**.

Cardinal Adjective: A type of determiner (also a limiting adjective) used to denote the specific quantity of a noun or pronoun (e.g., "*one* apple" or "*two* more").

Clause: A syntactic structure that contains a subject and a predicate; is either independent (main) or dependent (subordinate).

Collective Noun: A type of noun that names a group acting as a unit (e.g., *jury, committee, team*).

Common Noun: A noun referring to a general entity (e.g., *cat, beauty, box*).

Comparative Clause: A type of dependent clause that compares the information in the dependent clause with information presented in the independent clause; is introduced with the words *than* or *as*.

Comparative Degree: The form of an adjective or adverb that reflects a comparison of two entities; is typically formed by adding *-er* to the positive form of an adjective (e.g., *slow → slower*) or by prefacing the positive form with *more* or *less* (e.g., *slowly → more slowly*).

Complement: A word or group of words that follows copular verbs and provides further information about the subject (e.g., "She is *pretty*"). Also referred to as a **subject complement**.

Complete Predicate: A simple predicate plus all the modifiers that provide additional information about the simple predicate (e.g., "The mist *descended slowly*").

Complete Subject: A subject that consists of a simple subject and its modifiers (e.g., "*Intense curiosity* drives that cat").

Complexity: The state or quality of being intricate or complicated.

Complex Preposition: A type of preposition that consists of two or more words, usually an adverb with a preposition (e.g., *according to, outside of, across from*). Also referred to as a **phrasal preposition**.

Complex Sentence: A sentence consisting of one independent clause and one or more dependent clauses.

Complex Syntax: The use of advanced syntactic forms and functions so as to allow speakers to precisely communicate abstract thoughts and ideas.

Compound Adjective: An adjective formed by combining two words into one word (e.g., *pickup* truck), by hyphenating two words (e.g., "*mobile-friendly* website"), or by using two words together without combining or hyphenating them (e.g., "*child development* center").

Compound Adverb: An adverb formed by combining two words, by hyphenating two words, or by combining a prefix and a word (e.g., *clockwise, contra-laterally*).

Compound Clause: A sentence consisting of two or more independent clauses that are conjoined with a coordinating conjunction. Also referred to as a **compound sentence**.

Compound-Complex Sentence: A sentence consisting of two or more independent clauses conjoined by a coordinating conjunction as well as one or more dependent clauses.

Compound Conjunction: A type of conjunction consisting of two or more words that are combined to form a single word (e.g., *however, thereafter*).

Compound Noun: A type of noun comprising more than one word; can be closed (e.g., *stepfather*), open (e.g., *attorney general*), or hyphenated (e.g., *president-elect*).

Compound Personal Pronoun: A type of pronoun formed by adding the suffix *-self* or *-selves* to a personal pronoun (e.g., *himself, themselves*); is used when a person or entity performs an action on his-, her-, or itself. Also referred to as a **reflexive pronoun**.

Compound Predicate: A predicate that consists of two or more simple predicates (e.g., "The mist *descended* and *evaporated*").

Compound Preposition: A type of preposition that is a compound word (e.g., *throughout, within, alongside*).

Compound Sentence: A sentence consisting of two or more independent clauses that are conjoined with a coordinating conjunction. Also referred to as a **compound clause**.

Compound Subject: A subject that is conjoined via a conjunction (e.g., "*Intense curiosity and sheer bravery* drive that cat").

Concrete Noun: A type of noun referring to a tangible, physical entity (e.g., *box, spoon*).

Conjunction: A word or words that serve to join other words, phrases, and clauses; is generally one of three classes: coordinating, subordinating, or correlative.

Conjunctive Adverb: A type of adverb that serves as a conjunction to connect two or more independent clauses (e.g., *accordingly, hence, meanwhile*). Also referred to as an **adverbial conjunct**.

Contractible Auxiliary: A verb used as an auxiliary that can occur in a contracted form with the full meaning of the sentence still expressed (e.g., "Jen *will* come" → "Jen*'ll* come").

Contractible Copula: A *be* verb used as a copula that can occur in a contracted form with the full meaning of the sentence still expressed (e.g., "I *am* happy" → "*I'm* happy").

Coordinate Clause: An independent clause conjoined to another independent clause of equal weight and importance via a coordinating conjunction.

Coordinating Conjunction: A conjunction used to join two independent clauses such that each has equal weight and importance (i.e., *for, and, nor, but, or, yet,* and *so*).

Copula: A *be* verb when it stands alone as a main verb and does not require an object (e.g., "I *am* happy").

Copular Verb: An intransitive verb that functions like a copula (e.g., "He *feels* happy"). Also referred to as a **linking verb**.

Correlative Conjunction: A conjunction that is typically used as one in a pair (e.g., *both/and, either/or, neither/nor*).

Count Noun: A noun that refers to a countable entity (e.g., *letter, child, cup*); also has plural forms (e.g., *letters, children, cups*).

Declarative Sentence: A sentence type that informs by making a positive or negative statement or an assertion (e.g., "Jason isn't coming").

Definite Article: The article *the*, which is used to refer to a specific entity; typically considered a determiner but also a limiting adjective.

Demonstrative Adjective: A type of determiner (and a limiting adjective) that is a demonstrative in an adjectival role; it serves to identify or highlight a particular noun that it directly precedes (e.g., "*this* bowl" or "*that* spoon").

Demonstrative Pronoun: A pronoun that identifies or highlights a particular noun or antecedent (i.e., *this, that, these,* and *those*).

Dependent Clause: A clause that contains a subject and a predicate but must be combined with an independent clause to form a sentence; is typically introduced by a subordinating conjunction or a relative pronoun. Also referred to as a **subordinate clause**.

Descriptive Adjective: A type of adjective that describes a quality of the noun or pronoun it modifies (e.g., "the *tall* girl"); can be grouped into two types: attributive adjectives and predicate adjectives.

Determiner: A modifier that clarifies aspects of a noun; cannot exist outside of a noun phrase; major categories include: articles, possessive pronouns and nouns, demonstratives, quantifiers, and *wh-* words.

Direct Object: The recipient of an action in a clause or sentence (e.g., "Tommy hit *the ball*").

Essential Predicate: A verb that provides the principle information contained in the predicate and is usually the main verb of the sentence (e.g., "The mist *descended* slowly"). Also referred to as a **simple predicate**.

Exclamatory Sentence: A sentence type that expresses a strong emotion (e.g., "He's a fool!").

Finite: A part of speech (e.g., verb) that carries information about tense and number (e.g., "She is swinging").

Finite Clause: A dependent clause that serves as the subject or object of a sentence; always contains a subject. Also referred to as a **nominal clause** or **noun clause**.

Future Perfect Tense: A verb tense that references actions or states of being that will be or shall be completed before a particular time in the future; is formed by combining *will have* or *shall have* and the past participle form of a verb (e.g., "Ian *will have eaten* by the time you get home").

Future Progressive Tense: A verb tense that references actions or states of being that will be or shall be continuously happening in the future; is formed by combining *will be* or *shall be* and the present participle (e.g., "Carlos *will be jumping*").

Future Tense: A verb tense that describes actions or states of being that will or shall occur (e.g., Tom *shall go*).

Gerund: The present participle form of a verb used as a noun (e.g., "*Lifting* is difficult for him" or "*Cooking* helps me relax").

Gradable Adjective: An adjective that can be modified to compare two or more entities along a continuum (e.g., *tall, taller, tallest*).

Grammatical Morpheme: A morpheme that adds to the grammatical structure of a word or phrase, including the 14 free and bound morphemes Brown (1973) studied primarily because of the obligatory context each possesses. (See Table 12.3 for a list of Brown's 14 grammatical morphemes.)

Head Word: The central element of a phrase; is usually a noun in a noun phrase, a verb in a verb phrase, etc.

Helping Verb: A verb that is linked to or combined with a main verb to provide additional information about person, tense, or mood (e.g., "Timmy *was* hiding" or "She *will* help you"). Also referred to as an **auxiliary verb**.

Imperative Mood: A mood used when giving a command or making a request (e.g., "Tell that terrier to stop barking").

Imperative Sentence: A sentence type that has an overall function of making a request or giving an order (e.g., "Put that over there, please").

Indefinite: A word that has a general, unstated referent (e.g., *all, every*); can function as a pronoun or a limiting adjective.

Indefinite Adjective: A type of determiner (also a type of limiting adjective) that provides additional information about the noun or pronoun it modifies; is an indefinite pronoun in an adjectival role (e.g., "Share *both* cookies").

Indefinite Article: Either the article *a* or *an*; both are used to refer to nonspecific entities; typically considered a determiner but also a limiting adjective.

Indefinite Pronoun: A pronoun that has a general, unstated referent (e.g., *nothing, some*).

Independent Clause: A clause that expresses the main idea of a sentence and can stand alone and maintain full meaning. Also referred to as a **main clause**.

Indicative Mood: A mood used when stating a fact (e.g., "That dog is a terrier") or requesting information (e.g., "Is that dog a terrier?").

Indirect Object: The beneficiary of an action in a clause or sentence (e.g., "Jill gave *Jack* the bucket").

Infinitive: A verb form that is the bare stem of a verb preceded by *to* (e.g., "I want *to wait*").

Infinitive Phrase: A phrase that uses the infinitive form of a verb (e.g., "*To wait any longer* would be foolish").

Interjection: A word or phrase of exclamation that is used to express emotion or surprise (e.g., "Ouch!" "Oh my!").

Interrogative Adjective: A type of limiting adjective that is an interrogative (e.g., *whose, which, what*) serving an adjectival role (e.g., "*Whose* dog is that?").

Interrogative Pronoun: A pronoun that is used to ask a *wh-* question (e.g., "*Who* went to the party?").

Interrogative Sentence: A sentence type that asks a question to attain information (e.g., "Who taught the diagnostics class?").

Intonation Question: A declarative sentence that is presented with a rising intonation as though to ask a question (e.g., "Sharon will help me?").

Intransitive Verb: A verb that does not require an object (e.g., "He *sleeps*").

Irregular Noun: A noun that has a unique plural form that does not follow the general formation rule for pluralization of adding *-s* or *-es* (e.g., *mouse* → *mice, deer* → *deer, child* → *children*).

Irregular Verb: A verb for which the past participle is formed in a unique manner that does not follow the general formation rule of adding *-ed* (e.g., *sleep* → *slept, broke* → *broken*).

Irreversible Passive: A passive sentence in which the subject and the object cannot be interchanged based on the meaning (e.g., "The ice cream was eaten by the boy" is irreversible to "The boy was eaten by the ice cream").

Limiting Adjective: An adjective that modifies a noun by focusing on how much, how many, whose, etc.; can be grouped into nine types: definite and indefinite articles, possessive adjectives, demonstrative adjectives, indefinite adjectives, interrogative adjectives, cardinal adjectives, ordinal adjectives, proper adjectives, and nouns used as adjectives.

Linking Verb: An intransitive verb that functions like a copula (e.g., "He *feels* happy"). Also referred to as a **copular verb**.

Main Clause: A clause that expresses the main idea of a sentence; can stand alone and maintain full meaning. Also referred to as an **independent clause**.

Main Verb: A verb serving as the principle descriptor of an action or a state.

Mass Noun: A noun that cannot be transformed from a singular to a plural form, nor vice versa; generally refers to an entity that is not viewed as comprising individual elements (e.g., *clothes, honesty, mathematics*). Also referred to as a **noncount noun**.

Modal Auxiliary: An auxiliary verb used to describe the intention and certainty of an action (e.g., *can, could, might*).

Modifier: A class of words that provides additional information about nouns, pronouns, and verbs; is generally either an adjective or an adverb.

Mood: Refers to the verb function (or sometimes form) that indicates the state of mind or intention of a speaker.

Nominal Clause: A dependent clause that serves as the subject or object of a sentence; always contains a subject. Also referred to as a **noun clause** or **finite clause**.

Nominal Form: A word that represents a person, place, thing, or idea (e.g., *Henry, Florida, water, freedom*). Also referred to as a **noun.**

Nominal Predicate: The information in the predicate slot of a sentence that provides more information about the subject and follows copular (linking) verbs; can be a predicate adjective or a predicate nominative (e.g., "It is *I*" or "Ginger will be *famous*").

Nominative Pronoun: A type of personal pronoun used when the pronoun is the subject of a clause or sentence (e.g., *I, they*). Also referred to as a **subject pronoun**.

Noncount Noun: A noun that cannot be transformed from a singular to a plural form, nor vice versa; generally refers to an entity that is not viewed as comprising individual elements (e.g., *clothes, honesty, mathematics*). Also referred to as a **mass noun**.

Nonfinite: A part of speech (e.g., verb) that does not carry information specific to tense or number (e.g., "The kids like to swing").

Nongradable Adjective: An adjective that cannot be modified into comparative or superlative forms (e.g., *square* box).

Nonrestrictive Clause: An adjective (or relative) clause that provides additional information about a particular referent, but the information is not necessary for recognizing the referent (e.g., "I called Bill, *who wanted to come over*").

Noun: A word that represents a person, place, thing, or idea (e.g., *Henry, Florida, water, freedom*). Also referred to as a **nominal form**.

Noun Clause: A dependent clause that serves as the subject or object of a sentence; always contains a subject. Also referred to as a **nominal clause** or **finite clause**.

Noun Phrase: A phrase that has a noun or pronoun as the head.

Object: Either the recipient of an action in a clause or sentence (direct object) or an object that indicates who or what is the beneficiary of an action in a clause or sentence (indirect object).

Objective Pronoun: A type of personal pronoun used when the pronoun is the object (the recipient of the action) in a clause or sentence (e.g., *me, them*).

Ordinal Adjective: A type of determiner (also a limiting adjective) that denotes the order of a noun or pronoun in a series (e.g., "the *first* issue" or "the *fourth* point").

Participle: A verb form created by adding *-ing* to a verb stem (present participle) or *-d* or *-ed* to a verb stem (past participle) (e.g., *walking, walked*).

Participle Phrase: A phrase in which either a past participle or a present participle is the main verb.

Passive Voice: A sentence in which the subject is acted upon (e.g., "The door was opened by John").

Past Participle: The past tense form of a verb, which is formed by adding *-ed* to the bare stem of a verb (e.g., *walk* → *walked*).

Past Perfect Continuous Tense: A verb tense that denotes events or activities that happened continuously in the past (e.g., "We *had been driving*"). Also referred to as the **perfect progressive tense**.

Past Progressive Tense: A verb tense that references actions or states of being that were in progress in the past; is formed by combining *was* or *were* and the present participle (e.g., "Carlos *was jumping*").

Past Tense: A verb tense that denotes actions or states of being that occurred in the past.

Perfect Progressive Tense: A verb tense that denotes events or activities that happened continuously in the past (e.g., "We *had been driving*"). Also referred to as the **past perfect continuous tense**.

Perfect Tense: One of the three basic verb tenses; used to describe actions or states of being that happened in the past or that will have happened before some other action; can be present, past, or future; uses the past participle form of a verb.

Person: The information contained in the verb of a clause or sentence that denotes who or what is completing the action.

Personal Pronoun: A pronoun that replaces a noun in a clause or sentence (e.g., *I, you, it, we, them*).

Phrasal Conjunction: A type of conjunction that consists of two or more words (e.g., *in other words, that is, even if*).

Phrasal Preposition: A type of preposition that consists of two or more words, usually an adverb with a preposition (e.g., *according to, outside of, across from*). Also referred to as a **complex preposition**.

Phrasal Verb: A verb that is formed by combining a verb with a verb particle (e.g., *allow for, insist on, believe in*). Also referred to as a **prepositional verb** or **two-part verb**.

Phrase: A syntactic structure that contains one or more words but does not contain both a subject and a verb; may fill the subject or predicate slot in a sentence and be combined with other phrases to form a sentence.

Positive Form: The form of an adjective or adverb that can be inflected to create comparative and superlative forms.

Possessive Adjective: A noun functioning as a limiting adjective; is used to signify possession (e.g., "the *man's* car" or "*John's* hair").

Possessive Noun: A type of noun used to signify possession (e.g., "That book is *John's*," or "Those are the *children's*").

Possessive Pronoun: A type of personal pronoun used to signify possession (e.g., *mine*); is also a type of determiner (e.g., "How's *my* hair?" or "That's *her* doll").

Predicate: A major sentence element following the subject slot that is made up of the verb and other constituents following it; describes the action, state, or condition that is stated, asked, ordered, or exclaimed by the use of a verb (e.g., "Allison *is sleeping*" or "The cows *are in the pasture*").

Predicate Adjective: A type of descriptive adjective that follows copular verbs; modifies the noun or pronoun serving as the subject in the clause or sentence (e.g., "The girl is *tall*").

Preposition: A word that links a noun or pronoun to another sentence element by expressing direction, location, time, or figurative location (e.g., "Put the butter *on* the table"); usually serves as the first word in a prepositional phrase.

Prepositional Adverb: A preposition that provides additional information about verbs in a sentence (e.g., "We walked *across* the bridge").

Prepositional Noun Predicate: A type of nominal predicate in which a prepositional phrase follows a copular verb (e.g., "The dog *is in the car*").

Prepositional Object: A type of verbal predicate that contains indirect objects or that complements a verb with information about place, time, or manner (e.g., "You *tell her the story now*" or "She called *with his phone number*").

Prepositional Phrase: A phrase that begins with a preposition (e.g., *in the basket*).

Prepositional Verb: A verb that is formed by combining a verb with a verb particle (e.g., *allow for, insist on, believe in*). Also referred to as a **phrasal verb** or **two-part verb**.

Prepositionless Noun Predicate: A type of nominal predicate in which the main verb is copular and the information following the verb is a noun or pronoun with no prepositional information included (e.g., "Those *are not your black gloves*").

Prepositionless Object: A type of verbal predicate in which a direct object or an indirect object follows a verb with no prepositional modification; includes predicates that contain information about manner, place, or time (e.g., "The pan *hit the floor*).

Present Participle: A verb formed by adding *-ing* to the stem of a verb (e.g., *walk → walking, ride → riding*).

Present Perfect Tense: A verb tense that references actions or states of being that were started in the past and have recently been completed or are continuing up to the present time; is formed by combining *have* or *has* and the past participle of the verb (e.g., "Ian *has eaten*").

Present Progressive Tense: A verb tense that references actions or states of being happening right now; is formed by combining *am, is,* or *are* and the present participle (e.g., "Carlos *is jumping*").

Present Tense: A verb tense that denotes actions occurring right now (e.g., I *eat*).

Progressive Tense: One of the three basic verb tenses; used to denote the duration of an ongoing action or state of being; can be present, past, or future; uses the present participle form of a verb.

Pronominal Form: A word that takes the place of a noun (e.g., *he, she, his, her*). Also referred to as a **pronoun**.

Pronoun: A word that takes the place of a noun (e.g., *he, she, his, her*); major categories of pronouns include personal, demonstrative, indefinite, relative, and interrogative. Also referred to as a **pronominal form**.

Proper Adjective: A type of determiner (also a limiting adjective) that refers to a specific entity (e.g., "*Spanish* class"); is typically capitalized.

Proper Noun: A noun that refers to a specific entity (e.g., *Louisiana, Grandma Beth, Bigfoot*); is usually capitalized.

Qualificative Predicate: A type of nominal predicate in which the subject is followed by a copular verb and the predicate provides qualitative information about the subject (e.g., "The fish *is simply delicious*").

Quantifier: A type of determiner that provides additional information about a noun regarding quantity (e.g., "*more* coffee" or "*another* green bug").

Referent: The noun to which a pronoun refers. Also referred to as an **antecedent**.

Reflexive Pronoun: A type of personal pronoun used when a person or entity performs an action on his-, her-, or itself (e.g., *himself, themselves*). Also referred to as a **compound personal pronoun** because it is formed by adding the suffix *-self* or *-selves* to a personal pronoun.

Relative Clause: A dependent clause that modifies an independent clause; it includes its own subject and predicate, but it cannot exist alone outside of an independent clause; is introduced by a relative pronoun (e.g., "The boy *who I like* is here"). Also referred to as an **adjective clause**.

Relative Pronoun: A pronoun that refers to a noun and embeds or conjoins a clause to the rest of a sentence via subordination (e.g., *who, why, that, which*).

Restrictive Clause: An adjective (or relative) clause that serves to narrow down the noun phrase it modifies; deletion of a restrictive clause changes the meaning of the independent clause.

Reversible Passive: A passive sentence in which the object and subject can be interchanged and the sentence still carries meaning (e.g., "The girl was hit by the boy" or "The boy was hit by the girl").

Sentence: A syntactic structure containing at least one independent clause with one complete thought; includes a subject and a predicate.

Simple Adjective: An adjective that occurs as a single word (e.g., *blue, silly*).

Simple Adverb: An adverb that occurs as a single word (e.g., *slowly, quickly*).

Simple Conjunction: A conjunction that occurs as a single word (e.g., *and, nor, so*).

Simple Noun: A noun consisting of a single word (e.g., *peach, paper*).

Simple Predicate: A verb that provides the principle information contained in the predicate and is usually the main verb of the sentence (e.g., "The mist *descended* slowly"). Also referred to as an **essential predicate**.

Simple Preposition: A preposition that occurs as a single word (e.g., *about, beyond, toward*).

Simple Sentence: A sentence containing one independent clause.

Simple Subject: A subject that is one word, typically a noun or pronoun (e.g., "*Curiosity* drives that cat").

Subject: A principle element of a sentence that frequently occurs at the beginning of the sentence; information comprising the subject slot defines who or what is the instigator of the action or state reflected in the verb (e.g., "*Nancy* held her closely" or "*The window* is being fixed").

Subject-Auxiliary Inversion: The movement of the auxiliary verb to precede the subject in *wh-* questions.

Subject Complement: The information in the predicate slot of a sentence that provides more information about the subject and follows copular (linking) verbs; can be a predicate adjective or a predicate nominative (e.g., "It is *I*" or "Ginger will be *famous*"). Also referred to as a **complement**.

Subject Pronoun: A type of personal pronoun used when the pronoun is the subject of a clause or sentence (e.g., *I, they*). Also referred to as a **nominative pronoun**.

Subjunctive Mood: A mood, used in dependent clauses that follow independent clauses, that express wishes, demands, or conditions that are improbable, doubtful, or contrary to fact; often reflects fantasizing and hypothesizing (e.g., "I wish that I *were* taller").

Subordinate Clause: A clause that contains a subject and a predicate but must be combined with a main clause to form a complete sentence; is typically introduced by a subordinating conjunction or a relative pronoun. Also referred to as a **dependent clause**.

Subordinating Conjunction: A conjunction used to connect a dependent clause with an independent clause (e.g., *after, although, when*).

Subordination Index (SI): A measure of clausal density, calculated by summing the total number of independent and dependent clauses and dividing by the total number of T-units.

Superlative Degree: The form of an adjective or adverb that reflects a comparison of three or more entities; is typically formed by adding *-est* to the positive form or by prefacing the positive form with *most* or *least* (e.g., pretty → *prettiest*, seriously → *most seriously*).

Tense: Information depicted by the verb in a clause or sentence that refers to time.

Terminable Unit: One independent clause plus any dependent clauses and embedded phrases (also termed "T-unit").

Transitive Verb: A verb requiring an object, such that the action or state of the subject carries over to the object (e.g., *kicked* is a transitive verb requiring an object in the following: "Jason *kicked* the can").

Two-Part Verb: A verb that is formed by combining a verb with a verb particle (e.g., *allow for, insist on, believe in*). Also referred to as a **prepositional verb** or **phrasal verb**.

Uncontractible Auxiliary: A verb used as an auxiliary that cannot be contracted in a clause or sentence due to the loss of or unclear meaning (e.g., "We *were* eating" → "We're eating").

Uncontractible Copula: A *be* verb used as a copula that cannot be contracted in a clause or sentence due to the loss of or unclear meaning (e.g., "He *was* mean" → "He's mean").

Verb: An "action word" in a sentence; describes what is done to a noun or pronoun or describes a state of being or existence.

Verbal: A word derived from a verb; includes infinitives, gerunds, and participles.

Verbal Predicate: The information comprising the predicate slot in a sentence in which the verb is not of a copular nature (e.g., "The test *was given last Thursday*"); types of verbal predicates include a verb standing alone; a prepositionless object; and prepositional objects, adverbs, and adverbial clauses.

Verb Particle: The part of a prepositional verb that modifies the verb (e.g., allow *for*, attend *to*, believe *in*). Also referred to as a **particle**.

Verb Phrase: A phrase that is the main structure of a predicate and includes the main verb of the sentence or clause and any auxiliary forms attached, as well as any modifiers.

Verb Standing Alone: A type of verbal predicate in which the verb is freestanding (e.g., "I *understand*").

Voice: The voice of a verb is modified to indicate whether a subject is doing the action or receiving the action in a clause or sentence; can be active or passive.

References

Aarts, F., & Aarts, J. (1982). *English syntactic structures: Functions and categories in sentence analysis.* New York: Pergamon Press.

Arndt, K., & Schuele, M. (2013). Multiclausal utterances aren't just for big kids: A framework for analysis of complex syntax production in spoken language of preschool and early school-age children. *Topics in Language Disorders, 33(2)*, 125–139.

Baldie, B. (1976). The acquisition of the passive voice. *Journal of Child Language, 3,* 331–348.

Bates, E. (2003). On the nature and nurture of language. In R. Levi-Montalcini, D. Baltimore, R. Dulbecco, F. Jacob, E. Bizzi, P. Calissano, & V. Volterra (Eds.), *Frontiers of biology: The brain of homo sapiens* (pp. 241–265). Rome: Istituto Della Enciclopedia Italiana Fondata da Giovanni Trecanni.

Berko Gleason, J. (1993). *The development of language* (3rd ed.). New York: Macmillan.

Bloom, L. (1973). *One word at a time.* The Hague: Mouton.

Bloom, L., Tackeff, J., & Lahey, M. (1984). Learning to in complement constructions. *Journal of Child Language, 11,* 391–406.

Braunwald, S. R. (1995). Differences in the acquisition of early verbs: Evidence from diary data from sisters. In M. Tomasello & W. E. Merriman (Eds.), *Beyond names for things: Young children's acquisition of verbs* (pp. 81–111). Hillsdale, NJ: Erlbaum.

Brown, R. (1973). *A first language: The early stages.* Cambridge: Harvard University Press.

Burchfield, R. W. (1996). *The new Fowler's modern English usage* (3rd ed.). Oxford, UK: Clarendon Press.

Carlson, K. (1997). *Miller-Yoder test of grammatical comprehension: Norms for three- through eight-year-olds.* Unpublished manuscript, University of Wisconsin at Madison.

Carroll, J. B., Davies, P., & Richman, B. (1971). *The American Heritage word frequency book.* Boston: Houghton Mifflin.

Caselli, M. C., Bates, E., Casadio, P., Fenson, J., Fenson, L., Sanderl, L., & Weir, J. (1995). A cross-linguistic study of early lexical development. *Cognitive Development, 10*(2), 159–199.

Clark, E. V., & Sengul, C. (1978). Strategies in the acquisition of deixis. *Journal of Child Language, 5,* 457–475.

Cole, M. L., & Cole, J. T. (1989). *Effective intervention with the language impaired child.* Rockville, MD: Aspen.

Crystal, D., Fletcher, P., & Garman, M. (1974). *The grammatical analysis of language disability: A procedure for assessment and remediation.* New York: American Elsevier.

Curenton, S. M., & Justice, L. M. (2004). African American and Caucasian preschoolers' use of decontextualized language literate language features in oral narratives. *Language, Speech, and Hearing Services in Schools, 35*(3), 240–253.

Darling, C. (2001). *Guide to grammar & writing.* Retrieved from Capitol Community College website: http://webster.commnet.edu/grammar/adjectives.htm

Davis, E. A. (1938). Developmental changes in the distribution of parts of speech. *Child Development, 9,* 309–317.

deVilliers, J. G., & deVilliers, P. A. (1973). A cross-sectional study of the acquisition of grammatical morphemes in child speech. *Journal of Psycholinguistic Research, 2,* 267–278.

deVilliers, J. G., & deVilliers, P. A. (1978). *Language acquisition.* Cambridge, MA: Harvard University Press.

Diessel, H. (2004). *The acquisition of complex sentences.* Cambridge, UK: Cambridge University Press.

Dodds, J. (1998). *The ready reference handbook: Writing, revising, editing.* Needham Heights, MA: Viacom.

Emslie, H., & Stevenson, R. (1981). Preschool children's use of the articles in definite and indefinite referring expressions. *Journal of Child Language, 8,* 313–328.

Feagans, L. (1980). Children's understanding of some temporal terms denoting order, duration, and simultaneity. *Journal of Psycholinguistic Research, 9*(1), 41–57.

Gopnik, A., & Choi, S. (1995). Names, relational words, and cognitive development in English and Korean speakers: Nouns are not always learned before verbs. In M. Tomasello & W. E. Merriman (Eds.), *Beyond names for things: Young children's acquisition of verbs* (pp. 83–90). Hillsdale, NJ: Erlbaum.

Gordon, K. E. (1993). *The deluxe transitive vampire: The ultimate handbook of grammar for the innocent, the eager, and the doomed.* New York: Pantheon Books.

Halliday, M. A., & Hasan, R. (1976). *Cohesion in English.* London, UK: Longman.

Hoff-Ginsberg, E. (1997). *Language development.* Pacific Grove, CA: Brooks/Cole.

Horgan, D. (1978). The development of the full passive. *Journal of Child Language, 5,* 65–80.

Hughes, D., McGillivray, L., & Schmidek, M. (1997). *Guide to narrative language: Procedures for assessment.* Austin, TX: PRO-ED.

Hunt, K. W. (1965). *Grammatical structures written at three grade levels.* (Research Report No. 3). Urbana, IL: National Council of Teachers of English.

Jacobs, R. A. (1995). *English syntax: A grammar for English language professionals.* New York: Oxford University Press.

Johnston, J. (1984). Acquisition of locative meaning: *Behind* and *in front of. Journal of Child Language, 11,* 407–422.

Justice, L. M., & Ezell, H. K. (1999). Knowledge of syntactic structures: A comparison of speech-language pathology graduate students to those in related disciplines. *Contemporary Issues in Communication Science and Disorders, 26,* 119–127.

Karmiloff-Smith, A. (1986). Some fundamental aspects of language development after age 5. In P. Fletcher & M. Garman (Eds.), *Language acquisition* (2nd ed.; pp. 455–474). New York: Cambridge University Press.

Kemper, S., Kynette, D., Rash, S., O'Brien, K., & Sprott, R. (1989). Life-span changes to adults' language: Effects of memory and genre. *Applied Psycholinguistics, 10*(01), 49–66.

Kemper, S., & Sumner, A. (2001). The structure of verbal abilities in young and older adults. *Psychology and Aging, 16,* 312–322.

Kent, R. D. (1994). *Reference manual for communicative sciences and disorders: Speech and language.* Austin, TX: PRO-ED.

Kessler, L., & McDonald, D. (1991). *When words collide: A media writer's guide to grammar and style.* Belmont, CA: Wadsworth.

Larsen, J. A., & Nippold, M. A. (2007). Morphological analysis in school-age children: Dynamic assessment of a word learning strategy. *Language, Speech, and Hearing Services in Schools, 38*(3), 201–212.

Leech, G. (1991). *An A–Z of English grammar and usage.* Quarry Bay, Hong Kong: Thomas Nelson.

Leonard, L. B., Eyer, J. A., Bedore, L. M., & Grela, B. G. (1997). Three accounts of the grammatical morpheme difficulties of English-speaking children with specific language impairment. *Journal of Speech, Language, and Hearing Research, 40,* 741–753.

Levy, E. T., & McNeill, D. (2013). Narrative development as symbol formation: Gestures, imagery and the emergence of cohesion. *Culture & Psychology, 19*(4), 548–569.

Lewis, M., & Ramsay, D. (2004). Development of self-recognition, personal pronoun use, and pretend play during the 2nd year. *Child Development, 75*(6), 1821–1831.

Limber, J. (1973). The genesis of complex sentences. In T. E. Moore (Ed.). *Cognitive development and the acquisition of language* (pp. 169–185). New York: Academic Press.

Loban, W. (1963). *The language of elementary school children.* Urbana, IL: National Council of Teachers of English.

Loban, W. (1976). *Language development: Kindergarten through grade twelve.* Urbana, IL: National Council of Teachers of English.

Lonigan, C. J., Burgess, S. R., Anthony, J. L., & Barker, T. A. (1998). Development of phonological sensitivity in 2- to 5-year-old children. *Journal of Educational Psychology, 90,* 294–311.

Mäkinen, L., Loukusa, S., Laukkanen, P., Leinonen, E., & Kunnari, S. (2014). Linguistic and pragmatic aspects of narration in Finnish typically developing children and children with specific language impairment. *Clinical Linguistics & Phonetics, 28*(6), 413–427.

Master, P. (1995). *Systems in English grammar.* Upper Saddle River, NJ: Prentice Hall Regents.

McDonough, C., Song, L., Hirsh-Pasek, K., Golinkoff, R. M., & Lannon, R. (2011). An image is worth a thousand words: Why nouns tend to dominate verbs in early word learning. *Developmental Science, 14*(2), 181–189.

McGhee-Bidlack, B. (1991). The development of noun definitions: A metalinguistic analysis. *Journal of Child Language, 18,* 417–434.

Miller, J. (1981). *Assessing language production in children.* Baltimore: University Park Press.

Naremore, R. C., Densmore, A. E., & Harman, D. R. (1995). *Language intervention with school-aged children: Conversation, narrative, and text.* San Diego, CA: Singular.

Nelson, K. (1973). Structure and strategy in learning to talk. *Monographs of the Society for Research in Child Development, 38*(149, Serial No. 260).

Nelson, K. E. (1974). Concept, word, and sentence: Interrelations in acquisition and development. *Psychological Review, 81,* 267–285.

Nippold, M. A. (2007). *Later language development: School-age children, adolescents, and young adults* (3rd ed). Austin, TX: PRO-ED.

Nippold, M. A., Cramond, P., & Hayward-Mayhew, C. (2014). Spoken language production in adults: Examining age-related differences in syntactic complexity. *Clinical Linguistics and Phonetics, 28*(3), 195–207.

Nippold, M. A., Hesketh, L. J., Duthie, J. K., & Mansfield, T. C. (2005). Conversational versus expository discourse: A study of syntactic development in children, adolescents, and adults. *Journal of Speech, Language, and Hearing Research, 48*(5), 1048–1064.

Nippold, M. A., Mansfield, T. C., & Billow, J. L. (2007). Peer conflict explanations in children, adolescents, and adults: Examining the development of complex syntax. *American Journal of Speech-Language Pathology, 16*(2), 179–188.

Nippold, M. A., Schwarz, I. E., & Undlin, R. A. (1992). Use and understanding of adverbial conjuncts: A developmental study of adolescents and young adults. *Journal of Speech and Hearing Research, 35,* 108–118.

Nippold, M. A., & Sun, L. (2008). Knowledge of morphologically complex words: A developmental study of older children and young adolescents. *Language, Speech, and Hearing Services in Schools, 39*(3), 365–373.

Opdycke, J. B. (1965). *Harper's English grammar.* New York: Harper and Row.

Orlansky, M. D., & Bonvillian, J. D. (1988). Early sign language acquisition. In M. D. Smith & J. L. Locke (Eds.), *The emergent lexicon: The child's development of a linguistic vocabulary* (pp. 263–292). San Diego, CA: Academic Press.

Owens, R. E. (2012). *Language development: An introduction* (8th ed.). Boston: Pearson.

Palmer, H. E. (1939). *A grammar of spoken English on a strictly phonetic basis.* Cambridge, England: Cambridge University Press.

Paul, R. (1981). Analyzing complex sentence development. In J. Miller (Ed.), *Assessing language production in children: Experimental procedures* (pp. 36–40, 67–71). Baltimore: University Park Press.

Peterson, C. L., & McCabe, A. (1988). The connective *and* as discourse glue. *First Language, 8*(22, Pt. 1), 19–28.

Radford, A. (1990). *Syntactic theory and the acquisition of English syntax: The nature of early child grammars of English.* Oxford: Basil Blackwell.

Rescorla, L., Alley, A., & Christine, J. B. (2001). Word frequencies in toddlers' lexicons. *Journal of Speech, Language, and Hearing Research, 44*(3), 598–609.

Retherford, K. S. (1996). *Normal communication acquisition: An animated database of behaviors* [Computer software]. Eau Claire, WI: Thinking Publications.

Retherford, K. S. (2000). *Guide to analysis of language transcripts* (3rd ed.). Austin, TX: PRO-ED.

Rispoli, M. (1998). *Me* or *my*: Two different patterns of pronoun case errors. *Journal of Speech, Language, and Hearing Research, 41,* 385–393.

Scott, C. (1988). Spoken and written syntax. In M. Nippold (Ed.), *Later language development* (pp. 49–96). Boston: College-Hill Press.

Scott, C. M., & Rush, D. (1985). Teaching adverbial connectivity: Implications from current research. *Child Language Teaching and Therapy, 1,* 264–280.

Shapiro, L. P. (1997). Tutorial: An introduction to syntax. *Journal of Speech, Language, and Hearing Research, 40,* 254–272.

Silva, M. N. (1996). *Grammar in many voices.* Lincolnwood, IL: NTC.

Skillin, M. E., & Gay, R. M. (1974). *Words into type* (3rd ed.). Englewood Cliffs, NJ: Prentice-Hall.

Stageberg, N. C. (1981). *An introductory English grammar* (4th ed.). New York: Holt, Rinehart, and Winston.

Turnbull, K. L. P., & Justice, L. M. (2011). *Language development from theory to practice.* Boston: Pearson.

Turner, R. P. (1966). *Grammar review for technical writers.* New York: Holt, Rinehart, and Winston.

Tyack, D. L., & Gottsleben, R. H. (1986). Acquisition of complex sentences. *Language, Speech, and Hearing Services in Schools, 17,* 160–174.

Wallach, G. P., & Butler, K. G. (1994). *Language learning disabilities in school-age children and adolescents.* New York: Merrill.

Weiss, C., & Lillywhite, H. (1976). *Communicative disorders.* St. Louis, MO: Mosby.

Wells, G. (1985). *Language development in the preschool years.* New York: Cambridge University Press.

Westby, C. E. (1991). Learning to talk, talking to learn: Oral-literate language differences. *Communication skills and classroom success,* 334–357.

Westby, C. E. (1994). *The effects of culture on genre, structure, and style on oral and written texts.* In G. P. Wallach & K. G. Butler (Eds.), *Language learning disabilities in school-age children and adolescents* (pp. 180–218). New York: Merrill.

Williams, J. D. (1999). *The teacher's grammar book.* Mahwah, NJ: Erlbaum.

Williamson, G. (2001). *Human communication: A linguistic introduction.* Bicester, Oxon, UK: Speechmark.

Windsor, J. (1994). Children's comprehension and production of derivational suffixes. *Journal of Speech and Hearing Research, 37,* 408–417.

Wing, C. S., & Scholnick, E. K. (1981). Children's comprehension of pragmatic concepts expressed in 'because,' 'although,' 'if,' and 'unless.' *Journal of Child Language, 8,* 347–365.

Yuan, S., Fisher, C., & Snedeker, J. (2012). Counting the nouns: Simple structural cues to verb meaning. *Child Development, 83*(4), 1382–1399.

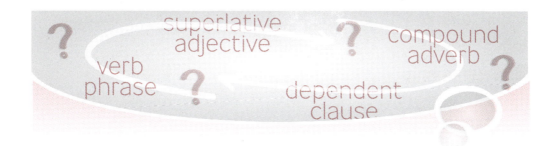

About the Authors

Laura M. Justice, Ph.D., is a clinical speech-language pathologist and applied researcher in early childhood language and literacy development, communication disorders, and educational interventions. Dr. Justice is EHE Distinguished Professor in the School of Teaching and Learning at The Ohio State University and Executive Director of the Crane Center for Early Childhood Research and Policy and the Schoenbaum Family Center. Justice has published more than 100 articles on early education and language/literacy intervention and has authored or edited 10 books.

Helen K. Ezell, Ph.D., CCC-SLP, is a speech-language pathologist who specializes in children's language and early literacy development. In addition to her clinical research, her experience includes preparation of teacher-scholars in speech-language pathology.

Mary Beth Schmitt, Ph.D., CCC-SLP, is an assistant professor at Texas Tech University Health Sciences Center in the Department of Speech, Language, and Hearing Sciences. Through her research, Dr. Schmitt investigates child-level and treatment-level aspects of language therapy that affect outcomes for children with language disorders. To date, Dr. Schmitt has authored and co-authored more than 16 peer-reviewed papers and six book chapters and commentaries related to children with language disorders. Dr. Schmitt currently serves as the editor for EBP Briefs, a peer-reviewed publication supporting evidence-based practice for practitioners.